42/50

KENYA

a holiday guide

Michael Tomkinson MA, FIL

London & Hammamet

First published 1973 by ERNEST BENN LTD
25 NEW STREET SQUARE, LONDON EC4A 3JA
Fifth edition 1981

© MICHAEL TOMKINSON 1973, 1981

Photographs pages 13, 29, 33, 81 by
AFRICANA/DAVID FANSHAWE, PETER SAW

Photographs pages 15, 39, 41, 87, 118 by
DAVID KEITH JONES

Photograph page 85 by ESMOND BRADLEY
MARTIN

Photographs pages 25, 37, 111 by PHILIP
POWELL

Printed by BALDING + MANSELL, WISBECH

Printed in Britain: ISBN 0 905500 08 3

INTRODUCTION

Few are the places left on earth today where scenery and peoples, climate and wildlife combine to create a land of beauty. Fewer still where politics do not restrict or wholly preclude travel. Kenya, happily, is one. From the tropical Indian Ocean coast through the Highlands and Rift to the lakes, a fascinating medley of tribes and races live – without most Western prejudices of colour, sex and status – in a land for the most part idyllic.

Though the last state in the region to attain independence, Kenya is unquestionably first for progress and prosperity. Its 225,000 square miles of panoramic wealth fully justify its pride of place with visitors from overseas. Which is why for this, our fifth edition, the General Introduction to East Africa has been dropped. Each previous revision since 1973 optimistically included Tanzania and Uganda in its Place, People, Past and Practical chapters. The facts, however, must be faced. With Uganda still struggling back from its lapse into the Dark Ages, with Tanzania – a land of natural plenty – reduced by politics to poverty, Kenya is sole survivor where sophistication, order and stability are concerned. Equal treatment with its hapless neighbours would be both anachronistic and unjust.

Some common features – history, tribes and wildlife – none the less remain. The history of the three states is frequently interlinked. Without the Uganda Railway we might never have had Nairobi; Nakuru, Kisumu and many Kenyan centres were the product of the British urge to penetrate Uganda. And without some description of German Tanganyika, my account of the Great War in East Africa would read like a commentary on a shadow-boxing match. Most of Kenya's boundaries were drawn in accordance with colonial politics, not tribal limits, in the 1890s. Civil servants in London and Berlin agreed convenient straight lines on maps (with bends as necessary to allow, for example, the Kaiser and Queen Victoria to have each one snow-capped African peak). Colonial governments having disregarded traditional 'native' territories, many tribes today ignore the arbitrary frontiers. Any summary of their distribution must do so too. Wildlife, naturally, pays no heed to boundaries political or tribal.

Its tourism promoted sensibly and successfully, Kenya is catering increasingly for the mass-market. The 'mass', though, applies to the travel trade's arrangements: you will not feel it means you. Apart from the often packed jet there and back, your holiday here, whether 'package' or private, will be just as individualistic as you choose. On the Indian Ocean's vast palm-lined beaches crowds seem to dissolve; hotels and lodges cater spaciously, and for your almost mandatory national park game drive or charter flight up country, the terrain is usually against vehicles and aircraft seating over six or seven.

In attempting to describe all the region's attractions, whether on or off the beaten track, I may have made the 'Holiday Guide' something of a misnomer. Kenya has many impressive tourist circuits with excellent hotels and competent personnel to fly, drive, guide and feed you. Elsewhere, however, conditions are different. Hotels are few, the terrain is tough and you, the *Wazungu*, still an unfamiliar sight. One quirk of East African English, moreover, is that 'road' means where cars do pass, have been known to pass or might at times be able to pass. The region's 'Road Maps' – most put out by petroleum companies, whose interest it is to see you motorized – thus display a deceptively inviting network of red-line 'roads', many of which I found to be sand-pits or skid-pans, to shatter steering, suspension or sump when used at any speed, or simply to vanish into swamp or forest. Following normal English usage, I have kept 'road' for bituminized surfaces only, and Kenya's more frequent thoroughfares – *murram* (earth) tracks, sand tracks and mountain tracks – are described as just that. A week or two's travelling on these, and a holiday is not what you have had but what you need.

For the 10,000 miles of travelogue that follow, the ingredients were gathered and the distances measured in the winter of 1979-80. And, with the Ministry of Tourism's help, in an indefatigable Ford Cortina hired by Hertz/UTC. (This with the exception of Maralal-Loyangalani, which requires not necessarily four-wheel drive but a vehicle with high centre clearance.) As with *Tunisia a Holiday Guide*, distances are given in kilometres and square brackets, and less worth-while sights denoted by indentation. With most maps inadequate, I have attempted to make the itineraries practicable by faithfully copying notice boards and road signs. These, however, are appreciated not only by travellers: in outlying areas they are sought after by locals as useful sheet-metal or fire-wood, and in national parks often rubbed illegible by itchy elephants, or flattened. There is seldom any lack, though, of the same light-fingered locals to point the way or explain, and in any event reroutings and detours are rarely a bore in Kenya's fascinating, panoramic outback.

When tourists call them tigers   *even lions laugh*

SWAHILI

Perrott's *Teach Yourself Swahili* is probably the best short work for serious students; Huseini's *English Swahili Phrase Book*, whose author remains understandably anonymous, contains useful word-lists as well as 'informations . . . pharses . . . and notes on Swahili grammer'; Wilson's *Simplified Swahili* is just that and Le Breton's *Up-Country Swahili*, recently reprinted, will help you muddle through convincingly. The following glossary is designed solely to keep you from starving, overpaying or losing your way. Swahili as a language is outlined on page 12. Its consonants are pronounced as in English: *g* is always hard; *f*, *s* and *th* always 'heavy' as in *fin*, *sin* and *thin*; *ng* as in *singer*; *gh* is the Arabic '*ghain*, and *m* + consonant a frequent Swahili prefix – best said simply as *g* and *mmm* respectively. The vowels – *a, e, i, o, u* – are pronounced as in our (English English) *bath*, *bay*, *bee*, *toe* and *too*.

Hello *Jambo, Jambo sana*
How are you? *Habari?*
Well *Mzuri*
Ill, fed up, awful *Mzuri*
  (Swahili greetings are never
  spoiled by facts)
Thank you (very much)
  Ahsante (sana)
Please *Tafadhali*
  (but often omitted – just
  sound polite)
Bring me *Lete*
I want/would like *Nataka/*
  Napenda
Now/Quick(ly) *Sasa/*
  Upesi, Haraka
Today/Tomorrow *Leo/Kesho*
Food *Chakula*
Beer/Coffee/Tea *Tembo/*
  Kahawa/Chai
Water/Milk/Bread *Maji/*
  Maziwa/Mkate
Meat/Fish/Fruit *Nyama/*
  Samaki/Matunda
Butter/Sugar/Salt *Siagi/*
  Sukari/Chumvi

Hot/Cold *Moto/Baridi*
Many/Big/Small *Mingi/*
  Mkubwa/Kidogo
Come in, Welcome! *Karibu*
Yes/No *Ndio/Hapana*
I, me/You/And *Mimi/Wewe/*
  Na
Here/Later *Hapa/Bado*
How much? many? *Ngapi?*
  (*Shilingi, senti*)
One/Two/Three *Moja/Mbili/*
  Tatu
Four/Five/Six *Nne/Tano/Sita*
Seven/Eight *Saba/Nane*
Nine/Ten *Tisa/Kumi*
Eleven etc. *Kumi na moja* etc.
Twenty *Ishirini*
Twenty-one etc. *Ishirini na*
  moja etc.
Thirty/Forty *Thelathini/*
  Arobaini
Fifty/Sixty *Hamsini/Sitini*
Seventy/Eighty *Sabini/*
  Themanini
Ninety/Hundred *Tisini/Mia*
Two hundred etc. *Mia mbili* etc.

Thousand *Elfu*
Two thousand etc. *Elfu mbili*
  etc.
Where is? *Wapi?*
  – the WC *choo*
  – a good hotel *hoteli*
    mzuri
  – a police station *stesheni*
    polisi
  – the nearest doctor
    daktari karibu
  – a telephone *simu*
  – a petrol station *garage*
  – a mechanic *fundi*
  – a chemist's *duka la dawa*
    (medicine *dawa*)
  – the main road *barabara*
Slow(ly) *Polepole*
I don't understand *Sifahamu*
  If you still do not understand, just hold out for:
Left *Kushoto*
Right *Kulia*
Straight on *Moja kwa moja*
Watch out! *Angalia!*
Good-bye *Kwaheri*

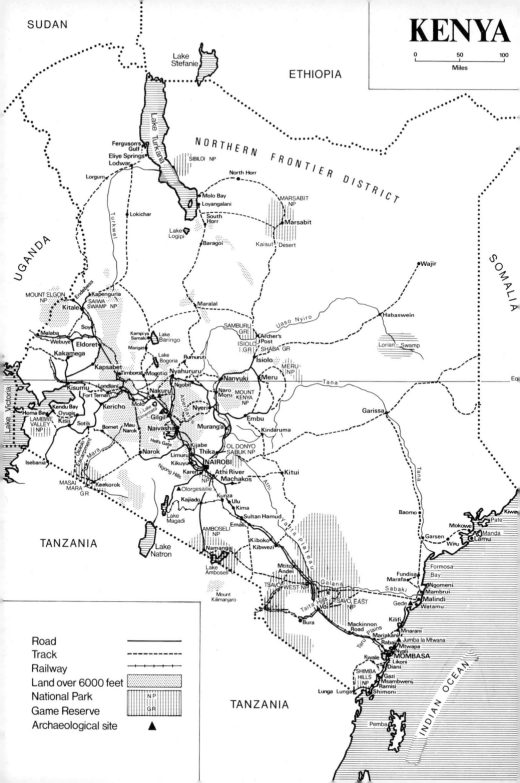

PLACE

Geography. Kenya is a compact if immense geographical entity. It is bounded to the north by the deserts of Somalia, Ethiopia and the Sudan, to the east by Somalia and the Indian Ocean and to the south and west by Tanzania and Uganda respectively. The country lies, as the guidebooks say, astride the **Equator** – and almost exactly so, with five degrees of latitude north and 4°40 south. Visitors envisaging a quick drive round might also note that its total area, though varying from one official source to the next, is about 225,000 square miles (582,644 km²).

From Lamu to Lunga Lunga run some 270 miles (430 kms) of **Indian Ocean coast**. This as the crow flies, for promontories and inlets prolong the Kenya littoral to almost 1000 kms (c. 600 miles). Temperamental rivers – the Tana, Sabaki and Ramisi – meander through to the shore's mangrove swamps and countless coconut-palms; the former yield frequently to sand and coral beaches, and to the more extensive bays or creeks of Mombasa, Malindi and the Lamu archipelago. Off shore the coral reefs, sand-banks and spits, exquisite green when seen from the air, broaden into islands some seasonal and small, others as substantial as Lamu, Manda and, not least, Mombasa itself.

North-west from Lamu and the Tana River valley the desert of Kenya's **Northern Frontier District** reaches to Lake Turkana (the former Lake Rudolf), interrupted only by Marsabit's mountain-oasis. No less an obstacle to early explorers, the dry Taru Plains lie due west of the 30-mile/50-km. littoral. Westward they rise, beyond the Taita and Akamba hills, to Tanzania's Kilimanjaro and to **Mount Kenya**. The former 19,341 feet (5895 metres), the latter 17,058 feet (5249 metres), the two perennially snow-capped peaks are Africa's highest. West from Mount Kenya, beyond the Aberdares' rugged forests and the gentler Ngongs, lies 'The Rift'.

The **Great Rift Valley**, if not the last word in geographical spectaculars that schoolroom-minded writers make it, is none the less a remarkable phenomenon. Through a fault in the earth's crust the adjacent land can either be forced volcanically upwards or sink. Here there were two parallel faults and the land between them, viz. 4000 miles from Beira to the Dead Sea, sank – over 2000 feet and 1 million years ago. The near-sheer walls of this cataclysmic ditch, sometimes 50 miles wide, are a stupendous sight. Clouds on the highlands around disperse, as clear-cut along the Rift's two lips as though Moses had intervened. Volcanoes, often only dozing, lie scattered along the Rift-floor. The lakes – Turkana, Baringo, Bogoria and Nakuru, Elmentaita, Naivasha and Magadi – are said to be vestiges of one vast inland sea.

West of the Rift Kenya climbs, through the forests, stark escarpments and well-cultivated slopes of the ex-White **Highlands**, to the massif of Mount Elgon, half in Uganda, and – at 3860 feet (1134 metres) above sea-level – to **Lake Victoria**. 'Victoria Nyanza' is second only to Superior in the great-lake stakes (the Caspian excluded) and covers 26,828 square miles (10,480 km²). Which, be it said without *arrière-pensée*, is just enough to sink Ireland in. Territorially, the three states share its waters, and the islands, papyrus beds, creeks, bays and beaches that make up its much-praised loveliness are legion.

Climate. Although generally speaking – if one dare generalize with the weather – the Coast is a place of tropical sunshine and the highlands bracingly clear, the country's jungles and lush cultivation do not, obviously, thrive on Scotch Mist. The rain, however, tends to fall considerately: not as London's often listless drizzle but in short heavy downpours or violent storms, with a blackening sky as fair warning. The theory is that the **Long Rains** fall between late March and June and the **Short Rains** in November, but not for nothing, the locals say, has the British influence prevailed for 50 years. The rain comes early or late or never – as predictably as Wigan's. And even when with us, it appears to work part-time; in none of the 'wet' months mentioned above have I known rain stop play the whole day.

For the motorist, it pays to be weather-wise. As many 'roads' turn to mud when it rains or thick dust in a dry spell, it is not just a question of packing your mac but of whether you ever arrive. **Temperatures** everywhere depend on the altitude, from an all-year average of 83° fahrenheit on the Coast to eternal sub-zero atop the snow-capped Mount Kenya. The Northern Frontier District is perennially warm and Nairobi's July can be cold. Although Western winters make December-March the peak tourist season, Kenyans themselves like September and October.

The Coast, though literally tropical, is cooled by the **monsoon winds** that blow steady north-east – the *Kaskazi* – from November to March, and south-east – the *Kusi* – for the rest. The fact that they dictate the region's weather and vary only twice each year leaves the forecasters little room to be wrong. With the sun perpendicularly above, remember: suntan lotion and adequate cover outside, more drink – even than usual – inside, good sunglasses for your eyes and a UV filter for your camera.

The weather, however, should never be called 'unseasonal': with the Equator so close there are no seasons as such. Daylight lasts, all year round, from six a.m. to seven p.m. (local time and with a little leeway). **Local time** is, incidentally, three hours ahead of GMT, and Swahili-speakers, like the Bible and Arabia's Beduin, take sunrise/sunset as zero. Seven a.m. is thus their '*saa moja*', 'one o'clock' – which may explain the occasional untimeliness of your 'early morning' call. Sunrise and sunset are often glorious but invariably short, and, if you do have a Boy Scout badge for finding your way by the sun, remember that sunset wanders from south-west in March to north-west in August with the sunrise, too, correspondingly off.

Access. Early in 1977 the last shipping line to carry passengers to East Africa paid its last call at Mombasa, and so made ship-to-shore sorties on round-the-world cruises (or your private yacht) the only means of reaching Kenya **by sea**. You can drive down from Europe as I did, once but never again: given the developments since in Uganda, Ethiopia and the southern Sudan, respect for the reader prevents my recommending the trip **by land**. So – as the flight from Europe or even the States takes less hours than the land or sea journey did days – it is no surprise to find 99% of Kenya's visitors arriving **by air**.

Of these a large, unpublished percentage come as '**all-inclusive packages**'. The pros of such airfare-&-accommodation arrangements far outweigh the cons. For the need to book well in advance you are rewarded by inclusive 'package' prices by charter that often cost little more than the one-way fare alone by the scheduled service. Apart from the herd factor, there are no hidden snags. The Association of British Travel Agents, now aided by the Trade Descriptions Act, ensures that tour operators in the United Kingdom provide the services paid for. An additional assurance has always been that, as your respective tour operator is responsible for meeting your hotel bill in Kenya, he is loath to let the return flight leave without you.

Many utilize the country's national airline, **Kenya Airways**. As do those, too, who find **scheduled flights** 'smarter than charter'. The first company to fly a British monarch (as East African Airways in 1952), 'KA' will fly you nightly save Monday to Nairobi and, on Friday, Saturday and Sunday, to Mombasa also: departure from Heathrow's terminal 3 at 6 p.m., arrival the next day in Nairobi at 6.45, 7, 8, 8.15, 9.05, 9.20 or 10.20 depending on the routing. An extra service operates on Friday and Saturday – departure 7 and 9.15 p.m. respectively – and the latter flight, like Friday's at 6 p.m., is not by 707 but by 747 Jumbo. Within Kenya, the airline's exceptionally smart and smily cabin crews are pleasant company on the half-dozen daily flights, by Fokker or DC-9, between Nairobi and Mombasa.

Information on travel to and in the country can also, usually, be obtained from the **Kenya Tourist Offices**: 13 New Burlington Street, London W1X 1FF, tel. 839 4477; 60 East 56th Street, New York, NY 10022, tel. 486 1300; 9100 Wilshire Boulevard, Doheny Plaza, Suite 111, Beverly Hills, Ca. 90212, tel. 274 6635; Ger Jarlsgatan 37, 2nd Street, 111 45 Stockholm, tel. 51006/9/19.

PEOPLE

Population. Kenya was subjected to a census in August 1979. From the national total of 15,320,000, 0·4% are Europeans, 1·5% have Arab or Asian origins, and 2% pay income tax.

While any remarks about the last class would be rash, it is no secret that the minuscule **European** percentage represents the tail-end of the large-scale white immigration in the first half of this century. First the Germans in Tanganyika; next the Boers, poor but experienced pioneers from South Africa; then in the 1910s the first shipments of wealthier British immigrants to follow Lord Delamere's colonizing lead: 'British East Africa – Winter Home for Aristocrats' fast became the permanent home of some 80,000 Europeans. Developments in Europe – wars, depressions, international gerrymandering – made the influx cosmopolitan.

Independence put an end to this 'white exploitation', which was far more beneficial and far less unscrupulous than Africa's hotheads insist. Unlike America's reservation Indians, East Africans now control their territory entirely. Large numbers of European landowners, feeling themselves increasingly to be a foreign body and unused to the tenor of new African trade unions, sold up and left. But in other fields many remain, 'settlers' of second or third generation, East African citizens

Kenya Airways' Boeing 707

perforce. Kenya in particular has benefited sensibly by barring discrimination: 'Europeans' here still run the best hotels and lodges, manage the national parks, operate travel agencies and occupy sensitive Civil Service posts. Along with the still numerous missionaries, the older generation continues to display the secondary pioneer talents that choral concerts, amateur dramatics, fêtes and flower-shows imply, while their offspring are more for motor rallies, race-courses and drive-in cinemas.

Tighter and more tradition-minded is the **Asian** community. The British, everyone will tell you, brought in some 32,000 Indians to build the Uganda Railway, just as the Germans used Greeks in Tanganyika. Da Gama, however, met Indians at Malindi; two Muslims from Surat were in 1825 the first non-Africans to penetrate Tanganyika, and 6000 Hindu *banyans* – merchants – were financing expeditions from Zanzibar in the 1860s, long before the Railway builders decided that importing Asian labourers was a better bet than trying to enlist the Masai. Many Indian coolies died in exile, 28 between the jaws of the Man-Eaters of Tsavo that Colonel Patterson's book describes. Most went home with their wages, but others foresaw that prosperity would follow the railway they had helped lay. All along the line their *dukas* multiplied. Today these tin-roofed, small-time stores, like the mosques, temples and churches of some 30 Asian communities, are a feature of every township from Zambia to the Sudan – Wajir was the only one I found without Asians. Their stake is considerable, too, in most spheres of trade. But African resentment, largely of their prosperity but also of their near-Masonic cliquishness, has prompted government measures against Asian non-citizens. Amin's 'final solution' of the Asian question has made ghost-towns of some Ugandan suburbs; it has also accelerated the voluntary exodus of Asians from Tanzania and Kenya, with some demonstrating for Entry Vouchers at British High Commissions and others being shuttlecocked intercontinentally.

Arab penetration predates both the above. Throughout the nebulous Middle Ages, Muslims from Arabia came to the Coast not, as in France and Spain, to conquer, but to trade, convert and settle. Their dhows sailed in on the north-east monsoon, laden with glass, ironware, wheat and wine: to return with tortoise-shell, rhino horn, ivory, spices and slaves. Zanzibar's Kizimkazi Mosque dates from 1107; the ruins of 14-15th-c. mosques, houses and palaces show that Arab influence was by then paramount. More important, Arab settlers were interbreeding admirably, the outcome being the fine 'Afro-Asian' race – and the mulatto language – of **Swahili**. Why no equivalent 'Afro-Europeans' ensued from the attentions of first the Coast's Portuguese settlers, then the mass of Europeans everywhere, is the subject of much indecorous speculation: because of Nature's preventative grace, say some, the European head being too much for the African pelvis. By 1832 the Arabs of Oman regarded Zanzibar as so much a part of metropolitan Arabia that

9

they made the island their seat of government. Arab influence grew inevitably – for the worse in the unmerciful expansion of the slave-trade, for the better in the opening up of the interior and the civilizing spread of Islam. Though Kenya is now no closer to the Arab states than many other of its 'Third World' bloc-mates, the Arabian way of life at the Coast and the mosques and African Muslims everywhere testify to its Middle Eastern heritage.

For all this the three countries are and always have been **African**. The Leakeys' discoveries have made it probable that our first post-ape predecessor – if you accept Evolution – lived in present-day East Africa. Which might make you wonder, fatuously, if beneath the shag his skin was black or white. The first historians' African contemporaries were unquestionably ebony: Herodotus, 'The Father of History', calls even the Egyptians *melanes*, 'black', and in the works of every century's travel writers, whether authoritative or early arm-chair, the Nubians' southern neighbours have been Negro.

East Africa's peoples, like melodies and smells, have thwarted the experts' attempts to define. With blood-ties, origins and religion all found wanting, language is the yardstick now usually accepted. The linguistic criterion gives the region five main African strains. Or four. Or three, depending on which expert's work you prefer.

Those tribes known as and speaking **Bantu** – a group of languages itself ill-defined – are the most numerous. (The word enlighteningly means 'people'.) Their supposed origin is West Africa, whence their *Drang nach Osten* took them first to Uganda, where they settled as the peoples of Buganda, Bunyoro, Toro, Ankole and Busoga, then, interbreeding to some extent with the Hamites, to Kenya as the Kikuyu, Akamba, Taita, Embu, Meru and Giriama.

The older-established **Hamites** must, if they really are nephews of Japheth and Shem, have come to Africa from Arabia. They moved south, perhaps in the 10th and 11th centuries, and today survive principally in Kenya as the once-powerful Galla and the picturesque if primitive Samburu, Boran, Rendille and Somali of the Northern Frontier District.

The **Nilotes** (because they travelled up the Nile) remained en route as the north Ugandan Acholi, Jonam and Alur, settled north and east of Lake Victoria as the Ja-Luo and spread south and east as the Masai of Kenya and Tanzania. The Masai, whom ethnologists recently promoted from the Nilo-Hamitic to the Nilotic class, live astride several main tourist routes and have thus come, disproportionately, to the forefront of many a visitor's ken.

The **Nilo-Hamites** (a term which the language yardstick makes as meaningful as *Franglais*) were originally Hamites that merged and migrated with the Nilotes. Having pressed southward in the 18th and 19th centuries, the group is represented in Kenya today by the Kipsigis, Tugen, Nandi and Turkana, and in Uganda by the advanced Iteso, the Langi and Sebei, and the backward Karamojong. Little remains of the putative fifth group, aboriginal and perhaps prehistoric: Tanzania's Kindiga of Lake Eyasi, akin to the Bushmen and speaking a 'click' language; Lake Rudolf/Turkana's fish-eating Molo, whom student expeditions and letters to *The Times* revived for the West in the 1950s, and the Dorobo, a fragmented and secluded community who live bittily off hunting, grubbing and honey but who are, in their mastery of jungle lore, the nearest thing to Tarzan.

It is customary to call East Africa's peoples 'agriculturalists', 'pastoralists' or 'hunters'. While large uniform communities in outlying areas, the Masai, for example, or the Karamojong 'cluster', retain these occupational name-tags, they are made increasingly inapt by improved communications, steady tribal disintegration, intermarriage and economic progress. Peoples of particularly flamboyant interest to visitors will be described as they occur in the itineraries. They are lavishly portrayed in Mirella Ricciardi's masterpiece, *Vanishing Africa*; less selective, more aesthetic documentary, is the 'comprehensive record of Kenya's peoples' which the Kenya government commissioned Joy Adamson to paint in 1948-57. 'Peoples', incidentally, is the word you use for 'tribes'. As the government is trying with remarkable success to quash tribalism for the sake of national unity, few authorities will acknowledge that Kenya has an approximate total of 52 tribes/peoples.

Religion. Officially, Catholics number 4 million and Protestants 2·5, Muslims more than 4 million, Hindus and similar 250,000 and pagans are known to exist. Simple arithmetic shows that the existence is considerable: nowhere have I met so many people, from suave MPs to primitive villagers, who openly claimed to be pagan.

This is not to discredit the missionary effort. For almost a century the Western churches have been sending men so active and versatile that 'missionary' has in most cases meant not only evangelist, but teacher, doctor, explorer, mechanic, farmer and builder to boot. Even when, as in

Tanzania, their religious work is circumscribed, they continue to run their clinic, printing-press, orphans' home, experimental farm and even the local lay school – each mission's bright school-uniform is a characteristic splash of colour in many a rural area. Everywhere Africans flock to, and preach in, churches of all denominations and orders.

Nor is it to suggest you will see 'tribesmen' horizontal in front of sticks and stones. Fetishism does exist – Black Magic *qua* 'native medicine' too – but practising pagans you are, on a short visit, less likely to encounter in the flesh than in the Nairobi, Kampala and Dar museums' collections of dried voodoo debris. Tribes of Bantu origin (p. 10) usually vested divinity in their king,

On-the-spot hotgospelling – every Sunday everywhere around Lake Victoria

whence the need to kill him and so 'save God' as soon as his health (viz. sexual energy) failed. With others the godhead was also seen as the source of rainfall and fertility, but might inhabit, or even be, a mountain. Though tourists today may clamber all over their holy places, many sick Africans have still as much faith in the spells and incantations of their native witch doctors as in the proven power of the modern *daktari*.

None of which means more for your holiday than an undercurrent of titillating mystery. You are free to enter and admire the Hindus' temples, wondrous with images all heavily symbolic. Muslims, whether orthodox Sunnis, schismatic Shi'is, 'heretic' Ahmadis or the Aga Khan's Isma'ilis, will usually welcome you in (with shoes off). The abundance of churches, temples and mosques is in fact an architectural attraction, and the peaceful coexistence of so many beliefs a lesson for Ulster. Only League football teams that still place spells on the ball, spend £10 per match on witch-doctor predictions and nail fetishes to goal-posts to stop opponents scoring, mar the impression East Africa gives of being as diversely devout as the West, only more so.

Language. East Africa's ethnic Tower of Babel made a *lingua franca* indispensable. Uganda's is English, Kenya's English and Swahili equally, and Tanzania's nationalistically Swahili. Although all educated Africans speak English remarkably, even ebulliently well, you may need to adjust to the pace and intonation: of the radio-announcer's 'It is 1900 hours Greenwich. Meantime here is the News', or the waiter's directions, when you desperately ask for the loo: 'Yes, I see. Now you go, let me see, yes, we might say, go first to the left hand (raising right arm) then . . .'. **English**, whatever accent-free sort you speak, will serve you impeccably on all the tourist circuits. Elsewhere some Swahili will help, and even in the towns a few simple words will evoke

11

such smiles – admiring, not derisory – that the effort of learning page 5 is worth while. Be careful to falter: any show of fluency will bring down upon you a colloquial maelstrom, unintelligible, embarrassing and somewhat defeating the object.

Swahili, which the language's protagonists call 'the World's Twelfth Greatest Tongue' (but which by numbers of speakers ranks 44th), is basically Bantu with very many borrowings, originally from Arabic and recently from English (*Kiplefti* for a roundabout and *Picha la Cowboy* for a Western amongst numerous examples of its linguistic promiscuity). It varies from the pure, deeply inflected dialect of Zanzibar, through sundry up-country patois to *Ki-settler-i*, the Europeans' kitchen lingo. In Uganda Swahili – which means Coastal – was traditionally disdained as the speech of immigrant workmen, while Tanzania is so self-consciously encouraging its use that officials, though speaking English well, sometimes refuse to do so.

Names and Appellations. Politics impinge here too on modes of address. 'Boy' for the hotel staff is taboo, you are told, because of colonial connotations. Tourist boards and guide-books suggest 'Steward', and Tanzanians preach '*Rafiki*'. (This supposedly only means Friend, but as it is also the Swahili for Comrade the authorities must smile up their communistic sleeves when Western capitalists use it with the waiter.) The issue is rather a storm in a teacup. Most visitors have no colonial connections and will surely do as they would at home and call the waiter 'Waiter'. Room-boys, I found, appreciate being called by name – a useful memory test.

With personal names religion, not politics, dictates. Muslims everywhere reveal their creed by the same timeless selection: Ahmad, Mahmud, Mohammed and Abdullah, Fatima, Aisha, Jamila and Zohra – the Prophet's family and the Qoran's cast still set the tone. Amongst the Christian majority the Bible's hardy annuals recur universally: John, Peter, Paul and Philip, Mary, Sarah and Ruth, but also found are such Old Testament *trouvailles* as Ariodh, Aaron and Nahum. Some parents favour the classico-heroic: Julius, Jupiter and Apollo, but most frequent of all are the popular English names of a generation ago – or was it two?: William, Ernest, Albert and George, Constance, Florence, Edith and Lil. Purely tribal names go their own unfamiliar and often unpronounceable way.

Dress. Clothes to a greater or lesser extent are now worn by a majority of the inhabitants. If you can live in Nairobi or Mombasa today and never see one 'native' private part, it is half because Islam is anti-naturist, half because the Christian missions, failing at first to inculcate the Eucharist, worked instead on the more glaring aspects of their congregations' 'ignorance'. Shirts with shorts or trousers, lengthy dresses, *khangas* or skirts with blouses are thus standard garb around civilization everywhere. Shoes are not *de rigueur*; many, like Hemingway, boggle at underwear, and when the women's khanga is worn as a single knee-length wrap, held tight across the buttocks by a bustle of coir and in a rolled tuck across the torso, not only bras but often breasts, too, are conspicuously out. Muslim women and girls cover their heads and their dated Western-style dresses with the black *buibui*, which may mean 'web'.

Europeans, Arabs and Asians dress much as *chez eux*. The Coast Muslims' full white *kanzu* is despised as 'colonial' by some Kenyan house-boys. In Uganda it is worn by married men of any creed. Equally often Swahili men sport a *longhi*-skirt or *kikoi* and ordinary shirt. Their limp embroidered skull-cap is called *kofia*. Amongst better-class men in the towns the 'Kaunda Suit' is popular: a smart, usually collarless, short-sleeved shirt with cotton trousers matching.

Babies everywhere start life tightly swaddled on their mother's back, to bob head-down as she digs the family *shamba*, then, with navel often monstrous, to toddle through infancy naked or at most bare-bottomed in a short, unisex dress.

Despite the missions' influence, many stay unconvinced. Masai men, like their fellows in Karamoja and the Northern Frontier District, may be draped in a toga-like *suka*, but 'so carelessly that they by no means fulfil our ideas of propriety', and spears, knives and bows and arrows are accessories more usual than shorts.

Their womenfolk's skirts, sometimes separately two-piece front and back, will be cloth near the townships; crinkly, odorous goatskin amongst the Turkana and Pokot, or even barkcloth, beaten and stretched from the bark of the *bongi* tree. Elaborate beadwork, high and tight on the throat, as a broad ruff around it, or hanging low from the sagging, pierced ear lobes, completes the ladies' attire. Some African women have their tight curls straightened, or grow them long in a striking, tidy 'Afro', but most keep them cropped short, hide them in a turban of cloth often two yards long, or shave them hygienically off (which does not cause problems of a constantly embryonic crew cut because Negro hair – which Livingstone called 'wool' – grows far more slowly than

Kakindu church murals. African-Asian marriages are no rarity, and African-European increasing. Usually the bride is white, perhaps because of Burton's assertion that Negro husbands are coveted 'for reasons somewhat too physiological for the general reader'.

True communism will, they say, make theft irrelevant, and some tribes' social systems have done as much for permissiveness and incest. Young Masai live not in families but in 'age-sets', adolescents leaving their parents to share a *manyatta*-home until the age of approximately 30 with their circumcision contemporaries and sisters. Other tribes modify the pattern – with an excess of social and sexual variations too diverse, I regret, to mention – but with most pre-marital promiscuity is accepted and normal.

Which may lie – somewhere – behind the pre-War jibe of 'Are you married or do you live in Kenya?'. Now however it does not give you, the tourist of 21, a free hand with the same-aged local ladies. Africans pagan and Christian can be as jealous as Arabs of sisters and daughters, and Asians even more so. One Giriama father recently took the relevant revenge on an over-impulsive German tourist (whom prompt hospitalization failed to re-equip with spare parts). So before you risk making your liaisons a misnomer, be sure your attentions are unmistakably welcome. As happily they often are.

Traditional in buibui
Nubile in the NFD
Sophisticated in Nairobi
Lake Turkana fisherman

PAST

A straight account of the region's past would make the ideal school essay. 'See that it starts with something striking,' my English master would say, 'and give it a good ending, then it doesn't much matter what goes in the middle.'

If no one book does justice to Kenya's prime contribution to man's early history, it is because the Further Recommended Reading of even popular works runs to over 300 titles. Recent times are equally well documented – in relative conciseness by Ingham's *History of East Africa*, Alan Moorehead's *The White Nile* and C.P. Kirby's *East Africa* – but of the intervening vacuum the chapter-headings of the OUP's *History of East Africa* are a good indication: 'The Coast AD 100-1498' and 'Discernible Developments in the Interior c.1500-1840'.

Prehistoric. Man, if the evolutionists are right, descends from the lemurs, primates which now survive on Madagascar mainly (and which Linnaeus gave the Latin name for 'ghosts' because of their large eyes and nocturnal habits). Apes and monkeys, our relatives *not* ancestors, have followed a separate line of descent for many millions of years, and the 'apemen' of popular science also turned off from the human mainstream before the appearance of any true hominid (thus the upright but ape-like PROCONSUL whose 25-million year-old remains Dr Leakey discovered on Rusinga Island). Our historical start in life is marked not by when we stopped crawling and walked, but by our manufacture of tools.

In 1911 one Professor Kattwinkel, a German entomologist, was chasing a butterfly across the Serengeti when he stumbled upon, or rather into, the world's finest palaeontological site. **Olduvai** (the Swahili corruption of the Masai's *Oldupai*) is a clean-cut gorge 300 feet deep, in the stratified sides of which some 2 million years of human evolution are illustratively piled. From Kattwinkel's booty of bones and fossils, and that of a 1913 German expedition, the Berlin Museum realized that at Olduvai the usual archaeological problem of co-relating the chronological evidence of many scattered sites was overcome. The study of the gorge that **Dr Louis Leakey** and his future wife, both British Kenyans, began with an expedition in 1931 appears almost as awesome in its decades of painstaking research as the aeons of history they uncovered. In July 1959 Mrs Leakey found the 400 fragments of the skull of ZINJANTHROPUS BOISEI, now reassembled in the Dar es-Salaam Museum. 'Zinj' – the 'Nutcracker Man' – was found to be an important early 'apeman', and the American National Geographic Society took over financial responsibility for all subsequent excavations. The Leakeys' son Richard then in 1960 discovered the skull and bones of a ten-twelve year-old HOMO HABILIS, 'Handy Man' or, less glibly, 'Man having the ability to manipulate tools'. Though geologically a contemporary of Zinjanthropus, this hominid had a larger brain and a gripping thumb, and the Leakeys saw him, despite some opposition, as Man's true prototype. Since his father's death in 1972, Richard Leakey has made even more significant discoveries in the vicinity of Lake Turkana. Finds by American archaeologists near by, *Newsweek* hastens to add, appear to confirm that the *ab quo* of modern man should be put back to 2·6 million years ago and that 'two or even three manlike creatures coexisted with the original homo for more than a million years'. In any event, East Africa had replaced the Middle East as mankind's most likely cradle.

Besides plentiful other early human relics, animal fossils found throughout East Africa reveal the quondam existence there of sabre-toothed tigers and METASCHIZOTHERIA, huge antelopes with claws for hoofs; short-necked giraffes – SIVATHERIA – with a massive spread of antler; pigs and sheep the size of rhinos and ponies, and the monstrous GORGOPS, a hippo with periscope eyes above the skull.

Indefinitely African. By the fourth millennium before Christ the distant offspring of homo habilis were hunting big game on East Africa's plains, cooking the meat, sewing the skins into clothes, and piercing and chipping the bones for ornaments. If the Garden of Eden was really here, the descendants of its African Adam subsequently boomeranged: the light-skinned races that came to flourish in the Nile Valley and Mesopotamia returned south, as the Hamites and Nilo-Hamites (p. 10), to oust East Africa's aboriginal 'Bushmen'. And a human strain of which nothing is known produced the true black 'West' Africans that spread east as the Bantu (p. 10).

These peoples have no written record of their past. Whatever material culture they had has rotted and vanished, victim of the climate and the tidy, all-destroying termites. Even tombs are absent for – even today – African pagans leave their dear departed out to feed the hyaenas.

Being a Biblical and mediaeval *terra incognita*, East Africa could conveniently be accredited with King Solomon's mines and the Queen of Sheba's kingdom, the Egyptians' fabled Land of Punt and the Book of Kings' Ophir, the unicorn of Deuteronomy and the petrifying basilisk. The only hard fact we have in centuries of fancy is that a Roman empire Greek, living in Egypt and called Diogenes, returned from a voyage of exploration south around AD 110 to write East Africa's first guide-book. In *The Periplus of the Erythraean Sea* ('Erythraean' being any waters east of Suez), Diogenes gives a flimsy description of the coast of 'Azania' (whence 'Tanzania'?), where he landed at Rhapta (perhaps Pangani) and 'travelled inland . . . to . . . two great lakes, and the snowy range of mountains whence the Nile draws its twin sources'. Ptolemy incorporated this in his 'Map of the World' of *circa* AD 150, and there the matter rested for the next 1350 years. Arab geographers refer, vaguely and usually once every century, to their 'Land of Zinj', which means negroid (viz. *Zinj*anthropus and *Zanzi*bar). Only ruins recently studied along the Coast prove the existence of flourishing towns from the 12th century on. As evidence of their African-ness some scholars point to the unique 'phallic' pillars (p. 80), but all else supports the traditional 'colonial' view: that this civilization was of alien inspiration, its architecture and administration from Arabia, its furniture and other creature comforts from India, Persia and even China. (Chinese traders had long been importing African slaves and ivory, with India as entrepôt, when in 1415 Malindi sent the gift of a giraffe to the emperor of China, with an ambassador to feed it, and the emperor in 1417 sent his Muslim eunuch-admiral Cheng Ho, with a fleet of 62 ships and an escort of 37,000 men, to bring the ambassador back.)

Arab and/or Portuguese. While Columbus sailed the ocean blue, Portugal was sending others to circumnavigate Black Africa. Bartholomew Diaz reached the Cape in 1486, and in 1498 **Vasco da Gama** Mombasa and Malindi (p. 79). The 16th-century Portuguese, like the Allies in 1940, were determined to circumvent the obstacle to Far East trade caused then not by the Axis but by the Ottoman Turks. A flanking attack on Islam; exploration; propagation of the Gospel and

Pillar tombs – exclusive to the Coast

a fillip to Portuguese prestige were side attractions, like spices and the gold of Sofala. Da Gama made a second voyage in 1502, sometimes befriending but usually bullying, beating or double-crossing the sultans into paying tribute. The main Portuguese onslaught started when Francisco d'Almeida's African armada set sail with 23 ships and 1500 men in 1505. Sofala (now vanished) was sacked, Kilwa garrisoned and Mombasa taken in hand-to-hand fighting. Malindi alone proved friendly, perhaps because of da Gama's PR groundwork, probably because of the contemporary proverb: 'Any Enemy of Mombasa is a Friend of Malindi'. The northern towns then fell in 1506-7 to Tristan da Cunha.

There follow two centuries of petty colonial politics. The profusion of minor sultanates along the Coast enabled the Portuguese to play one against the other, but it also meant that somebody somewhere was always in open revolt. Ali Bey, a Turkish emir, sailed down the Coast in 1585 and 1589 preaching Holy War amongst the Muslim Swahili. Apart from trusty Malindi, the sultans' loyalties lay with whichever power could get there first with a punitive fleet, the Turks from Arabia or the Portuguese from Goa. After another Portuguese sack of Mombasa in 1589 strange allies arrived in the **Zimba**.

This Bantu horde, cannibal and all-male ('except for such women as were taken along as food'), had eaten its way through Kilwa in 1587 then up to Mombasa, which it offered to 'mop up'. The Portuguese agreed; but when the Zimba then turned on Malindi, it was the neighbourly Segeju, not the Portuguese, that saved the townspeople from serving as cannibal fare – and this in 'one of the decisive battles of African history'.

In 1593 **Fort Jesus** was built in Mombasa as the quite literal stronghold of Portuguese power on the Coast (p. 66). The supposed impregnability of João Batista Cairato's construction, which represented the quintessence of the century's military architecture, was not symptomatic. Already subject to Spain since 1580, Portugal lost ground steadily. Its tiny crews continued to fight, trade and parley but, save in Fort Jesus, its settlements along the Coast were held nowhere as tenaciously as, until recently, Angola or Mozambique.

The monsoon winds that first brought the Arabs took the Portuguese away. To ply between their more lucrative territories of Mozambique and Goa they found that the ideal southerly monsoon made the ports of call further north unnecessary. By the 1740s little remained save the maize, cassava, cashews, tomatoes and tobacco they had brought in from the Americas.

Arab and Individually British. The coastal towns were soon subject to Arabs again. Omani dynasties became entrenched throughout the 18th century, the Bu Saidi, Harithi and Mazrui reflecting in their African rivalries the internecine intrigue at home. It was the Bu Saidi sultan **Sayyid Said** who, by stabbing the ruler and seizing power in 1805, co-operating with Britain in restricting the slave-trade and moving the Omani government to Zanzibar (p. 10), started the odd, often problematical and wholly disproportionate part that Zanzibar played in Britain's 19th-century policies.

Their unholy link was principally **slavery**. Ardent Swahilis insist that Negroes were first enslaved by an early 15th-century Portuguese explorer who took back ten to Prince Henry as proof of how far he had been – a premise sufficiently demolished by the fact that in classical Arabic 'negro' is synonymous with 'slave'. From the Prophet's time onward *nakhudas* – dhow-captains – had made regular deliveries of their fellow men to the shaikhly households of Arabia. With the need for cheap labour to exploit new western colonies,

this small-time barter trade became international big business. Britons like Hawkins helped keep the Americas stocked with West Africans. On the east coast the French settlers' demand for slaves to work their Ile de France outstripped supplies from nearby Madagascar, so American, Dutch and Portuguese shippers joined them in 'tapping' Kilwa and Zanzibar.

It was left to Arabs to produce the goods. At first they simply sold off, as expedition surplus, Nyamwezi porters who had carried down to the Coast their booty of ivory from the interior. The changing market meant that manacles and forked-stick yokes replaced ivory as the Africans' burden. And their numbers multiplied. Some 10 million Africans are altogether thought to have been enslaved. Chiefs were persuaded with beads, cloth and guns to surrender their subjects; and guns, plus the tribes' almost unbelievable torpor, enabled handfuls of traders to force-march caravans of over 500 slaves at a time down to Bagamoyo, Lindi and Kilwa. Stragglers, shot or left to die, were scarcely the usual army afterthought: if only 25% of the caravan reached the Coast it was enough to make a profit.

Zanzibar was then entrepôt for some two thirds. After being paraded naked in the public market and handled by prospective buyers, writes Captain Smee in 1810, 'in the most indecent manner', the happy few would be bought for £4 or £5 and employed locally. The majority were reloaded on to dhows – packed tightly upright or flat between decks only two feet apart – to be freighted in the tropical heat, in utter privation and in their own filth, to Arabia, Persia and the Indies East and West.

News of this reached the West partly through British naval reports. Although the young United States could not yet afford to feel humane, the Revolution – for Liberty, Fraternity and Equality – was recent in France; and Britain, having officially liberated her 15,000 Negro 'servants' in 1772, was moving towards Chartism, Cobden and Queen Victoria. With a massive but remote home chorus of support, a surprisingly small number of Britons negotiated slavery out of existence – usually by personal pressure (plus the Navy's presence) on the sultans of Oman. Though now universally outlawed, slavery was the subject of a special UN convention as recently as 1956.

Slavery, though hideous, was not wholly negative in its effect. The Arab slavers spread Islam (p. 10), introduced coconut-palms, casuarinas and bougainvillea, and planted in their scattered trading stations the mango trees that today shade many a village in the East African interior. Moreover, those slaves that survived, like their descendants, must have found life on the plantation no worse than at home. Black Power has noticeably never preached any Israel-like exodus to Africa.

Most important of all, the anti-slavery movement prompted **exploration**. To 'enlighten darkest Africa' was one of the Victorians' best aims and achievements; but we should not overlook one African view that the Age of Exploration is, in a sense, just the European view through an imperialistic telescope. To Europe the explorers' feats seemed momentous: Lake This was 'discovered', Mount That found and named, but from the African end this was just the *Bourgeois Gentilhomme*'s prose. Their fathers had fished in these waters and farmed those slopes since time immemorial. It is only the West's still unparalleled lead in researching, reporting and publicizing that stultifies any comparison with a Hottentot's 'discovering' Trafalgar Square today.

The name of **David Livingstone** is of course synonymous with African exploration. But apart from his last, personally epic journey, the Scottish doctor's searches for a healthy site for a Christian mission station were made largely outside our area. Only in 1866 did he return to explore for exploration's sake, commissioned by the Royal Geographical Society for £500 (and as first 'HM Consul for Central Africa'), to travel up the Rovuma to Lake Tanganyika and 'perhaps reach the still unknown sources of the Nile'. For seven years he wandered in southern Tanganyika, witnessing countless slave-trade atrocities but often obliged by failing health to accept the slavers' help. In 1871 Stanley found him 'a ruckle of bones' at Ujiji; in 1873, 'knocked up quite', he died at Chitambo's on May Day.

Apart from Arab and Indian explorers, Livingstone's little-known precursors were German. **Ludwig Krapf**, sent by the British Church Missionary Society, reached Zanzibar in 1844 whence, with the help of Sultan Sayyid (p. 18), he moved to Mombasa. His wife and child succumbed rapidly but Krapf went on to convert, translate the Gospels and explore. In 1849 he confirmed the existence of snow on Kilimanjaro which had been reported in 1848 by **Johann Rebmann**, similarly German and CMS, but unfortunately myopic – whence the cold water poured on his discovery by European 'experts'. Their

travels – north to the Tana River, west to Mount Kenya and south to the Usambaras – is too little known and acknowledged. It was the publication of their 'Slug Map' in 1856 that gave European geographers an interest in further penetration as great as the Anti-Slavery Society's. The *Sketch of a Map of a Part of East Africa* showed a single inland sea and, largely to test its existence, **Richard Burton** and **John Hanning Speke** set out from Zanzibar in 1856.

The White Nile sifts best the voluminous diaries, correspondence and contemporary articles that describe – and distort – this *enfant*

Lake Victoria, source of the Nile

terrible of an expedition. Given the two wholly different temperaments – Burton mercurial, brilliant and Speke prosaic, correctly 'Victorian' – the sickness and other ordeals they endured were scarcely needed to ensure a clash. They sailed round Lake Tanganyika together, Speke 'deaf and almost

Coconut plantations

found, acknowledged Stanley's most celebrated byline 'with a kind smile, lifting his cap slightly'.

After a regal reception in London as Livingstone's saviour – and many a private snub as an upstart Yankee hack – Stanley was commissioned jointly by the *New York Herald* and the *Daily Telegraph* to settle the Nile once and for all. Better equipped than any of his predecessors and devoid of Livingstone's scruples, he succeeded in getting his half-mile column complete with the *Lady Alice* from Zanzibar to Lake Victoria in 1874. Riding roughshod over the losses his 356 escorts sustained, Stanley circumnavigated the lake and reached Uganda in April 1875.

Colonial by Force and Default. That they should have won through single-handed, converting, influencing, outwitting or defeating whole peoples in a vast and often hostile land, speaks tremendously for the early explorers. But it says as much for the peoples. There was rarely any cultural tradition to unite and inspire; the slave-trade had depopulated widely and demoralized everywhere, and the region's endemic diseases needed no exaggeration by glory-seeking explorers. Cholera eradicated 10,000 Zanzibaris in 1859; sleeping sickness emptied large areas; smallpox still ravaged Uganda in the 1900s; bilharzia remains unconquered; malaria makes your holiday prophylactic a necessity, and venereal disease still runs rife. In the Great War 3443 British soldiers died in battle, 6558 from disease.

Such are the motives of colonial politics that this major obstacle to exploration diminished in importance when East Africa proved to be exploitable. While Britain, as some say, had been pushed backwards into Uganda, the German empire acquired the Coast more brazenly. An imperialistic con man called Carl Peters persuaded unsuspecting and usually illiterate chiefs to 'sign' Treaties of Friendship. On the strength of these he founded the German East Africa Company and Bismarck declared a protectorate. German gunboats ensured the sultan's approval. Britain then accepted the Agreement of 1886: what today is Tanzania became the German 'sphere of influence', modern Kenya and Uganda British.

The Germans experienced straight away what for Britain came later: loyal to the dispossessed sultan, Bagamoyo, Pangani and Tanga rebelled. Anti-German campaigns were put down in 1889; another, the Maji Maji Revolt, was quashed in 1905 at a cost of

blind and I paralytic', wrote Burton; and though they found no effluent river to prove it Burton insisted, like Livingstone, that the Nile rose here. Speke alone followed Arab reports of a great lake further north. Arriving at Mwanza on 3 August 1858, he saw the 'Victoria Nyanza' and there and then assumed this to be the source of the Nile – a conclusion rash, unproveable and quite correct. Burton, thwarted, led the attacks on Speke in the controversy that followed. Speke's discovery of the Ripon Falls (whence his telegram home: 'The Nile is settled') only slightly stayed the criticisms amidst which he died – by accident or suicide? – in 1864.

Helping repeatedly if inevitably to fill dead men's shoes, the RGS then commissioned Livingstone to complete Speke's work.

The next name on the explorers' Roll of Honour is **Henry Morton Stanley**. Stanley, like Churchill, Americans claim conjointly. Though hailing from Wales, né Rowlands, he worked his passage to New Orleans and took the name of his American adopter. Then, having fought on both sides in the Civil War, he came east again in 1869 as correspondent of the *New York Herald*. His assignment would have delighted, or daunted, today's foreign correspondents: 'Proceed up the Nile. Send us detailed descriptions of everything likely to interest American tourists. Then go to Jerusalem, Constantinople, the Crimea, the Caspian Sea, through Persia as far as India. After that you can start looking round for Livingstone'. The 'looking round' resulted in their historic meeting at Ujiji. Dr Livingstone, who had needed but not asked to be

and sisal estates

Aspects of the colonial inheritance

120,000 African lives. The German government took over: Arab *akidas* were appointed to administer the vast and in fact ungovernable interior. Modern Dar es-Salaam was built as capital; new railways linked Tanga with Moshi in 1912 and Dar with Morogoro in 1907, then with Lake Tanganyika in 1914. Coffee, sisal and rubber estates were started, and clinics and missions established. Defeat in 1918 lost Germany the harvest of this vigorous if ruthless colonial sowing.

Britain showed less haste with her 'sphere of influence'. Only Uganda, it seemed, offered any prospect of profit, and even there only ivory justified the high cost of transport to the Coast. Sir William Mackinnon's **Imperial British East Africa Company** of 1888 pressed for a railway link with Mombasa but the government boggled at the cost. Only when Captain Macdonald had completed the £25,000 railway survey of 1892 – and Whitehall had debated it interminably – was work begun in 1895. Expenditure snowballed: from the £3 million estimated in 1896 to the final total of £7,909,294. Nairobi was reached – and founded – in May 1899, 'Port Florence' – Kisumu – in 1901. Because, however, the protectorate boundaries were adjusted in 1902, the **'Uganda Railway'** still did not reach Uganda. Only in 1931 was it completed to Kampala – to Kasese and Pakwach in 1956 and 1965. Charles Miller's *Lunatic Line* gives the background and the best account, albeit frequently in American journalese, of the hostile game, terrain and tribesmen that the pioneer railwaymen faced and overcame. Relics of the 'Iron Snake', and of much of

East Africa's early network, are admirably displayed in Nairobi's Railway Museum (p. 48).

The railway opened up Kenya to European farmers and settlers (p. 8) who, until the reservation of the exclusive 'White Highlands', mostly took over unoccupied inter-tribal areas. It also became an Allied soft spot when **World War I** broke out. With the German and British East Africas adjacent, confrontation was unavoidable. At sea the German *Königsberg* made the Indian Ocean hazardous for merchantmen; she took 276 rounds to sink HMS *Pegasus* in Zanzibar harbour on 20 September 1914. With the British cruisers *Astrea* and *Hyacinth* threatening, she retreated up the Rufiji River where, blockaded for ten months then bombarded, her crew removed her guns and blew her up. If your pilot is obliging you can extend your Dar-Zanzibar flight slightly south to see her still unsalvaged hulk. The *Schutztruppe* on shore used part of the armament until 1918, and a 'Koenigsberg Gun' has now been mounted at the entrance to Fort Jesus, beside one of the eight that the *Pegasus* fired back.

On Lake Victoria armed tugs and steamers served in a bitty campaign of bombardments and small landing parties. To dominate Lake Tanganyika the British man-handled two gunboats overland from the Cape – an epic trek which inspired *The African Queen* and is described in Shankland's *Phantom Flotilla*.

On land, settler volunteers soon swelled the member-lists of local Rifle Clubs, coalesced into the East African Mounted Rifles and, with African recruits like the Baganda Rifles and their ponies camouflaged as zebras, set off to 'lay Lettow-Vorbeck by the heels'.

General **Paul von Lettow-Vorbeck**, an unjustly little-known German worthy, countered by leading the Allies a brilliant military dance. With British, Belgian and Portuguese territories on each of his borders, he started, Lawrence-like, to harass the Mombasa Railway. A British landing force attacked Tanga on 3-4 November 1914, while a land detachment moved south around Kilimanjaro. Having reconnoitred Tanga by riding his bicycle through the British lines, Lettow-Vorbeck defeated the first force as soundly as the second was then routed at Longido. A third British army surrendered at Jassini. But soon the reinforced Allies were pressing south under Smuts; the Belgians occupied Ruanda, and General Northey was advancing north with his Rhodesia/Nyasaland troops. Lettow-Vorbeck's hit-and-run response has made military history. Living off the land, minting money in the railway workshops, making bandages from bark and medicaments from herbs, he engaged much superior Allied forces in a three-year goosechase through Tanganyika, Mozambique and Northern Rhodesia. The Armistice bell caught him still in the opponent's corner: at Abercorn on 25 November 1918, Lettow-Vorbeck's 155 Europeans, 3408 Africans and 819 women surrendered as heroes. Of the several non-official, more 'journalistic' histories of this 'last of the gentleman's wars', Charles Miller's *Battle for the Bundu* is the most complete and readable.

At the outbreak of **World War II** Tanganyika's 3205 German nationals were quickly interned, but although Nazi groups had formed throughout the country the real enemy was the 'Italian Empire' on the Kenyan border. Settlers in all three states contributed to Britain's war effort by accepting to pay income tax. In Kenya all 'white male British subjects between eighteen and forty-five' were conscripted into the Kenya Defence Force which, with officers from the existing Kenya Regiment of British volunteers and contingents from the King's African Rifles and the South African Brigade, began raids over the Ethiopian frontier on the very day that Italy entered the War. Superior forces soon repelled them, but in January 1941 began the campaign, master-minded by Wavell and commanded by Cunningham, that has been called 'a feat of spontaneous exploitation unsurpassed in war'. Within one month 30,000 Italians had been killed or captured; army engineers were forcing through roads and drilling wells that still serve this desert today; Nigerian troops were advancing 60 miles daily, outpacing supply lines 1000 miles long. In five months the Allies occupied one million square miles of enemy territory, captured 250,000 better-trained and better-armed opponents, and ended Italy's African empire. Twelve thousand East African troops helped seize 'Vichy' Madagascar in 1942, and Negro contingents fought not only on Burma's 'Jambo Hill'. Their headstones far outnumber those of their 428 British comrades in the Commonwealth War Graves Commission's 82 East African cemeteries.

Independent. Between the Wars Kenya became the white settlers' virtual fief, admirably farmed but bigotedly administered (and in 1920 officially designated the 'Kenya Colony and Protectorate'). Receiving little support and even less finance from Whitehall, the Convention of Associations – the 'Settlers' Parliament' – pressed for Ian Smith-style self-government (p. 116). Africans and Asians grew predictably resentful. Symptomatic in the grievances it voiced was first Harry Thuku's Young Kikuyu Association, then the Kikuyu Central Association, with **Jomo Kenyatta** its secretary. Having spent the War in Britain lecturing for the Workers Educational Association, the *Mzee* returned in 1946 to become president of the soon-proscribed Kenya African Union. Constitutional talks and changes continued, but Kikuyu tempers were not stayed by negotiation. The horrors of the eight-year 'Emergency' are well known; the Mau Mau Oaths, in their sexual, faecal and bestial extremes, nauseate the least squeamish; but the fact that Mau Mau victims totalled 11,500 fellow Africans to some 30 Europeans is wrongly ignored. Though still in detention, Kenyatta was elected president of the **Kenya African National Union** in 1960, and he and that party took Kenya through its first polls to independence.

From that first Uhuru Day – 12 December 1963 – until his death on 22 August 1978 Kenyatta led his country unchallenged and well. In the eyes of his people *Mzee* – the Old Man, in official publications *Taa ya Kenya* – Light of Kenya, he first proscribed the Kenyan African Democratic Union, preached reconciliation to the white population, practised tolerance towards the Asian community (the source of much support in his anti-British struggle) and so welded three races and threescore tribes into a single successful nation.

PRACTICAL

Customs. Though your usually long wait for the airport Customs may make you wonder where the jet age stopped off, you will find them welcoming at Nairobi and Mombasa. Your accompanied personal effects for an up to six-month stay, your tape recorder, binoculars, cameras and film, one litre of alcohol, a ¼-litre of perfume and 50 cigars, 200 cigarettes or 250 grammes of tobacco do not bother them. They may raise queries, but are easily placated, over obviously new electrical appliances, but blatant **gifts** they charge duty for and obscene literature they retain for closer inspection. **Animals** are allowed in with a recent health certificate . . . into the country, that is, not into the national parks or, since the Swahili are Muslim, into many coastal restaurants. Back home, the British/US Customs show an interest only if the value of your booty exceeds the permitted £28/$100.

Postal parcels you receive in Kenya only by reporting – and usually paying duty and sales tax – to the post office Customs (who need confronting firmly on even used clothes). **Cars** for temporary importation come in duty free for as long as their carnet or triptyque is valid (but no longer than two years). Permanent importation entails duty based on the vehicle's age (which is why smart safari men fit the latest, best-equipped bodies to a small outmoded chassis).

Visas and Visitor's Passes. Tourism is, after coffee, Kenya's most lucrative industry; it brings in annually and approximately £74/$178 million. Entry requirements are understandably few. Only certain fellow Africans can arrive without a passport. Like Danes, Norwegians, Swedes and West Germans, all British and Commonwealth citizens (except of Asian origin) receive on arrival a free three-month visitor's pass. US citizens and other officialese 'visa-prone' persons pay for their passes: $3·15 plus postage to a Kenya Tourist Office (p. 8) or the nearest British consular office or Kenyan High Commission/Embassy (45 Portland Place, London W1N 4AS; 2249 R Street NW, Washington DC 20008; Kungstiolmstorg, 611221 Stockholm; E-27 Defence Colony, New Delhi).

Currency. East Africa's first postage stamps were printed, or rather typed, by Uganda missionaries with their value as five or ten cowrie shells. As the rate of exchange of this rather cumbersome currency was 100 shells to one blue bead, tax-collectors found their work literally too heavy: in 1901 Indian rupees, in 1906 'East African Protectorate and Uganda' cents were substituted. This metal issue was replaced in 1921 by the notes and coins of the East African shilling; Kenya's first independent emission came in 1966; in 1969 the common East African currency was ousted by each state's separate shilling and in 1972 withdrawn as legal tender.

The **Kenya shilling** (Ksh.) breaks down into 100 **cents**, has picturesque notes in denominations of 5, 10, 20 and 100 and, being 'tied' to the dollar, retains a give-or-take value of thirteen US cents. The Mother Country may go decimal, but shillings remain 'bobs' and ten-cent pieces 'coppers' for East Africans black and white. I obviously cannot disclose that taxi-drivers and hotel touts tend to overlook our currency decline and offer you twenty shillings to the pound sterling and nine or ten to the dollar. To hamper such 'illegal' transactions, the authorities now require you on arrival to complete in duplicate a declaration of all monies held. As you may be the subject of a spot check on departure, you should ensure that what you have left adds up, with your receipts for money changed, to what you originally declared. You may not re-export shillings (and should not have brought any in) and reconverting those you have left is permitted only upon production of your exchange receipts.

Health. You should arrive certified for yellow fever, smallpox and cholera. Also required, though not mandatory, is an adequate constitution. Few travel agents are brave enough to tell you that even mini-safaris can be tough. The thrill of seeing wildlife so close makes even a bumpy, dusty 'game run' unforgettable, but too many senior citizens, often with heart conditions, reach their night-stop exhausted and far from help. Excellent as the 'Flying Doctors' are, summoning their services can mean a costly set-back (unless you take out temporary membership which, for one month and Ksh. 15/-, guarantees you free air transport from anywhere in East Africa to a suitable medical centre; Nairobi POB. 30125, tel. 501301).

Though doctors may not agree on the region's most widespread disease, they have no doubt about the second: 'Venereal disease is completely out of control in developing countries', according to a recent International Health Congress. One especially virulent breed makes

Malindi hazardous for some and, untreated VD being illegal, the authorities here and elsewhere occasionally order likely suspects to be clinically checked – and fine those found infected. City pharmacists are sophisticated in their stock of penicillin, prophylactics, contraceptives and the Pill.

Widespread dysentery makes raw vegetables undesirable. Otherwise visiting tummies run far less risk here of open-ended upsets than in the Middle East, say, or Spain.

At the Coast show the tropical sun due respect (p. 8). Here more than anywhere a malaria prophylactic is required. The likes of Paludrine and Nivaquin are cheap in Kenya, but the dosage prescribed on the packet is best commenced ten days before you travel and continued similarly after your departure.

The tsetse – in its 21, or 22, or 26 African species – is both a curse and a blessing. All can carry the 'Rhodesian' or 'Gambian' sleeping sickness (*Trypanosomiasis*) that kills men and domestic cattle alike. But by thus deterring human settlement – 60% of Tanzania is affected – they have left vast areas free for wildlife to flourish. With most free of disease, the cross-tailed tsetse-flies that become so attached to you in many national parks are no danger. Their Latin name is GLOSSINA SPP., but squash them just the same.

Bilharzia infects most African lakes and rivers – resist the temptation to strip off and swim. Despite the hope that Ethiopian endod-plants hold out, no immunization yet exists for bilharzia, carried by water snails and causing years of lethargy and internal decay. Ancient Egyptians, now mummified, died of it; acquaintances of mine have caught it from a few seconds' paddle; Ambilhar cures but does not stop reoccurence.

All of which is more bark than bite. Kenya has a fine public health tradition and a generally benign climate, so that you are unlikely to need the good doctors and well-equipped hospitals, government and private, that serve every centre.

Insomnia and East Africa are, however, literally bad bedfellows. In park lodges and camps the animal chorus of shrieks, roars and grunts is a nightly, non-optional extra. Many lodges have generators, often diesel, which vary in resonance from a subdued roar to a steady vibrato, and air-conditioning in Coast hotels can likewise crescendo from an all-night hum to a battery of units that in one Mombasa establishment measured 80 decibels. After which the staff – in Hilton or youth hostel – can be noisy early.

Souvenirs and Spending. Besides the photographic mementos, East Africa offers several colourful and still off-beat souvenirs. But as the beaten track of tourism reaches out to more and more tribes, the problem of misguided charity becomes increasingly acute. Every old Turkana will be pleased, if puzzled, that you should want his head-rest or ivory lip-plug, but anything more than a reasonable few shillings may make him wonder whether pestering tourists may not be more lucrative than much-needed work on the land. The best souvenir sources – for both your pocket and your conscience – seem to me to be the centres run by governments and charities: the National Christian Council of Kenya's 'Cottage Crafts' in Standard Street, Nairobi, and 'Tototo' Home Industries Centre in Msanifu Kombo Road, Mombasa, the 'Prison Industries' shops wherever there are prisons, and local bodies from the Lorgum St Joseph's Fathers to Mazeras and Bombolulu Gardens (p. 74) – all selling cheap and genuine local work.

Amongst the Nilotes **beads and shells** have traditionally been a much-coveted form of currency (p. 23). And/or sexual symbols (p.109). Early explorers came loaded with cowries and 'Rosetta' or 'Trade Wind' beads as *hongo*-tribute to pay their way. Nowadays beadwork and shells strung as necklaces, albeit colourful and intricate, often look as cheap as they are. Selling sea-shells by the sea-shore, or even collecting them, is forbidden in Kenya's marine parks and frowned upon elsewhere, so Nairobi boutiques now tend to have less – and ask more. Conservationist legislation prevents your emulating the Mzee with his famous elephant-hair fly-whisk, and explains why that matter has been replaced by plastic in the luck-bringing talismans worn round many wrists and touted on every street corner. When plumes went out with Marie Lloyd, the ostrich was saved: its feathers you now see in tribal regalia and, cheaply, in souvenir shops (where, in spite of a ban on their sale too, there is no lack of ostrich eggs either).

Stone-carving is pretty in Kisii soapstone, the flesh-pink or black steatite. Less of an excess weight problem are pipes of Arusha **meerschaum**, sturdier than Turkey's.

In war the Masai never throw or let go of their **spears** (their motto warns 'Do not arm your enemy'), but they hand them over promptly if your price is right. **Shields** too are for sale. African **instruments** are displayed by the museums or jealously kept by their maestros. **Drums**, however, are mass-produced souvenirs. Akamba and Zaramo craftsmen can turn out ten a day,

Bananas, abundant up country

No lack of Akamba wood-carvings

diving have in recent years been so extensively developed that almost all Coast hotels now have, or share, an instructor and equipment . . . and Tanzania has had to ban spear-guns.

Riding is no longer confined to up country – where hotels near Nairobi hire for hacking, and companies like Safaris Unlimited (Ltd) have horses available for half-days on the Ngongs or sterner nine-day 'saddle safaris' to the Mara (Nairobi POB. 20138, tel. 332132). The climate at the Coast precludes anything so strenuous, but shorter rides can be enjoyed at Nyali (tel. Bamburi 268) and at Malindi (p. 83). If you are in the habit of riding to hounds, a cap for the day costs only $2 with the Limuru Hunt which, every Sunday from April to November, holds drags for fields of up to forty. Gymkhanas and **race meetings** – both horse and motor – are frequent in Kenya (see the press and p. 52).

Those keen on **climbing** here usually set their sights highest, on Kilimanjaro (little more than a long scramble to Uhuru Peak/Kibo, more testing to Mawenzi) and Mount Kenya (for experts only, except for the 'Tourist Peak' of Point Lenana, p.106). The Mountain Club of Kenya's *Guide-Book to Mount Kenya and Kilimanjaro* covers its subject adequately, while Robson's *Mountains of Kenya* – and the MCK (POB. 45741, tel. 501747) – can advise on expeditions to 97 other 'recommended peaks'.

If spectator sports are more your forte, watching African **football** gives the game a new perspective (and see p.11). **Athletes** maintain the Kipchoge Keino tradition at frequent meetings in the big-city stadiums. **Boxing** is popular (guests v. staff in some hotels), not only Sikhs play **cricket**, and charity walks and 'nature trails' are attended commendably well.

Entertainment. Evenings out are confined to the towns. 'After a day's game viewing on these tracks, all people want is food, drink and sleep,' every lodge manager explains. Most of Nairobi's **cinemas** have Leicester Square standards with fair suburban prices; Mombasa's tend to be cheaper in every sense. Films are either one step behind London or standard Indian song-and-dance romance.

The principal cities have their share of visiting **concert** virtuosos, announced in the press and hotel lobbies, and often sponsored by the British Council or the Goethe Institute. The Donovan Maule Theatre Club is a permanent attraction in Nairobi (p. 44), the Kenya National Theatre there houses regular repertory companies, and Mombasa's Little Theatre maintains an Arsenic and Old Lace tradition.

Some city hotels have resident bands; though African instrumentalists have adapted well to electric guitars, lamé jackets and the Top Twenty, not many of their numbers end without a bum note. De luxe hotels have built-in **night-clubs**, and in Nairobi and Mombasa one or two independents flourish respectably. The mood is usually uninhibited African; lights and prices are low, and anything Olde Tyme or even loosely Ballroom they leave to the Country Clubs.

Congolese groups, tunes and dances are favourite; Africans dancing are fish in water, and to hold your own you should know how to manage the Sex Machine (and similar numbers). Most villages' 'High Life' or 'Day & Night' clubs are just bars with juke boxes. And bar often means brothel.

Wholesome **tribal dancing** is a popular tourist attraction. Apart from the Bahimas', who dance sitting down, most are of a kind to give youths sleepless nights or wild dreams. Flutes, plumed lyres, rattles, 'thumb pianos' and xylophones are used – the Dar, Nairobi and Uganda museums have good displays – but most numbers are vocal with drum accompaniment. Or rather *vice versa*. *Ngoma* in fact, which merely means 'drum', is the generic term for any 'musical' occasion. Though the rhythm is always evocative and most of the dances' symbolism obvious, Westerners may, when listening for the melody, suspect that the needle is stuck. Tribal costumes, when worn, are photogenic (with soap-packet shin-guards and oil-can spurs somewhat odder accessories). Sunglasses, James Bond belts and running shorts are equally *à la mode*, and dancers who mark time with a whistle may make the performance nostalgic for football fans. Well represented by the Harambee Dancers (and best seen at the Bomas of Kenya, p. 52), Kenyan performances are vigorous and varied: the Kikuyu impress with their flair; the Akamba, Meru, Embu and Chuka are known for their drumming, and the Masai astonish with Freudian leaps.

Food. Most hotels and restaurants disprove the half-witticism that British cuisine is a contradiction in terms. The quality, quantity and cost of what you eat is a pleasant surprise – and one of East Africa's less publicized attractions. Though well-provisioned Indian, Chinese, Italian, French and even Japanese chefs excel, with Wimpys, fish-and-chip shops, 'Kentucky Frieds' and pubs around too, it is the hearty but *bon viveur* settler tradition that still sets the gastronomic tone.

If your hotel does not start the day with a self-service sideboard of fruit juice, cereals and fruit – papaws, bananas, pineapples or prunes – it will be because the waiter brings them. Fish or eggs with fried etc. follow; thereafter toast, marmalade and coffee. Kenya's is in fact a full-blown British breakfast. Lunch in the lodges is often a succulent buffet; even in cheaper hotels it will run to three courses, with meat and two veg. There is British standard Afternoon Tea (Early Morning Tea too).

Dinner menus often read like the near-best in London, Paris, Delhi or Rome, but all combined, and cheaper than each. *Tilapia* seems to be ubiquitous: mostly frozen or smoked from Lake Victoria, this bream-like delicacy provides half of Uganda's and Tanzania's catch. Trout in many a mountain stream is as good for the gourmet as for the angler (p. 26). The Coast hotels' sea-fare is predictably delicious. Amongst the full range of familiar meats, Kenya's Molo lamb is outstanding – and, like Aylesbury duckling, now often from anywhere but. The bread in many distant lodges is crisp and delicious home-baked, *kitumbua* a tasty round of fried-rice bread, less well known than its compatriot popadom and chipatee. Though *samosas* are also originally Indian, these oily patties filled with nondescript meat-matter are now sold in every local café and eaten eagerly by African workmen. In Mombasa and Kisumu especially, the backstreet Asian cafés offer some unusual gastronomic oddities: the sweet *farshans* – *mesub, mithai*, nutmeg *barfi, halwa* and *jalebi* (the Arab *zalabia*); the non-sweet (read pepper-red hot) *bhajia, chevra, gathia* and *chana-dall*; Bombay chowder, tasty to take away, and all the fiery varieties of *pan*, washed down viz. extinguished with *maziwa lala* – whey – or passion-fruit juice.

Desserts and cheeses are mostly familiar, and the cakes blessedly more pastry than *pâtisserie*. **Fruit**, however, is exotic and excellent. If Cape gooseberries and tree tomatoes are staider oddities, papaws, passion-fruit and pineapples are tropically luscious. And if eating peaches in public prompts letters to *The Times*, mangoes deserve a Special Supplement. Most hotels serve them tamed, as neat cubes on the inside-out skin, Lamu's are reckoned to be best and in Mombasa a score sell for ten shillings, rightly underripe and packed ready to take home.

Bananas, too, are unbelievably cheap. Introduced from south-east Asia, they are now Uganda's staple diet, and eaten *passim*. The gangly plant with its weird-obscene flower and massive leaves (which they use to wrap food in or as umbrellas) dominates almost every shamba. The taste is familiar with the yellow and red fruit, the smaller the sweeter, but the green banana they boil or steam then mash into *matoke*.

African cooking is scarcely epicurean. Beside bananas and *ugali*, maize/sweetcorn is staple. *Posho* is made from it and used almost everywhere, often with fruit or meat to flavour. Maize is ground into meal and flour; as corn-on-the-cob it is often boiled old, and sold still in the husk to keep in the heat and the tastelessness. Millet, sorghum, beans, yams and cassava roots byways. And two thirds of the cars, entered by works or private enthusiasts, all expertly raced and maintained, drop out. If you do disregard this initial deterrent to independent driving you find yourself between the Scylla and Charybdis of chauffeur or self-drive. **Hire charges** are usually calculated per kilometre: a test-run first along a road with distance-signs will help you spot dishonest milometers. While these were true in vehicles hired from the United Touring Company, certain other firms had made such lucrative 'adjustments' that, by the distance clocked up in the hiring time, I must have been sightseeing round Nairobi at some 50 mph.

UTC *qua* Hertz have the biggest and probably best selection (Muindi Mbingu Street, Nairobi POB. 42196, tel. 331960; Moi Avenue, Mombasa POB. 84782, tel. 20741; Malindi POB. 365, tel. 40; at Nairobi and Mombasa international airports and the Norfolk, Mombasa Beach, Nyali Beach, Serena Beach and Tradewinds hotels). Wherever hiring, make a check and a test-drive before leaving: spanners/wrenches and jacks tend to vanish, and punctures to occur miles from anywhere by night. And before hiring, ensure that your travel plans might not be better met by one or more of the minibus safaris organized by every travel agent. The driving that writing this book entailed cost £3000/$7000 in cheapest hire charges.

In some courts, they say, the accused are guilty till proved innocent and, in my experience, car dealers crooks till proved honest. It is advisable to supervise everything done to your car, not least at filling stations. (The petroleum companies confess defeat in their running war with the petrol-pump 'fixers'.) Driving conditions encourage break-downs; as at home, the best cheap quick work is done by backstreet mechanics, here mostly Sikh and Goan *fundis*.

Driving in sand, mud and notorious 'black cotton' is a question of speed- and wheel-control, which bitter experience teaches quickly. The essential is to maintain momentum, in second or third gear best. Kenya's tracks, to a dreadful extent, consist of corrugated 'washboarding': tight, solid waves of packed sand and mud. The accepted theory that these are caused by wind, rain or pounding lorries would be credible if only they did not exist in Arabia's Empty Quarter, windless, waterless and where never a car tyre has passed. You must force yourself over them

Traffic jam in Lamu

Outside catering on the Mombasa Railway

fast: surprisingly they tend to level out at 30-40 mph from a juddering, nerve-searing thunder to a steadier, less vibrant rumble. Surprisingly, too, most cars stand up to them longer than their drivers. Driving, wherever conditions permit, is on the left; road signs and number plates look similarly British. Insurance is compulsory. Your home licence is accepted for up to 90 days; speed limits are 30 mph/50 kph in towns and, on the open road, 60 mph/100 kph.

In local Letters to the Editor Kenyans ask themselves: 'Where are our road manners?'. Though the 'roads' may explain if not excuse the manners, Africans make immaculate pedestrians, always standing aside and waiting at the first distant strains of your horn. For up-to-date news on particular routes contact the **Automobile Association of Kenya** (Nairobi POB. 40087, tel. 742926-9; Mombasa POB. 86250, tel. 26778; Nakuru POB. 7307, tel. 2314; Kisumu POB. 1831, tel. 41361; Eldoret POB. 494, tel. 2700). Its information is often accurate, and on a board in the Westlands headquarters the state of most main thoroughfares is chalked in day by day.

With so many deterrents to self-drive, it is all in all best to suppress the inner pioneer. Nairobi has some 190 **safari tour operators**, Mombasa rather less but still plenty. All advertise enthusiastically in local hotels and newspapers; most use comfortable VW minibuses or four-wheel-drive vehicles like Land-Rovers; few employ couriers *per se* (though these the home 'package' operators sometimes provide) but all have English-speaking drivers – usually unpunctual but too charming to chide.

In a raid to demolish the key Tsavo Bridge, German commandoes in 1914 used British **maps**, thereby missing the bridge completely, running out of supplies and having to surrender. Today East Africa's vast network of tracks is better charted, but unpredictable conditions make the oil companies' 'Road Maps' unreliable (p. 4). More sparing in their use of 'All Weather Road' red, and otherwise more authoritative, are the official maps put out by the Land Survey offices (Survey of Kenya, Harambee Avenue, Nairobi, and obtainable from the Visitors' Information Bureau, p. 41).

Photography. Whether you hire drivers and guides or take pot-luck in a national park, Africa is a photographer's dream. With abundant animals and colourful birds, picturesque peoples, magnificent scenery and regular sunshine, it is hard to come home without something to show the folks. Professional standards are high. On the other hand do not look down on your Instamatic: game on occasions can be so close to your car that these idiot-proof automatics are as good as expensive telephotos (which at that range give you all of an elephant's toe or a lion's eye). Zooms are useful, however, and telephoto lens essential for birds and shier mammals – susceptible Africans too. *National Geographic* photographers use fixed 300 mm, lesser men usually 200 mm; many-sectioned lens of 500 mm plus tend to work loose on East Africa's tracks.

If you meter, through the lens or manually, remember to expose for not the terrain but the animal itself (often much the colour of your neighbour's safari suit). Negroes, usually sitting inconsiderately in the shade, also need one stop extra exposure. A UV filter is necessary everywhere, and a lens hood helps reduce glare which, from silver-sand beaches, dried-grass plains, volcanic dust and white safari-car roofs, is a regular hazard.

If not already equipped – ideally with two 35 mm cameras plus one 50 mm and one 200 mm lens – and if coming home to the Customs does not daunt you, remember that cameras are cheap in Nairobi. The **Expo Camera Centre** (POB. 44402, tel. 21797, 336921) has a good selection for sale or hire; the cine specialists are the **Pioneer Audio-Visual Centre**, also in Mama Ngina Street (POB. 46513, tel. 26846); they and the **Sapra Studio** in Kaunda Street (POB. 45882, tel. 24165) can arrange repair of most makes too, while the Ebrahim Camera House is lower in price. And principle.

Film costs more than in Europe, and photogenic tribesmen wise to Western tourists demand from one shilling to 50 for posing. On the 'road' you should stop in advance to shoot them: once passed they have disappeared in your cloud of dust. Experts recommend a polythene bag to protect your camera from this, but extricating the thing just as the rhino charges I found fiddly, and prefer a loose towel or cloth over the cameras. Photographing the national flag, the president, state lodges, soldiers, prisons or convicts costs you a fine or time inside.

If you have expensive equipment you also have a problem. Though most Westerners are in no position to criticise other countries' crime rates, the armed guards and alsatians outside every bank, large business or classier residence, and a prospering Securicor are facts that speak for themselves. Every hotel warns against valuables left in your room, but even money entrusted to the management I have had stolen, and cameras found the night-staff playing with to wile away the small hours. You may leave your camera in an unlocked car, but the locals won't.

WILDLIFE

The sight of so many wild animals at large is the highlight of most East African holidays. To expatiate is pointless: the visitor can no more be oblivious to the wonderful flora and fauna here than to snow in the Alps or sunshine in Spain. The briefest game run gives new significance to the *Human Zoo*: rhinos and elephants may charge you off, giraffe, zebra and buffalo raise their heads to stare, others ignore you – for they are at home and you the intruders, caged in your car.

Once the initial excitement is over, most of us to feel a strange, atavistic sensation that the world is righter, more 'natural', this way. Stay long enough to take that for granted and home, when you get there, will seem distressingly bare. Then, perhaps for the first time, you may well stop to wonder what happened – and why – to the big game of Europe and North America.

That danger faces East Africa too. The railwaymen in 1900 found game in Serengeti-profusion where Nairobi's Industrial Area now spreads; 50 years have brought animals like the Cape Lion from abundance to extinction. Understandable if unforgiveable motives explain this wholesale slaughter: fashion makes skins and tusks big business; fancy – that it acts as aphrodisiac – maintains the sale of rhinoceros horn. Perhaps better motivated in his war on game is the farmer whose crops it tramples and eats, or the rancher whose herds it infects with rinderpest, ticks and East Coast Fever. Large, well-armed poaching parties are the greatest immediate threat (p. 95; Kenya's elephant and rhinoceros populations reduced in a decade by 70% and 90% respectively). An indirect but increasingly insidious menace are the charcoal-burners who cut trees for fuel and thereby destroy many species' natural habitat. But the ultimate verdict on wildlife survival lies with the common man. Larger populations mean pressure on land; many tribes – like the Masai in the Mara – are beginning to resent that pastoral or farm country be set aside for game; politicians are publicly denouncing the stress on conservation and, in local wildlife/farmland conflicts, the latter usually wins. The question posed by all concerned is whether Kenya's people can succeed in making these pressures compatible.

President Nyerere's 1961 *Arusha Manifesto* is a frequent sermon text of those who preach conservation: 'The survival of our wildlife is . . . not only important as a source of wonder and

33

inspiration but an integral part of our natural resources and of our future livelihood and well being . . . We look to other nations to co-operate'. Your contribution comes in national park gate fees and membership of the **East African Wildlife Society** (POB. 20110, Nairobi). This admirable organization was founded in 1961; its gift shop and art gallery are well worth a visit in the Nairobi Hilton; its Review appears under the aegis of *Swara*, a well-produced quarterly report on the region's wildlife scene, and its conservationist activities range from financing anti-poaching units and educational projects to helping feed hungry hippopotami.

Already in 1894 Sir Harry Johnston foresaw the need for **national parks**. Kenya now has 34, including **game reserves** (the USA, incidentally, 35 and Britain ten). Here wildlife is sovereign: human habitation is forbidden or minimized; no organism – not even your dog – may be introduced or removed; on the vehicle tracks not only the elephants have right of way, and regulations are strict. You may not exceed the respective speed limit – 20 mph/30 kph or 30 mph/50 kph – and will miss most of the best sights at much over ten; you may not drive by night, use your hooter, light fires or leave litter; you may not disobey the generally excellent and easily recognized rangers and you may not, save in certain rare instances, leave your car. Inside it your human odour is masked by petrol fumes, which the animals ignore. With a companion on look-out you can safely change a tyre, but if your break-down is major, *wait*, do not walk (which makes some food-and-drink forethought wise if you travel remotely or in one car only). In marine national parks and forest reserves the underwater and arboreal contents are respectively sacrosanct.

For **preliminary reading** and on-the-spot identification animal books are as two-a-penny here as recipes in France. Good maps of most Kenyan parks have appeared – and repeatedly increased in price – and Collins' *Field Guides*, with one a summary of the *National Parks of East Africa*, are good for the ardent amateur. The Shell *Wildlife Guides* are attractive introductions. Coffee-table Africana is catching on, but mostly too fancy for your safari, and – *The Mystery of the Flamingos*, *The Book of the Giraffe*, *The Year of the Gorilla* – many species are the hero of some separate publication.

Most guide-books' 'Wildlife Notes' are limited to academic details like the species' Latin name or its 'height at the shoulder' which, with individuals varying considerably, is as hard and fast a figure as a German's girth. Some areas are known for certain species, others move with the rains and the grazing. Rather than give each animal's putative habitats, of little help to holiday-makers, I mention those parks where I found them most consistently in evidence. Swahili names are *italicized*, SMALL CAPITALS are Latin.

Remember: however endearingly close they may come, these beasts are wild. Any liberty you take could be your last.

Of the hunter's 'Big Five', **elephants** are biggest. Just how big is brought home to you as you round a bend and find one in your track. You will not need telling to stop. Most browse on oblivious or trundle enormously off, in which case drive past slowly. If they trumpet at you or flap ears, reverse: having thus asserted their lordship of the jungle and made you defer, they should then give way. Called locally *tembo* (which also means beer), the East African bush elephant is a three-six-ton vegetarian, is born after 21 months' gestation, stays close to mother till twenty years old, dies at an average 60 and has neither 'elephant cemeteries' nor a phenomenal memory. Clustering protectively round their Dumbos, taking a trunk-shower at water-holes or scratching their rump on tree stumps, elephants are endearing monstrosities. Chipperfields will catch you one for a price. Read the Douglas-Hamiltons' *Among the Elephants* or Daphne Sheldrick's prize-winning *Orphans of Tsavo* – in English, French or German – for further details.

The **lion** – *simba* – is more ferocious in Hollywood than Africa. The 'prides' you see in the Serengeti, Ngorongoro or Nairobi National Park are less likely to be roaring than yawning or belching after their twice-weekly meal. Deadlier than the male, the maneless lioness stalks and leaps on to zebra, buffalo and antelope, to break the neck or suffocate. Tourists tell fishermen's tales of the 'kills' they have seen. Despite Tarzan tradition, lions climb trees at Lake Manyara, Ishasha and Semliki. They have on average a weight of 400 pounds, a gestation period of four months, a life-span of twenty years and a 'territory' of some 100 square miles. Joy Adamson's books are the by-word.

Another unlikely vegetarian, the **rhinoceros** – *faru* – seems to win many visitors' (long-range) affection, being absent-minded, unsociable, short-sighted and thick-skinned – all qualities which never won me any kudos. The poor sight supposedly explains their irascible ever-readiness to charge. The much-publicized probability that (a) they will forget you en route and stop to graze or (b) not see you and charge right past, are of little comfort when you see two armour-plated tons coming at 30 mph. Black rhinos have been so poached that the total of 2000 reckoned left alive in Kenya is tellingly described as 'less than one year's supply of horns to North Yemen'. White rhinos, just back from the brink of extinction and second in land-mammal size to the elephant, are easily seen, under guard, in Meru National Park. They are not white but have a wide – Dutch *wijd* – and hippo-like square jaw. And the rhino's two horns are not horn but close-packed hair – overrated, I am told, as an aphrodisiac.

Buffalo – *nyati* – are sharper dangers. The African or Black buffalo grazes everywhere in docile and cattle-like herds, or looks up and stares as you disturb his mud-bath wallow. But even a walk on Ol Donyo Sabuk or along the Ngongs requires caution: with keen scent, sight and hearing, a lone buffalo at bay attacks cunningly and lethally, charging not head-down blindly like the rhino

Tree-climbing lioness

Wallowing hippos

but with eyes fixed radar-firm on his target. Then a sidelong sweep of his butcher's-hook horns and . . . buffalo account for more hunters than any other game. On average one poacher dies for every five buffalo caught. Old bulls – often rejected by the herd – can weigh up to a ton.

Last of the Big Five is *chui*, the **leopard**. As they leave their lair in thick bush or rocks only singly and warily by night, sighting leopards is a challenge (except at Lobo, where they sometimes dine at the lodge, and Secret Valley, where they feed floodlit on platforms). Their favourite food is baboon but, immensely strong for their 100 plus pounds, they can drag dead gazelles (and goats) into trees, where they like to eat them not only several feet but also three or four days 'high'.

The **cheetah** – *duma* or Hunting leopard – is distinguished by longer legs, smaller head and marked 'tear drops'. It hunts by day but elusively and fast – 60 mph in reliable time-trials. The fact that they cannot retract their claws may explain why the world's 750 surviving cheetahs are sought after, elitely, as pets.

A more sizeable outsider is the **hippopotamus**. In Swahili *kiboko*, in Greek 'horse of the river' (but really of the even-toed pig family), hippos can wander up to ten miles for the nightly 90 pounds of grass they need to sustain their two tons. Though often submerged to the snout by day, they grazed diurnally along the Kazinga Channel . . . until the arrival of the Tanzanian army. With huge tusks and jaws, these stumpy-legged, pink-grey leviathans can outrun a man and kill lions and crocodiles. Hippos give birth on land, suckle underwater and live some 30 years. Around Lake Victoria they often munch into suburbs at night; at some lodges you will hear them at your window; from Mzima Springs' underwater tank you can observe them eyeball-to-eyeball, and how they got into Ngorongoro Crater no one knows.

Related to the hippo – by the zoologists' curious expedient of counting toes – is the **giraffe**, *twiga*. The frequently seen groups of two or three will often interrupt their acacia-tree feed to stare back at you; their flowing, slow-motion, ground-stroking gait you will never forget. Though mild-natured and almost voiceless, they have when frightened a pile-driving kick. Of the Common giraffes, the Masai – GIRAFFA CAMELOPARDALIS TIPPELSKIRCHI – you see south of the Athi River in Kenya, and in Tanzania; and the Rothschild's far less often – only 150, the *Daily Nation* says, now survive in Kenya. The former has two or three vestigial horns, the latter three or five, and in Olduvai Museum are illustrations of the SIVATHERIUM ancestor whence these remnant antlers derive (p. 16). The smaller Reticulated giraffe, merely fifteen-seventeen feet high, lives north of Kenya's Tana River – try the Samburu/Isiolo reserves. Its neck-network of white lines distinguishes. Between the Tana and Athi rivers the two races, and their markings, mix to confuse the observer. Spinage's *Book of the Giraffe* might help.

The rhino's equally unlikely, 'odd-toed ungulate' relative is the **zebra**, *punda milia*. Presumably designed to blend with the natural chiaroscuro, these plump and conspicuous oddities are everywhere. Commonplace, except in Uganda, is Burchell's zebra; Grevy's, distinctive with its bat ears and closer stripes, you may well see at Samburu/Isiolo or the Mount Kenya Safari Club park. Both types graze in family groups of twelve or so alongside giraffe and antelope but, the only BOVIDAE with sharp incisors, they eat the toughest grasses and, overfed and overweight, sometimes suffer coronaries when lions close in.

While nobody bothers about the Burchell's two races – Grant's strikingly black and white and Boehm's with greyish shadow-stripes – **gazelles** head your wildlife catechism. What stands 32-35 inches at the shoulder and has buttocks white above a black-tipped tail? Answer Grant's gazelle. What stands no more than 27 inches, has buttocks white below an all-black tail and should never be confused with the above? Answer Thomson's gazelle. Both *swala tomi* – 'Tommies' – and *swala granti* are ubiquitous in Kenya and Tanzania, twitch their tails apparently incessantly and make tasty chops. Uganda has only the suspect sub-species called Bright's gazelle – GAZELLA GRANTI BRIGHTI – and this only in Kidepo. Ample compensation is the fine **Uganda kob**. On most plains you will see them en masse, the males guarding their breeding ground and locking their horns so doggedly in combat that lions walk up and kill both. Larger too is the **impala**, *swala pala*, one of the several animals that movement more than appearance helps identify: its fast, graceful leaps and bounds – often 30 feet by ten – make it easily if fleetingly recognized.

Dikdik, twelve pounds and in pairs, and the long-necked **gerenuk** – not 'Walley's' or 'Walter's' but Waller's gazelle, *swala twiga* – are common sights in Samburu/Isiolo. **Reedbuck** and **bushbuck** complicate your 'deer' identification further, but their remaining small antelope relatives – suni, oribi, duiker, puku, steinbok, grysbok and klipspringer – you will not so often encounter.

While dikdik are the smallest, **eland** are the largest antelopes. With *pofu*, I feel, the Swahili sums up its dewlap-breasted, dowager-look. Eland, though usually docile grazers, can use their horns to hara-kiri effect on those who keep them – illegally – for their fine beef-like meat. **Waterbuck** – *kuro* – occur frequently; less lady visitors would have soft spots for the males, with their cuddly, baby-donkey coat and well-formed horns, if they knew their harems numbered some twenty does.

Hartebeest are unmistakable and everywhere. Coke's, the *kongoni*, you see in southern Kenyan and Tanzanian parks; the Jackson's of Uganda is taller and tawnier with longer horns. Both slope to the rear, have a long face like Fernandel's, and graze in herds while one stands sentinel. A more deserving figure of fun is the gnu – 'White-bearded' or 'Nyanza Blue', *alias* wildebeest or *nyumbu*. Why this 'Clown of the Plains' will stare at you then frolic off, half gambolling bronco, half overgrown lamb, no one knows. Its herds abound in southern Kenya and Tanzania, but are primarily

Common giraffe, gerenuk and Burchell's zebra

Wildlife eyeball-to-eyeball

vast on the Serengeti where, over one million strong, they star in the Migrations' annual animal saga. Then, with the predators close, newly born gnus must join the headlong stampede and run for their lives when only seven minutes old.

The striking **oryx** – Africa's BEISA not Arabia's rare LEUCORYX – is found in southern Kenyan and northern Tanzanian parks. From the side you will see why it gave rise to the unicorn myth. **Topi**, handsome in blue-black and brown, come in sizeable herds or not at all. Most other large antelopes remain hunter's hopes: the Greater and Lesser **kudu**, *tandala*; the **bongo**, seldom, but increasingly seen in herds of up to 30 at The Ark (p. 104); the **Roan** and **Sable antelopes**, elusive specialities of Kenya's Lambwe Valley and Shimba Hills respectively, and 'Speke's'

sitatunga, whose squeegee feet enable it, so they say, to survive immersed to the neck in Uganda's swamps. Passers-by seldom light on it (but may on occasions sight it high and dry in the Saiwa Swamp National Park near Kitale).

Baboons abound, 'Olive' or 'Yellow'; the **Vervet, Patas** and **Sykes/Blue monkeys** too – old males ape-patriarch, babies clinging to their mother's back or under-carriage. At Mzima and Treetops they pose, pester or pilfer. Their depredations are in fact often so great that farmers petition Game Departments for permission to shoot them. Avoid fraternizing – their scratches can turn septic.

There is no such risk with the **colobus**, *mbega*, 'Black and White' or 'Red'. You may well glimpse the former in Jadini Forest or the Aberdares, Lake Nakuru and Mount Elgon national parks, gargling in high treetops or leaping like Batman with mantle flowing and limbs outstretched. Those on Kilimanjaro often lost this magnificent mantle to Chagga hunters, who used it in tribal head-dress: a thumb the colobus lacks naturally. The red species being officially classed as 'Endangered', one favourite habitat was recently converted into the 68-square-mile Tana River Primate Game Reserve (p. 90).

Bush babies, not the outcome of romantic safaris but nocturnal curiosities, are, like **pottoes**, 'Slow Lemurs' – and so remotely our relatives (p. 16). You can rarely hope for more than the saucer-shine of their eyes in your headlights at night. Wait until dark, too, for aardvarks, caracals, servals, civets, wild cats, genets and zorillas. (Touch the civet inadvertently with your bumper and the skunk-like stench will be with you for miles.) **Mongooses**, in some dozen varieties, scamper across your track everywhere, both day and night, and, as you pass, yard-long **monitor lizards** slip into the Tana and 'Lake Vic'.

Snakes, chameleons, iguanas and lizards are in fact countless. **Chameleons** come in twenty un-earthly but harmless species; **lizards**, often large and gorgeous *agamas*, practise their press-ups on many a lodge wall and terrace. But you will be lucky, or unlucky, to see **snakes** anywhere outside the Nairobi, Malindi and Mtwapa snake parks, the Mnarani Serpentarium or the Coast hotels' snake-milking shows. Some 170 species inhabit East Africa but, *The Standard* reassures, no tourist has died of a bite in over ten years.

The small furry creatures that at many lodges scamper disconcertingly up trees and round rocks are not rats but 'Rock' and 'Tree' **hyrax**. These *pimbi* are like nothing so much as overgrown guinea-pigs. Save that their similar digestive system and hoof-like feet make them the elephant's closest kin.

True rats – like otters, bats, hares, rabbits, foxes, badgers, squirrels, porcupines, dormice, mice, moles and shrews – are often exotic variations on the homely theme. **Hyaenas** thank Goodness are unique. In animal films the *fisi* plays the cowardly scavenger; Africans endow it with the Evil Eye; cat-lovers resent its primaeval kinship to their pet; lions, whom it finally eats alive, plainly despise it; old hunters standardly chill your spine with stories of jaws that 'remove half your face as you sleep'; even 'experts' have probed and pronounced it hermaphrodite. If its jaws are monstrous and its shoulders Quasimodo, they help the hyaena scavenge hygienically. Though you may not be able to verify this as they skulk in a mud-bath beside your track or lope cringing and low-rumped away, the 'bisexual' fallacy arises from labials swollen to scrotum dimensions. Hyaenas, 'Striped' or 'Spotted', not only filch the lions' prey, but kill independently, often in turn having their meal pilfered. They have a penchant for shoe-leather, and the unnerving laugh – all part of 'Wild Africa's Silent Call'? – has, they say, possible sexual significance.

Like hyaenas, **hunting dogs** do not kill then eat, but devour alive. Rather like a blotchy, tan alsatian (but in no way related), the 'African wild dog' – *mbwa mwitu* – hunts in well-organized packs and its puppies, like yours, are prone to distemper. **Jackals**, with their long legs, bushy tail and pointed nose, are recognized easily, feeding on sufferance at a lion's kill or crossing your track by day or night, less in Uganda than elsewhere. The *Innocent Killers* contains the Van Lawicks' account of their research on these species.

The **crocodile**, too, is unjustly despised. For all its reputed blood-lust, the *mamba* will lie and stare beadily at you on your launch or canoe, or sleep on oblivious, jaws ajar. You may see some in Lakes Baringo and Turkana; none at Nakuru or Naivasha, but certainly those that they summon by name on the banks of the Tana at Crocodile Camp (p. 98). Reaching fifteen feet in length, mother mambas lay up to 100 eggs, incubate from December to March, help their squeaking monster offspring break from the shells, then safeguard them – sometimes – from mongooses and monitors. Unlike the elephant, who dies when his sixth set of teeth is too worn to chew, crocodiles grow new sets until the age of eighty. Egyptian plovers peck at their backs – not, *pace* Herodotus, in between their teeth. (Oxpeckers also keep watch atop the buffalo and piapiac crows on the rhinos.) Fish are eaten fresh and whole; gazelles and other small animals

Elephant, reflecting
Waterbuck – 'extended family'
Buffalo wallow
Wildebeest – 'Migrations' in the Mara
Black-faced Vervet

are swept in from the water's edge by a blow from the crocodile's tail, held under and drowned by its jaws, then hidden on the bank and eaten later, very 'high'. Alistair Graham and Peter Beard's *Eyelids of Morning* is a coffee-table compilation of crocodile photographs, anecdotes and data.

To the crocodile's seemingly gruesome malevolence, **warthogs** are comic relief. You will see them everywhere, half portly Dickensian, half Dr Doolittle: on their knees grubbing or trotting podgily away with their tails alarm-erect, the family in scale-model order of importance. They back into holes for the night; here too they breed, six or so piglets appearing twice in three years. Warthogs are said to lead exemplary family lives, but do occasionally get drunk on rotten apples. The 'warts' may or may not protect eyes when grubbing; cornered warthogs, like wild-boar everywhere, frequently attack.

Like the above, warts and all, is the rarer, larger **Giant forest hog**, so elusive that Science discovered it only in 1904; also the nocturnal **African bush pig**, *alias* Red hog or Red river hog. All for Swahili-speakers are *ngiri*, 'pig'.

We can, they say, discern 200,000 colours. Most of them you will surely see in East Africa's **bird life**, insects and flowers. Of the first there exist here about 1000 species. Familiar migrants may have got here before you, but all the more striking beside them are the variegated weaver birds; gorgeous bee-eaters, sunbirds, rollers and touracos; whydas hovering long-tailed, hornbills top-heavy and superb starlings everywhere, their colours as bold as their manner.

Ostriches are unmistakable. With feet often bigger than their heads they can run at 45 mph but not fly. The Somali ostrich – found north, as it happens, of the Mombasa Road – has male legs and neck blueish-grey; in the Masai, everywhere south, these are pink. Females of both types are indistinguishable; several even pool their eggs in one male's nest. Heads are not buried in the sand, but peck continually and lie low to avoid lions. Between 1900 and 1930 more than a million birds were killed for their feathers, but 'ostrich farms' meet present-day demands.

Guinea-fowl, spurfowl and francolin gather on your track everywhere at dusk. Vultures, hawks and eagles you will see, but more often hoary marabous by the lodge refuse-pits. And unmistakable secretary birds are so known because of their quill ears and Dickensian, frock-coated stride.

If you must identify all you see, works like Mackworth-Praed and Grant's *Birds of Eastern and North Eastern Africa* will be indispensable. The Nairobi Museum's Aga Khan Hall contains ample stuffed proof of how rich Kenya's bird life is (p. 50). And for those who prefer their captive specimens on the wing, or almost, Malindi's Birdland is ornithological bliss (p. 82).

If birds are legion, **insects** are myriad. As thousands of species of this, Nature's largest realm, are not only unnamed but unknown, I shall not attempt anything comprehensive here. Suffice it to say that, after your day viewing big game, its lesser night colleagues turn to you, but given mosquito-netting or an insect repellent, the countless creatures that share your room will ignore you and quietly proceed to eat the furniture and/or each other. **Ants** – *siafu* – do this remarkably – Coast settlers stood chair- and table-legs in deterrent tins of water – and columns of carnivorous driver-ants crossing your track after rain are an eye-eating terror of the animal kingdom. The conspicuous 'ant-hills' you see everywhere, in humps, hillocks and pinnacles, are not ant-hills but termite-mounds, of sun-baked earth bound with the half-digested cellulose of blind, soft-bodied TERMITIDAE. 'Worker termites' build and fetch the colony's food of dead wood and straw; 'soldier termites' bide their time to resist, with powerful jaws and poison glands, the onslaught of ponerine ants and the occasional aardvark, or 'earth-pig'; 'reproducer termites' fly forth in thousands after rain to breed or be eaten (p. 29), while the 'king and queen' mate single-mindedly underground. When the queen ceases to be reproductive, the 'workers' lick her to death. East Africa's **butterflies** are colourful in some 100,000 varieties – see the pinned and named collection in the National Museum (p. 50) or the Western Kenya Museum's at Kitale (p. 124).

For **trees and flowers**, the interested layman will be happy with the Shell Guides; botanical pundits will enjoy Nairobi's Arboretum and City Park (p. 54). Joy Adamson's water-colours in Nairobi's National Museum depict the order's smaller species in all their minute beauty. Bougainvillea, frangipani, hibiscus, jacaranda and Nandi Flame make not only Nairobi a perennial delight. The flora contributes surprisingly to Africa's panoramas: the bamboo 'impenetrable forests' are just that; in the western swamps papyrus is both Biblical and typical; the Coast is typified by the palm (p. 62) and the savannah by the acacia, its branches level-spreading and its bark and boughs yellowish. In African stories the homely-monstrous baobab tree is doomed to grow upside-down because it would not stay where God placed it; in Alan Root's unparalleled film it is fascinatingly home to a hundred creatures.

NAIROBI AND ENVIRONS

NAIROBI, as capitals go, is a comely upstart. The Uganda Railway surveyors arrived at the turn of the century to find little more than the 'Swampy place' which the name in Kikuyu supposedly means. (Masai maintain that *Nairobi* is their word for 'Place of cool Waters' but Muthaiga, a suburb, may mean 'Place by the Swamp'.) Water, anyway, was why Sergeant Ellis RE in 1899 chose this site in the Masai-Kikuyu No man's land, and disease that the Nairobi River's water brought, in 1900 and 1902, explains the rapid replanning of the one-street, tin-shack 'Nyarobe/Nyrobi'.

The World Bank's recent K£3½-million loan for a new city water supply points to the contrast today. The central Avenue – first 'Sixth', then 'Delamere', now 'Kenyatta' – was built so broad that twelve-span ox-carts could turn: today you will see it a Big City thoroughfare, with zebra crossings and parking meters to clinch the modernity. The shanties, bazaars and marshalling yards have given way to clean streets and plate-glass façades; cinemas, stores and neon-glossy arcades; government offices and neat green lawns. Banks and insurance blocks dominate the skyline, for Nairobi's monuments are not to the past but to present prosperity.

Nairobi replaced Mombasa as capital in 1907, was developed – 'with more order and charm' – in accordance with a master plan after 1947, and received its City status by royal charter in 1950. Its 266 square miles rise discreetly from 5370 to 5850 feet above sea-level, and Africans are working harder than Asians and Europeans to bring the population total to 900,000.

Beside the Hilton, the **Visitors' Information Bureau** has become the African Tours & Hotels' Retail Reservations Office – well stocked, well staffed, friendly and informative; also open weekdays 8.30 a.m.-5 p.m. and Saturdays 8.30 a.m.-1 p.m. (POB. 30471, tel. 23285). It puts out the useful *Nairobi Handbook* every month. Also free, but weekly, is Nairobi's *What's On*, which tells you just that. The *Daily Nation* and *The Standard* do likewise for both town and country while *Joe*, Africa's answer to *Punch*, reviews the news monthly with satirical hilarity. Of the several 'tourist' periodicals, most are heavy with advertising but light on information, and only the bi-monthly *Safari* remains consistently readable and reasonably priced. The Esso *Map of Nairobi* is the best in print.

National holidays are New Year's Day, Good Friday, Easter Monday, May Day, Madaraka Day (1 June), Kenyatta Day (20 October), Independence Day (12 December), Christmas Day, Boxing Day and the moveable Muslim feast of 'Id al-Fitr (1 August in 1981).

Jomo Kenyatta International Airport makes a pleasant curtain-raiser. Named after Kenya's first, late president, it was inaugurated on 8 December 1978 by the second, Arap Moi – a starkly pretty, compact concrete city, all tiled floors and false wood ceilings inside, its décor blue and yellow. Snack bars, banks and part-time post office, a 'Bon Voyage' boutique and fifth-floor Simba Restaurant complement airline and car-hire counters. Composed of three separate 'units', the airport boasts an unusual (unique?) feature: illuminated boards along the approaches which, repeatedly warning you to 'Check Flight Number', must distract the sad at parting or further confuse the flustered.

From the airport [0 kms] you can reach town in style, in a red Kenatco Mercedes, for Ksh. 108/-; haggle and rough it in one of the clappity taxis (90/-, but for you maybe 70/-), or wait for a 20/- seat in the Kenya Airways' bus. All drop you wherever you want.

With the Ngongs like knuckles on the skyline ahead, you meet the Mombasa Road [4]. The Coast lies to the left, albeit 300 miles further. Turn right and you could keep straight on to Kampala. For the moment, though, you rise across the railway [7½], ordinary except for its history (p. 21). The Nairobi Motor Race Track is an occasionally noisy neighbour to the Nairobi National Park's East Entrance (also l.)[8½]. After the Belle-Vue Drive-in Cinema (l.)[12] the bleak plain yields to schools and ever-spreading housing estates. You dip across the meagre Ngong River and, with Nairobi spread before you (but its start here all car show-rooms), reach the first of its many roundabouts [14].

Off right lies the **Industrial Area**, its roads named unflatteringly after British cities until in 1973-74 they, like most street-names both here and in Mombasa, were subjected to 'Africanization'.

Langata Road runs off left to Karen and the national park, and the Mombasa Road becomes **Uhuru Highway**. Its bougainvillea centre beds, acacia and jacaranda borders and rock-garden roundabouts justify Nairobi's alias, 'City of Flowers', and this it owes largely to ex-Park Superintendent Greensmith's veteran attentions. Drive along Uhuru Highway 8-9 each morning, in the lunch hour, or 5-6 each afternoon and you have ample time to admire it.

Beyond the next roundabout, a corner of the Railway Golf Course (l.) is one of the city's cemeteries (a central enclave Jewish, its inscriptions Hebrew and topped by a star of David; civilian and military graves around, the latter mostly from World War I and, though tended by the Commonwealth War Graves Commission, lying not in the standard serried ranks but alongside Africans and Indians, civilians, missionary wives and Charles Ryall, p. 44). To the right spread the still-busy yards and sheds around which the first railhead township grew, then **Haile Selassie Avenue** crosses: left up **Nairobi Hill** to the Nairobi Club (1901) and the Kenyatta National and Forces Memorial **hospitals**; right beneath the bridge that links the **post office** (r.) with the massive **Central Bank of Kenya**, past the slanting-glass and concrete monolith of Co-operative House (l.) to the **railway station** (r.).

Sports grounds, flower-beds, boating pools and well-kept lawns cover the slopes of **Uhuru Park** (l.). Completed in 1971 and backed gothically by the twin towers of All Saints', it affords the best view of **City Square** (r.). The Kenyatta Conference Centre looms roundly over everything; Parliament, equally unmistakable, stands beyond **Harambee Avenue**, and this, the next thoroughfare (r.), runs broad and straight between business and government blocks to Moi Avenue, the late Government Road (p. 48). *Harambee* is Kenya's national slogan, 'Let's pull together', *Uhuru* the Swahili for Independence.

From Parliament to the university, from Uhuru Park to Moi Avenue, Nairobi can be sightseen fairly comfortably on foot. Beyond, the city is a spacious place, and its distances deceptive. **Taxis** stand outside the station, the Ambassadeur, the Excelsior, the Hilton, the Inter-Continental, the New Stanley, the Norfolk, the Sixeighty and the City Market. (Their *matatu* colleagues tout insurance-less but cheaply everywhere.) Most safari companies run daily **round-town tours** – for generally Ksh. 50-60/- and two-three hours. My general anatomy of the city below you should dismember as time and energy require. Less interesting limbs are shown by indentation, and the street-plan should help.

A tour of **Parliament Buildings** costs only a call to the Serjeant-at-Arms (21291 x 256). From the fine carved doors in Parliament Road, you cross the floor of Italian marble to the mural of shields, one from each of Kenya's top ten tribes. Left is the Seal of Independence, right the Commonwealth Parliamentary Association Room with its antique tapestry. (Newer and of more specific interest are those that hang upstairs: after the eye-catching table on the landing – each of its

32 segments made from a different East African wood, and by the boys of Kabete School in 1958-59 – you reach the Long Gallery. Here, in 49 picturesque panels of wool-and-canvas Douanier Rousseau, the East African Women's League has produced a unique pictorial history of colonial Kenya. The tapestries were presented to Parliament in 1968 and are available, reproduced with an explanatory text, in *They Made it their Home*.) Right of the ground-floor lobby: the old Chamber (1952-54), its two Despatch Boxes an independence gift from New Zealand. To the left the gallery culminates in the fine blue mosaics, presented by the Isma'ili community, that form the façade of the new Chamber (1963-65), where the National Assembly now sits. The Members' Chapel below contains a plaque commemorating those who 'died in service'; a lift brings you to the view from the 130-foot clock-tower above. Left of the entrance stands the prominent statue unveiled in 1968 to 'The Father of the Nation Jomo Kenyatta'. In the **mausoleum** (further r.) lie his mortal remains. Twenty-one flags flank the walkway; ceremonial guards, changed every two hours, keep watch day and night, while flames burn eternal on each corner.

Between Haile Selassie and Harambee avenues, beside the Professional Centre in Parliament Road, the 1958 **Donovan Maule Theatre** is East Africa's best. Its attractive auditorium, restaurant, bar and sporadic exhibitions crown the three decades of enterprising rep. effort that began in 1948 with Mollie and Don Maules' tiny 'Studio Theatre' in Government Road. Maintaining steadily high standards (and inflation-free prices), the theatre club welcomes visiting playgoers: Ksh. 10/- p.d. (40/- p.m.) with seats at 40/- (reservations tel. 22300).

From the **Inter-Continental**'s eight-storey landmark the road right – formerly Sergeant Ellis Avenue (p. 41) – was in 1973 renamed prosaically **City Hall Way**. It skirts the **Holy Family Cathedral** (Mass Sundays 7, 8, 9, 11 a.m. & 6 p.m., Saturdays 12.30 & 6 p.m., weekdays 7.45 a.m. & 5 p.m.). Founded on the Feast of Saints Peter and Paul in 1960 – and on the site of an earlier church, Nairobi's first stone building – the cathedral was consecrated on 6 July 1963. Inside it impresses, lofty and simple, its concrete walls offset by strips of stained-glass window. Detached, the campanile stands a stark 198 feet tall.

Beyond it is the fine **City Hall**, designed as 'an act of faith' during the Emergency (p. 22) and completed in 1957. Its halls and con-ference rooms house frequent assemblies – and nightly film-shows – while the restaurant is interesting daily at lunch-time, when the clientele is Coloured white-collar.

Opposite, the neo-classical **Law Courts** have since 1972 been quite literally over-shadowed by the **Kenyatta Conference Centre**, an imposing circular complex of 28 storeys that looks down even on the Hilton, and is linked with a conical conference hall – the world's second largest – by a zigzag of ramps. The **Restaurant La Tour** revolves on the top floor of the magnificent, K£4-million landmark. Jomo Kenyatta, monumental alongside, sits facing Parliament, and a forest of flagstaffs fills most of City Square. Across Wabera Street (l.), the **US mission** occupies part of Cotts House; Silopark House aspired to be a skyscraper until International House arose, adjacent, to dwarf it and, after Kencom House (r.; 1977) and the **Hilton** (l.) as Nairobi's focal centre, City Hall Way meets Moi Avenue (p. 48).

The central **Kenyatta Avenue** bestrides Uhuru Highway's next roundabout, rising (l.) between Uhuru Park and the Nairobi Serena to **All Saints' Cathedral** (Communion 10.30 a.m. 2nd Sundays and 7.30 & 11.45 1st & 3rd Sundays, Morning Prayer 10.30 and Evening Prayer 6.30). You approach by a bridge 'In memory of Charles Ryall killed by a lion at Kima Station 6th June 1900'. The lion in fact scented his prey in a railway sleeping compartment, stood on one of the terrified occupants and carried off this police superintendent from his bunk (p. 48). Its foundation stone laid in 1917, the 'Cathedral of the Highlands' was constructed piecemeal – in 1922, 1930 and 1934 as funds allowed – and consecrated, completed, in March 1952. Unique with a chancel far wider than the nave, it is otherwise very English-village: four-square towers, Gothic arches, brass plaques polished, choir-stall coats of arms and gargoyles the only absentee. Some windows are plain, some stained – for the McMillans (pp. 47, 61) and Lord Baden-Powell (p. 103). Stones embedded in the walls come from Lindisfarne, St Paul's and Canterbury Cathedral; two Bibles, presented in March 1946, from King George and Queen Elizabeth, and the seeds for two of the cypresses outside from the Garden of the Tomb and Gethsemane respectively.

Beyond the cathedral, Kenyatta Avenue rises to the popular **Panafric** (l., occasionally kept awake by the Starlight Club below) and forks right into Milimani –

formerly Craufurd – Road with (all r.) the 1959 Seventh-day Adventist Church and Medical Centre (Saturday 'Divine Service' at 11 a.m.), the Heron Court Hotel (plus London bus), the 1973 **Milimani** – 'On the Hills' – **Hotel** ('the only Nairobi hotel to give its name to a street') and the **Grosvenor Hotel** (uphill l. in Ralph Bunche Road). As **Valley Road** it climbs on past the 3rd Ngong Avenue turning to the **Fairview Hotel** (twice l.), the **Greek** 'Saints Anarghyri' **Cathedral** (1953; orthodox in both rite and design with its gigantic Christ in the high cupola and the customary gold-framed saints around) and the Nairobi Pentecostal Church (also r.), built in 1961.

Opposite All Saints' Cathedral, Nyerere – ex-Kirk – Road skirts the **Central Park**. Since 1975 the corner is impressively occupied by the **Nairobi Serena Hotel**. To the left the sign is self-explanatory: 'Private Road Freemasons' Hall'. This was built in 1936, its blocks correctly squared and its façade all pillars, orbs, 'astrologia' and Biblical inscriptions. A line of massive eucalyptus, the YWCA National Office and Nairobi's First Church of Christ Scientist (also l.; Sundays at 11), then comes an ecclesiastical cluster which irreverent locals call 'God's Corner': **St Andrew's** (l.) is Presbyterian and prominent, with plate-glass façade and wrought-iron arches (Sunday services 9.15, 10.45 & 6.30 p.m.). Below, the tin-roofed **Lutheran Church** of Kenya – the 'Old St Andrews' of 1910 – looks every bit its age; polyglot and packed, its Sunday services in English, Swahili and German will, however, in time be held in

Nairobi – the view from Uhuru Park

the new 'Uhuru Highway Lutheran Church' arising alongside. A stark contrast opposite is the low modernistic polygonal of **St Paul's** Catholic Chapel, completed in 1971 and celebrating mass daily at 6.15 a.m., Sundays at 7.30, 9.30 & 6.15 p.m. Across Uhuru Highway, Nairobi's Hebrew congregation meets in Vermont Memorial Hall, now renamed 'The **Nairobi Synagogue**': 'Sabbath Eve' at 6.15 p.m. and at 7.30 a.m. each 'Sabbath morning' viz. Saturday.

Meanwhile at the last roundabout back (enlarged in 1974 for more cars to join the jam), Kenyatta Avenue's better half makes a desultory start as the city's main street. The corner **Provincial Commissioner's Office** – 1913 and typical 'Kenya colony' – is at long last being reworked. The ubiquitous Kenya Commercial Bank is the latest of the many occupants of the fit-for-nothing edifice opposite, stylelessly pompous like a Yorkshire union chapel. The **General Post Office** (r.; 8-6, Saturdays 8-4.30, Sundays 9-10) is efficient in style and in fact, and Koinange Street questionably embellished by the **Galton-Fenzi Memorial** (r.). Raised in 1939 to the 'Father of African Motoring', this 'Nairobi Milliary Stone' stands 5474·37 feet above sea-level, gives a random selection of places and distances with relative accuracy but appalling calligraphy, and sports for good measure of idiosyncrasy a piece of wishful thinking from Isaiah: 'And an Highway shall be there'. The brass plaque on the back, like so much of the country's (commemorative) mineral wealth, was soon thieved . . . to be replaced by marble in 1972.

Opposite, beyond the **Excelsior**'s prominent corner, **Koinange Street** continues past the round New Florida Night Club – the late 'Maduni's', the former 'Acadia' – whence wrong notes emanate nightly. To the right, the long, yellow, steep-stepped edifice that runs through to Muindi Mbingu Street is not another Indian temple but the **City Market**. On its close-packed forecourt the basketware and pottery stands are cheap and photogenic; the main hall is colourful with fruit, vegetables and flowers; upper galleries sell souvenirs, adjacent stalls meat at remarkable prices; and Spitting, in several languages, is Strictly Prohibited.

Along left lies the **Kenya Airways' terminal**. Before it, unjustly inconspicuous in a corner of Caltex House, is **Alan Bobbe's Bistro**. Here, save on Sunday, you can have a cheap lunch or an exquisite dinner. The Visitors' Book, with Churchill first, reads like an autograph-hunter's dream, and for the admirable service of an all-African staff, an amusing menu and the *patron*'s affable attentions, there is no extra charge. Despite the restyling in 1975, pressure on the 60-odd seats makes a reservation wise (tel. 21152).

Cheaper, after the terminal, is the Laws' **Hong Kong Restaurant** (1971; tel. 28612), less central than its compatriot Pagoda, Mandarin and Dragon Pearl, but a cut above average Chinese with its 71 well-served dishes and authentic Canton décor. With the *Maison Française* – the fine French cultural centre (and restaurant) – on the one-time wasteland to the left, Koinange Street then abuts the **university**. Promoted from Royal Technical College to a constituent college of the University of East Africa, the University of Nairobi took its present name and shape in 1970. On this side of the campus' well-gardened eighteen acres, sculptor Foit's Yajnik Memorial Fountain was completed in 1962. To the left is God's Corner, to the right the **Central Police Station**. Alongside the latter, Harry Thuku Road honours the early 'freedom fighter' whose detention in 1922 prompted the homicidal 'Harry Thuku Riot' (p. 49). Flanked by academic blocks, it leads to the **Norfolk Hotel**, patronised now for over 70 years by presidents, nobles, stars, millionaires and writers – the 'great' whatever your viewpoint. Facing the hotel, the **Kenya Cultural Centre** and the National Theatre. The former, opened in 1960, houses such diverse concerns as the Orient Art Circle and Prince Philip's Outward Bound Trust, a school of ballet and the British Council library. The **National Theatre** opposite was endowed with a British Council grant of £50,000 and opened by Sir Ralph Richardson in 1952. The foyer boasts a stone 'from the original foundation of the house where Shakespeare was born' and the rosemary beside the door 'came from Shakespeare's birthplace garden at Stratford-upon-Avon, England, and was planted . . . November 1953' – all this on brass plaques that soon disappeared and have since been replaced in plastic. Harry Thuku Road runs on past the Norfolk Tower and the Voice of Kenya station to stop at the **Boulevard Hotel**.

Initially **Kenyatta Avenue** is a cultural and architectural *mélange*: the once half-timbered corner, an African Old Curiosity Shop (l.), now Rehani House, all rectangular concrete like the rest; a 'K & A' supermarket topped by a stucco coat of arms (r.); the **African Heritage**'s spacious shop and show-room (l.) – vaguely 'native' and arty-ethnic craftware; a 'USSR Show-room' closing, appropriately, as a 'Kentucky Fried Chicken' opened opposite . . . all overshadowed since 1972 by the **Sixeighty Hotel** and this in turn topped by Bruce House (**British High Commission**). The avenue improves after **Muindi Mbingu Street** (l. the City Market; r. the 680 and **UTC** viz. Hertz, Kuoni and Sovereign Holidays). The Bank of India (l.) was the 'Memorial Hall' where sat Kenya's Legislative Council from 1924 until 1951. Between this and the Standard Bank's Oxford-institution block stand the **War Memorials**. One is a simple cenotaph 'To Our Glorious Dead 1914-1918/ 1939-1945', the other done like Mombasa's and Dar's by 'Myrander, London' in 1924: with three *askaris* – African soldiers – and three inscriptions to the 'Native African troops who fought: to the carriers who were the feet and hands of the Army: and to all other men who served and died for their King and Country'.

Just before, **Wabera Street** crosses: right to the British Airways' office and Standard, Kaunda and Mama Ngina streets, left to the **McMillan Memorial Library**. In memory of the Sir William Northrup who farmed and lies buried on Ol Donyo Sabuk (p. 61), the 1929-31 edifice has a façade of columns, stone lions and steps all vaguely Trafalgar Square. It is open 9 a.m.-5 p.m. daily except Sundays, Saturdays 8.30-1, and many of its 120,000 books, some of them excellent Africana, can be borrowed (deposit Ksh. 10/-).

Far more flamboyant behind is the Sunni sect's **Jamia** (meaning 'mosque') **Mosque**. Built 1925-33, it is a model mosque, Arabian not Turkish in style, with two main minarets, three silver cupolas and a façade fancy with spirelets, inscriptions and arches. Inside hangs one painted ostrich egg; four antiquated clocks mark disparate time for the five daily prayers; the *mihrab* (the niche indicating the direction of Mecca) is sculpted and painted bright and ornate, like the backcloth of a 19th-c. roadshow, and the simple *minbar* (mosque pulpit) is covered with the standard silk prayer-mats made usually in Italy. 'Entry With Shoes Strictly Prohibited Tips Forbidden' says the sign. To the right the Saudis are financing an extension; to the left the ablution rooms share a block with the 'Sayed Abdullah Shah 1956 Memorial Library' and the Jamia Mosque Committee and Clinic.

Behind is an area of mostly lowly clothes shops and beside the mosque the Exotica, where they serve snacks by day and solicit by night.

Where Kenyatta Avenue is cut obliquely by Kimathi Street, the New Stanley's **Thorn Tree** pavement café is much frequented by the *beau* (and *demi-*)*monde* of Nairobi. The old **New Stanley Hotel** opened in 1911. Then, and for some time thereafter, hunters in town with friends on safari would pin 'to await arrival' notes on the trunk of the courtyard acacia (the original, that is, not the present replacement which was planted in 1961). In 1976 the then-management reintroduced such a 'hunter's board' – not so much for the sake of tradition as to stop its reception being pestered with left messages.

Formerly Hardinge Street, **Kimathi Street** has perhaps an incongruous namesake: the Mau Mau leader Dedan Kimathi who, after four years' fighting against the British, was captured, tried and hanged near Nyeri in 1955. **Standard Street** comes in right, all business-block back-doors and fashionable establishments – the **Bacchus Club** (r.), **Studio Arts 68**, Gallery Watatu and **Rowland Ward** (all l.). Likewise **Kaunda** – the former York – **Street**: the Steak House, Sapra Studio and Thorn Tree Safaris (l.). Elite House, the 'Old Mutual' and the Norwich Corner House are relics of older Nairobi, and by the broader Queensway – now **Mama Ngina Street** in honour of the former First Lady – Kimathi Street comes up against the Hilton (p. 44). The Air France, Alitalia, Kenya Airways' and Iberia offices face you; to the right lie International House (**Marino's Restaurant** on the mezzanine), the **Expo Camera Centre**, Kenya Coffee House and 20th-Century Cinema (further r.) and, well sign-boarded just before them, Nairobi's **Marine Aquarium**. This was built in May 1974 and opened to the public here in KCS House in September 1975 (for Ksh. 5/-, under 12s 2/-; 9.30-5.30 daily except Sunday). Its twenty attractively sea-scaped tanks, tended by two affable and well-informed Africans, contain some 40 species from Kenya's off-shore waters: well-named box-fish, clownfish, butterfly-fish and angler fish, puffers, poisonous lion and stone fish and solicitous cleaner wrasse, which they move from tank to tank to doctor each's inmates in turn. The rare harlequin shrimp you see fed on red starfish: when this PROTOREASTER LINCKI is half devoured it is removed to grow again . . . and be re-eaten twenty months later. Shrimps themselves are fed to the two common octopi which, like the green turtles and the small sand shark, the aquarium recently acquired. Feeding time for the fish is 4 p.m. every Monday, Wednesday and Saturday.

Beyond the Kimathi Street crossing – where a bronze Lord Delamere long stood, where the fountain that replaced him was recently removed and where the corner Woolworth's is distinctly *déjà vu* – Kenyatta Avenue runs bittily into **Moi Avenue**. 'Government Road' until 1979, this one-time 'Station Road' boasted the first home of both the old New Stanley and the Donovan Maule. It is now Nairobi's watershed: to the east, where the money flows, things are Middle-West chequer-board and more cosmopolitan; to the west, conversely, closer-knit Afro-Asian quarters sink to the Nairobi River. **Tom Mboya Street** is the busiest thoroughfare, parallel to Moi Avenue; River Road is local colour with no holds barred, and Uyoma – ex-Byramjee – Street a curiosity, with the 1963 **Siri Guru Singh Sabha Temple** yellow-fronted like an exhibition hall, the staider 'Swaminarayantemple E.A. Satsang Mandal' opposite, and **St Peter Claver's Church** (1930) on the corner of Racecourse Road.

Moi Avenue runs south between the 'sunken garden' of the Information Bureau and a lone, porticoed, ex-bank pile reminiscent of old Khartoum. Beside it, the unmissable **Ambassadeur Hotel** and behind it Hallian's Club, where temporary membership is available – and preferable. Then, with the Nairobi and Kenya cinemas, Arturo's, the Gourmet Grill and Pagoda restaurants (r.), Moi tops Harambee and Haile Selassie avenues and stops at the railway station.

The **Railway Museum** is well sign-posted (0·8 kms r. along Station Road then l. on to the murram; entrance Ksh. 4/-, children 2/-; 8.30 a.m.-4 p.m. daily except Sundays, Saturdays 8.30-12.30). The collection, started in 1971, is a tribute to its dedicated curator. Displayed in a large and well-installed hall and shunted on to the lines alongside is the railway bric-à-brac, from old bells to locomotives, that he painstakingly saved from the scrap-heap and restored. Of historical interest – see page 21 – are an original print of Macdonald's survey map, the captain's table and furniture from the *Königsberg*, and *Heller*-coins cast by Lettow-Vorbeck at Tabora, as well as a 3/- railway-lunch menu from 1935 and many photographs. Of questionable authenticity – see page 44 – is the Inspection Coach No. 12 outside, in which Charles Ryall may or may not have slept his last night.

Northwards from Kenyatta Avenue, Moi Avenue runs past Lavarini's Restaurant (r.) where, under a previous management, Bing Crosby 'enjoyed the meal', and the splendid **Lobster Pot** (r. in Cabral Street). Colonnaded shopfronts then add to the increasingly Asian appearance, which is heightened by the **Isma'ilia Mosque** (r.; 1920) and the **Jeevanjee Gardens** (l.), with an elder Queen Victoria at her mini-monumental best. Moi Avenue then turns into University Way.

SUBURBAN AND NEARBY. Nairobi's 'tribal' hinterland is well served by the safari companies' cut-and-dried trips. The various 'Kikuyu/Masai/Akamba Tours', with intelligent itineraries and usually good couriers, make a worth-while afternoon's experience. The pros are their conducted tours of craft centres, farms, estates and markets; colourful performances of dances and chants; the questionable pleasure of tasting local *nduma*, *ngwachi*, *njahi* and *irio*, and the chance to Meet the People. The cons are typical homesteads sign-boarded 'Typical Homestead'; full-fledged warriors who face single-handed a horde of snap-shooting tourists, and ornamental tribesmen who 'relive tradition and enact warlike scenes' to order once a week.

The National Museum. A popular drive or bus-ride (no. 18 from Moi Avenue) is out to the museum. From God's Corner (p. 45) follow Uhuru Highway – pre-independence Princess Elizabeth Highway – past the YMCA and university sports grounds (l.) and turn right at the first roundabout up Museum – ex-Ainsworth – Hill. First right after the Nairobi River bridge, the **Ainsworth Memorial Garden** is 'Dedicated to the memory of the men and women of Kenya who gave their lives in the war of 1939 to 1945'. Colonel John Ainsworth CMG, DSO, originally the IBEA's transport superintendent in Mombasa, was moved first to Machakos in 1892 (p. 94) then to Nairobi in 1899 as 'Her Majesty's Sub-Commissioner for Ukamba'. Through the Township Committee he set up in 1900 the capital's first trees and gardens were planted, and the corner of colourfully landscaped hillside here is thus an appropriate tribute.

Along right, the National Museum was founded in 1910 and rehoused here in 1930. It is open daily from 9.30 a.m. to 6 p.m. and costs Ksh. 10/- for adults, 5/- for children (5/-, 3/- for citizens and residents and, on week-ends and public holidays, 3/-, 1/50). From Monday to Friday, 9.30-12 and 2-4.30, guides are available at the door for free tours in English, week-ends in Swahili. The first corridor (l.) contains displays of 'Old East African Currency' and 'Wellknown Firearms of the Past' (British and German and some once belonging to Sir Frederick Jackson, who hunted and administered with humour in the 1890s). Then a well-stocked shop selling books, postcards and 'Joy's' reproductions; calabashes and banana-leaf caricature animals; tribal jewellery and knick-knacks in metal, wood, beads, soapstone and ostrich's egg-shell.

Beyond the shop, *al fresco*, stands an ersatz Ahmed (p. 128). As 'normal taxidermy techniques could not be applied in the mounting', the first temporary sign apologized, 'the skeleton and original tusks will be displayed at a later date' . . . and this they are in the hall behind, amidst a stuffed menagerie of whole animals and heads. (Note – as you may well not see them elsewhere – the okapi, nyala and bongo family.) The authorities occasionally stultify this Guide by rearranging the ground-floor cases here: by the time you arrive it may be 'Man and his Environment' – a frankly educational display of photographs and exhortatory text. Or the 'Kenya Coast 9th to 19th century': querns, thrones, model dhows and wood-carved doors, chinaware and brassware, Islamic inscriptions, ornaments, Swahili clothes and photographs of Lamu, Pate and Takwa. Or neither.

Less fickle – and quite fascinating – are the exhibits upstairs: photographs and prints featuring 'Early Maps', 'Slavery', 'CMS Missionaries', 'Nairobi', 'Traditional Homes' and 'Developing Transportation' viz. zebra-carts and rickshaws. Joy Adamson's portraits have been replaced by a graphically macabre, but quite artistic painting of the 'Harry Thuku Riot' (p. 46). 'Aspects of Colonial Administration' and 'Emergency' are starkly illustrated by cases of curtain-rod and inner-tube fire-arms used by the 'Kenya Freedom Fighters'.

However, the museum is 'In Memory of Sir Robert Coryndon' – whence its pre-independence name – 'and in honour of . . . his love of nature', and that subject initially prevails. Its entrance flanked by tusks, the central ground-floor hall contains elephant skulls and twelve attractive 'habitat cases' of stuffed animals, most in a three-dimensional *nature morte* of papiermâché, plaster and paint.

The upstairs gallery was once merely trophy-portraits of principally antelopes. Now it is utterly ethnic. Of the seventeen cases, many are excellent if prosaic documentation: on 'Musical Instruments', 'Basketry and Weaving', 'Woodcarving', 'Homes', 'Tools', 'Utensils' and 'Transport'. That the last should include a pair of sandals – which you beat on the ground to ensure a safe journey – is a token of the display's enjoyability. This is enhanced by 'Metal Personal Ornaments' that protect babies from anything that might make

'Voodoo' dancers – ritualistic for tourists

them cry and grown-ups from bad dreams; by 'Clothing' for Akamba ladies that only husbands and/or boy-friends may see, and by 'Personal Ornaments made of Natural Products' viz. ostrich's egg-shells halved to cover the navels of circumcised, unmarried females whilst dancing. For most, the exhibition's *pièce de résistance* is probably the show-case labelled 'Religion, Magic and Medicine': sandals soaked in donkey dung or urine, for divining; 'magic sticks' made from aluminium kettles, with which to talk to God; rituals for rain-making and/or stopping plagues or hairy caterpillars; charms of horn, shell, bones and beads, to protect from everything conceivable (or, adorned with pendants representing breasts, nipples and nether organs, to ensure conception), and not least 'Cursing Objects . . . used by anyone'.

To avoid retracing steps, turn by the stands of Joy Adamson's originals into the side-rooms displaying maps and photographs of Kenya's lake, volcano and hot-spring locations. Beyond the incongruous chamber of Apollo space-shot pictures comes the collection, 'In Memory of Harry Watts . . . 1950' and reputedly the world's largest, of African butterflies and bugs. Even more attractive, adjoining, is the Aga Khan Hall's array of East African birds. In case after well-labelled case, they are for laymen a colourful wonder, for ornithologists an excellent aid to identification.

Stairs here take you down to the Mahatma Gandhi Hall. This provides an introduction to Kenya and Tanzania's prehistoric treasure trove, its diagrams and reproductions quite as enlightening as the tool and fossil relics. Recent additions illustrate, dramatically, scale-model dinosaurs and extinct Kenyan creatures; prosaically, progress at the East Turkana site of Koobi Fora (p. 131). The adjacent gallery, its display changed repeatedly, is now devoted to 'Containers': sundry shapes, from horn, wood, skin, fibre, clay and calabash, for carrying, storing or pouring salt, grain, water, tools, fat, dried food, infants' milk or honey-beer. At the end is an ante-room tapestried with water-colour flowers which, despite the former-name alias, are further testimony to Joy Adamson's talents and munificence. To the right, the Winston Churchill Gallery is quite aquatic: plaster casts of sea- and freshwater fish, lacquered and painted lurid; crustacea and other 'Products of the Sea'; a pseudo-aquarium of sharks, marlin, dugong, rays and turtles; newer displays of shells and corals, chameleons, lizards and snakes all safely stuffed, and the skeleton of a 'toothed' or sperm-whale, the source of commercial spermaceti and ambergris.

Nairobi Snake Park. The museum's ornithological collection may far outnumber that of the small **Nairobi Aviary** opposite, but the latter's inmates are at least alive. The aviary, however, is dwarfed in size and visit-value by the Snake Park adjacent (entrance Ksh. 5/- for adults, 3/- for children, 3/-, 1/50 for citizens and residents; 'photographic ticket' 10/-; 9.30 a.m.-6 p.m.). Even those who do not perhaps take to snakes will like the humorous jam on this reptilian pill: 'Trespassers will be Poisoned', says one sign, and

another, above the crocodiles, 'Visitors throwing litter into this pit will be required to retrieve it'. Opposite the cash-desk is a room of snakes non-venomous but not for that less horrid. Frogs you see fed alive to them, others petrified by fright as the snakes approach, paralyzed by poison, then slowly swallowed whole. In and beside the aviary doze common Nile and Needle-nosed crocodiles. Tortoises and turtles live in their amphibious pits. Opened in January 1961, the park now houses about 200 species.

Across Museum Hill, the **International Casino** dominates the roundabout (tel. 742600/1). Here, nightly since 1969, the city's élite has been dining well and dancing, enjoying a cabaret of the near-best from Europe and gambling at roulette, blackjack, baccarat and craps.

Nairobi National Park. So unquestionably one of the Things You Must See, this is with many 'package' holidays not even an Optional Extra. It is automatically included, and no less indispensable if you travel independently. It was gazetted – ecologically consecrated as a national park – in December 1946. Only 44 square miles in area and six miles from the GPO, this former Masai/Kikuyu inter-tribal limbo on the Athi Plains had been part of the settlers' 'Southern Reserve', then of the Somali shepherds' 'Nairobi Commonage'; camp, training ground and road to the Front in the First World War, then army firing range in the Second. As in all national parks, the animals are free to come and go as grazing dictates; the usual 'faunal reservoir' adjacent is in this case the Kitengela Conservation Area and the Ngong Hills Game Reserve (p. 53), and the fences along the Mombasa Road, like the experimental 'exclosures', are a national park exception. A Survey of Kenya map is available at the gate – but scarcely necessary.

Entrance, as in most Kenyan parks, costs adults Ksh. 20/-, under 12s 1/-, vehicles 20/-. The park opens from 6.15 a.m. to 7 p.m. daily but the best game run for your money is made from opening time to mid-morning. Then the nocturnal creatures may still be up late and the lions not yet hiding from the heat of the day. They rise after 4 p.m., the next best time for viewing. Rangers keep the prides tracked with near-military accuracy, but the encircling cluster of sightseeing car-loads pin-points them equally well. An understandable delight, the lionesses and playful cubs steal the thunder of some 80 other species (elephants a notable exception). The park's list of birds now outnumbers Britain's. Near its long southern edge are the higher ridges and gorges; the rolling plain north towards the Embakasi Gate is more typically Athi, and the Kalembi Valley Circuit south of the Main Gate takes you through country better suited to cheetahs, leopards and some two dozen rhinos. Certain of the last have been 'imported' here; of the first, 'Patience' was the matriarch and star. Known to have produced 27 cubs since 1966, she was on occasions hospitalized in the orphanage, and passed on to her offspring the affable habit of jumping on visitors' cars.

Despite the drought of 1973-74, which reduced by three quarters the wildebeest and zebra population and eliminated the kongonis, and despite poaching from the Athi-Kipiti area, sometimes by Masai deprived of grazing, this compact wildlife community is unique in its natural survival so near to a capital city. For all its 'urbanity', remember the game is as wild as anywhere. National park rules apply rigidly (p. 34); speed-bumps on the often bituminized tracks physically enforce the 20 mph/30 kph limit; extra safeguards here are the ban on cars travelling off the tracks or with roof-hatches open. Entry is also forbidden after 6.15 p.m. – but to stay on and enjoy the park's wildlife by night you have the facilities of Masai Lodge (p. 140).

The Animal Orphanage. You can take Uhuru Highway straight to the East/Embakasi/ Mombasa Road Entrance (p. 42) but the Main Gate has added attraction in the Animal Orphanage and, if time permits, in Karen and the Ngongs beyond.

From the roundabout at which the Mombasa Road begins (p. 42)[0] Langata Road runs out between Nairobi's 'Thomas Barnardo's House' (r.) and **Wilson Airport** [2]. The original 'Nairobi Aerodrome' was constructed near Dagoretti Corner (p. 52) for the RAF's first Annual Service Flight from Cape to Cairo in 1926. Resited here in 1929, it became 'Nairobi West' when the larger airfield was completed at Eastleigh, and 'Wilson Aerodrome' in 1961. Base now for the air-charter companies (p. 30), the Flying Doctor Services and the Police Air Wing, this aeronautical hive takes its name from Mrs Florrie Wilson OBE, who nursed her 'happy little airline', Wilson Airways, from a one-Moth outfit in 1929 to an organization which, taken over by the RAF ten years later, was acknowledged as the starting-point of East African/Kenya Airways. The airport starts with the 'Dambusters' and ends with the

Aero Club of East Africa (l.)[2½]. Formed in 1927 and reconstructed here in 1947, it offers – besides a bar and restaurant, accommodation, squash courts, swimming-pool and back-slapping RAF atmosphere – the cheapest private flying in Kenya (POB. 40813, tel. 501771/2; membership Ksh. 200/- p.m.).

After the GK Prison (r.), complete with craft shop and nursery, the sign opposite the **Golf Range** (l.)[3½] reads 'NSC'. The former boasts also a popular disco, while the latter stands for the **Nairobi Sailing Club**, based on the **Nairobi Dam**. Its half-mile track forks right to the 'Public Beach', a sandless misnomer where bilharzia even bars swimming, and left to the club-house, where only by invitation may you sail as helm or crew (tel. 501250).

The extensive Onyonika housing estate, the Langata Barracks and a 'Women Prison', then the park's various headquarters functions are listed unmissably (l.)[6]. Recovering from the drive's hazardous speed-bumps, you see (r.) the orphanage and (l.) the **Wildlife/Conservation Education Centre**, 'a gift of the African Wildlife Leadership Foundation, Washington D.C.'. The latter shows films (2-4.30 p.m. on Saturdays, Sundays and public holidays) and houses a library and **museum**, small but well planned, mainly for small people, with push-button models and wildlife displays – what you might call Game games (entrance free: 8.15-12.45 & 2-4.30 daily).

The orphanage is open from 8.30 a.m. to 6.30 p.m. daily (adults Ksh. 5/-, children 2/50). It was founded in June 1963 according to the official pamphlet, but 'in 1965' and 'thanks to thousands of Dutch children' according to the 'Symbol of international Friendship' unveiled by the gate on 8 February 1973 . . . the contradiction being explained by the orphanage's removal in 1969 from its overcrowded original site to its present 25 acres. But such details are irrelevant, for the orphanage's *raison d'être* and attraction are its transient intake of animal waifs. Curing and re-equipping them, if possible, for life outside in the bush is its most worth-while work. Some unrehabilitable veterans are resident stars; visiting artistes are the two brown bears, from North America, the prolific Pygmy hippos, a gift from Liberia, and the 'paying-guest' pets left temporarily by owners on leave. The marabous have gate-crashed. Although, for the rest, the cages and enclosures may be just like your local zoo's, a sign warns 'This Orphanage is Not a Zoo': food you should not donate for, with many sick and on diets, the inmates suffer here more than anywhere from these ill-advised gifts. Official feeding time, except on Fridays, is usually 2.30 p.m.

Opposite the park drive lies Langata Cemetery (open 7 a.m.-7 p.m. daily, with graves of all the nations but most British and one small selection even Bahai). The cross-roads [8] is then sign-posted **'Bomas of Kenya'** and 'Olorgesailie Prehistoric Site 66 km'. By turning twice right you reach the first at once: a sizeable, circular auditorium complete with café, VIP gallery and cushions on the stone seats for 1200 lesser folks below. The centre, with its 'settlement' of lifelike *bomas* beyond, was opened in 1972 as a KTDC project – and as a pleasant place to acquaint oneself (at second hand) with indigenous ceremonies and life-styles.

Karen. For Karen carry straight on beyond the 'Bomas' cross-roads. Alternatively, from Nairobi, continue past the Nairobi Club (p. 42) along the Ngong Road. Or join it via Valley Road (p. 45), climbing past the Panafric [0] and turning right at the second roundabout. Here the **Nairobi Baptist Church** occupies the corner (r.; Sundays 11 a.m. & 6.30 p.m.). The **Ngong Road**, part of the pioneers' 'trunk track' to Uganda, runs out past the ageing Gaylord Inn (r.)[2] and the African Safari Club's **Ngong Hills Hotel** (l.)[2½]. After sports grounds, a 'Swedish School' (r.), the Impala Club and the Swedish-aided Kenya Science Teachers College (also l.), you turn left at Dagoretti Corner [6], leaving this 'Old Naivasha Road', and pass **Jamhuri** – ex-Mitchell – **Park** (off l.): the Agricultural Society of Kenya's annual **International Nairobi Show** and the Boy Scouts' 30-acre **Rowallan Camp**, where you may picnic, swim and camp (tel. 568111).

The Ngong radio station [7½] is followed by the **Nairobi Ngong Road War Cemetery** (also l.)[8]: the approach road impressive to the Cross of Sacrifice; graves and gardens rising to the central Stone of Remembrance and, left of this, an unusual but moving enclosure where pink stone columns 'bear the names of two thousand four hundred men and women . . . who gave their lives . . . but to whom the fortune of war denied a known and honoured grave'. The Commonwealth War Graves Commission tends 740 British tombs in Kenya's 34 World War cemeteries, and details are found in the registers kept (until pilfered) in each gate-post or vestibule.

Next left: the Jockey Club of Kenya's popular **Ngong Road Race-course** [9], where the offspring of imported English thorough-breds and local Somali mares race most Sundays from 2.30 p.m. (Ksh. 20/-, under 16s 2/-). After the Lenana School – the old Duke of York's – and the Ngong Forest Station (also r.) you dip and wind through woodland: 'Picnicing or Parking in this Forest is a Personal Risk'. Karen then starts with **St Francis' Anglican Church** (l.)[11½] which was built, spireless but otherwise English-village, in 1952 (Sunday HC 8 a.m., Morning Prayer 10.30).

By using Baroness Blixen-Finecke's Christian name *tout court*, Karen's tribute is far more endearing, if somewhat smaller-scale, than Titograd's, Nashville's or Bury St Edmunds'. The coffee estate she developed here was her Danish family's wedding-present in 1914; her husband (and cousin) Baron Bror Blixen-Finecke went off to write *African Hunter* and to figure in Hemingway's *Francis Macomber*; the 36-acre farm that coffee-slump bankruptcy forced her to leave in 1931 became Denmark's independence gift to Kenya, and *Out of Africa* was published in 1937 ('Isak Dinesen' being Karen's *nom de plume*).

The baroness died in 1962, but you may visit her farm-house and final home (an earlier residence surviving as the lounge of the Westwood Park Hotel). Turn either first left after St Francis' and follow Karen Road across Langata Road, or second left after St Francis', out past **St Mark's** (l.; Sunday mass 8.30 & 10 a.m.) – its twelve Stations inside as though done by a drop-out from the Wedgwood School – and so (1st r.) into Karen Road. After the Karen Country Club (l.), **Karen House** (r.) shares the delightful gardens with Karen College (another £125,000 Danish gift, which Kenya took over in February 1971 and allotted to the Ministry of Health).

The Ngongs are Nairobi's homely backdrop. From afar they are humps, the highest 7990 feet; close to, one stretch of green sloping erosion. The Masai revere them: the original name of *Ngongo Bagas*, they say, means the knuckles – of a giant that terrorized their forefathers. Ants, their allies, heaped earth over the sleeping ogre, over all but the knuckles, that is. Farther-fetched variants are that the giant was trotting across Africa when he tripped over Kilimanjaro and, to stop himself falling, clutched at earth – thus shaping the Ngongs. Alternatively, that they are the dirt that God flicked from his fingers as he finished off the Creation. Sir Charles Eliot demurs: the name, he says, did the

Masai but know it, comes from their *Eng-ongu-e-'m-Bagasi*, the Eye (or Source) of the Athi (or the Mbagathi).

Unarguably rich in game, the Ngongs were for all that changed from a national reserve to a Masai-controlled game reserve in July 1961. In *Out of Africa* Karen pays loving tribute to their landscape, 'that had not its like in all the world'.

The **Circular Tour** must for 40 years have been much as she left it in the 1930s. Grading, however, in 1978 removed its rocky outcrops

Preparatory School. **Langata** – the Masai's 'Wide plain' – ends. So does the tarmac, and officially Nairobi, as the **Ngong Hills Game Reserve** begins [14]. The seven-km. track to **Masai Lodge** lies promptly left. The main track, dreadful rock and murram, stumbles between sparse settlements and shambas, over partly farmed slopes of aloes, acacia and cattle. After the mission-village of Kiserian in its dip [26] – the '*Kanisa katoliki*' now run, but not built, by the Mill Hill Fathers – this C 58, welcome tarmac again, sidles steadily

Dikdik confrontation – in Nairobi's Animal Orphanage

and mud-filled dips, enabling you now to enjoy without discomfort the suddenly wondrous and pristine scenery. Follow the Magadi Road, left from the Bomas cross-roads (p. 52)[8], out past the Langata and Banda gates to Nairobi National Park (the latter restricted to staff). Soon the countryside is heavy with hills, all tightly overgrown; smart homesteads occupy clearings, a Consolata Seminary and (also r.) the Banda

nearer the Ngongs. You round their southern spur to the sudden panorama of a stark volcanic country; shambas and bandas yield to wandering donkeys and goats, and by the hamlet of Olepolos [38] a sign used to point (r.) to the 'Ngong Hills Circular Tour 16 miles'.

'Ngong Rifle Range' is indicated (l.) [53½]: the track – the E 415 to Mount Suswa (p. 119) – leads four miles alongside low cliffs and loops left around the range.

The main Circular Tour zigzags back rockily over the Ngongs to rejoin first good murram (r.), then the tarmac into Ngong village [67½].

This, though, is more easily reached by the road straight on through Karen [0]. From its police and petrol stations, post office and village supermarket, the Ngong Road rolls on past the turning (r.)[1½] to the **Westwood Park Hotel**, the Savannah Pot Club (sic), the Masai Technical Institute and the radio station on Nairobi's city-limit [3½]. The *Masjid an-Nur* – the Mosque of Light – makes **Bulbul** conspicuous [4½]. It is a standard Sunni mosque (p. 11), with white and green spirelets and the usual upturned-bedstead style, but the village is remarkable for being not only Muslim in this Christian/pagan district, but also predominantly Nubian – its founding fathers being disbanded troops resettled here. Turn right in Ngong village [8], fork left uphill and left past the track to 'Oloolaiser Secondary School'. A first sign directs you 'Straight on for Ngong Hills Circular Tour', past the police station and the administration boma, then right [9]: 'Be Aware of Theft'. The track (l.) climbs steep and scenic, to curl to an end around the radio station [13].

The one-way, two-hour walk along the ridge is scarcely more strenuous than was the old Circular Tour drive. Residents recommend that your party divide into two cars, one to be left above the southern spur, the other above Ngong police station. You then cross paths en route, perhaps picnic *ensemble* on the **Lamwia** 'summit', and descend to take the other car home. If you find horseback better than both, contact Safaris Unlimited (p. 27).

The Arboretum. From God's Corner (p. 45) follow State House Road up past the **YMCA** (r.; POB. 30330; its pool open to visitors for Ksh. 10/- p.d.), the university's residential blocks and the Girls' High School (formerly the Delamere – and the 'Heifer Boma' in Nairobi schoolboy slang). The hill climbs on (l.) to the president's **State House** (photography forbidden), but follow the signs before (2nd r.) into Arboretum Road. The pink, dovecotted cottage (r.) was installed in 1946 as the 'King George V Memorial Girl Guide Headquarters' – a function it now shares with a private tutorial college.

Ahead, the Nairobi Arboretum Forest Reserve is an 80-acre pleasance of lawns and neatly labelled trees, some Kenyan, some foreign, and some 270 species in all. Entrance,

from sunrise to 30 minutes after sunset, is free, and 'It is an offence to climb trees shoot with guns or catpults throw stones ride horses or be guilty of indecent behaviour' . . . in English, Swahili, Farsi or Urdu.

City Park. This, even more than the arboretum, is one of Nairobi's aesthetically functional amenities: gardens, maze and orchid collection, pools and children's playground, nursery and cemeteries, sports grounds and dog pound. Take a no. 11 or 12 bus from Tom Mboya Street or, by car, climb Museum Hill on past the Ainsworth Garden (p. 48) and follow Forest Road out through Parklands to **St Francis Xavier's Church** (1933; mass Sundays 8, 9.30 & 5.30 p.m., weekdays 6.30 a.m. & 5.45 p.m.). Here turn on to Limuru Road (2nd l.). A sign-posted park drive (r.) – speed-bumps and bougainvillea – leads first to the **Nursery**, on each side of which paths descend to the 'Sunken Garden, Bandstand and Maze' (swings and slides for youngsters and ponds for fish and frogs). In the **Boscawen Memorial Collection** (further l.) the orchids originally raised by 'The late Lt. Col. The Hon. M.T. Boscawen D.S.O., M.C.' and 'Presented to the City of Nairobi by his Sister' are attractive if esoteric (admission 1/-; 12-6 p.m., Mondays 10-6, Fridays 7-2). Beyond lie the **cemeteries** (open 7 a.m.-7 p.m., with the 97 British military graves mostly World War II, but some from 1950 and five from World War I in a low-hedged area downhill). It is recommended that in the 300 acres of often pristine parkland around or especially, I suppose, in the **Maze**, 'ladies should have male escorts'.

The Rift View can be a spectacular attraction, but both rain cloud and heat haze can make it a misnomer. So only on a clear day should you keep straight on from the museum roundabout (p. 48)[0]. A fine dual carriage-way, **Chiromo** – formerly Salisbury – **Road** runs out between (r.) the Devon Hotel, the Chiromo Hotel's 'Swiss Grill', the Club 1900 and **Safarilands Hotel** and (l.) the head-quarters of the **Consolata Fathers**. The activities of these mainly Italian missionaries have been widely beneficial to Kenya. Here, beside a Caltex station, stand their hostels and offices, nursery and primary school, and **Lady Consolata Catholic Church** (mass Sundays in Italian at 12, in English 8.30, 9.30 & 11 a.m., Saturdays 5.30 p.m.). Archi-tecturally it appears to be polygonal in every direction, its concrete campanile an army-camp watch-tower, its interior a contrast of modernistic grey and colourful stained glass. The Italian image for a long time lingered also over **Westlands**, right of the next roundabout [2], with its 'Italian workshop', Agip Restaurant and Agip Motel. Two Agip stations and a 'Pizza Garden' remain, but the motel has become the **Jacaranda** and, with supermarkets plus a 'Kentucky Fried Chicken', the atmosphere – if not the efficiency – is now near-miss American. The **Automobile Association**'s busy tourist centre; bookshops, banks, butchers, bakers and drapers, chemists and cheap, persistent peddlers of flowers and fresh fruit; all these – and the problems of parking down town – have made Westlands a successful shopping centre.

Off left beyond the West View Hotel, Groganville commemorates the colonel who in 1897-1900 walked, and later wrote, *From Cape to Cairo* to prove himself to his loved one's father. Coming in right, the former Sclaters Road honoured Sergeant Ellis' CO (p. 41) and followed the line of the railway surveyors' track (p. 21). After Westlands, and since 1973, it is known as **Waiyaki Way**. Further right, **St Mark's Anglican Church** was built in 1958 (Sunday HC 8 a.m., Matins 10.30). A long winding rise, then the signs point left [3½] to 'St Austins Catholic Church 2nd right 1 Mile'. **St Austin's** was completed in 1912 by the initially French, then increasingly Irish **Holy Ghost Fathers**. Having established a first mission on Zanzibar in 1800, the fathers moved first to Kibwezi then here to 'Simonisdale' in 1901, where they developed an impressive educational (and coffee-growing) complex that has since been largely redeveloped as the Lavington and Bernhard estates. Karen regularly attended mass here – writing of St Austin's in *Out of Africa* – and you can do so too on Sundays at 7.30, 8.30, 10 & 11.30 a.m., at 7 a.m. on weekdays.

Kabete remains academic and ecclesiastical: left and right of the road, the Aga Khan and Nairobi high schools and government research institutes, the 'All Africa Conference of Churches Training Centre' and Apostolic Nunciature. Kabete was the site of the Church Missionary Society's first up-country station. Established in 1901, it was in 1902 taken over by Canon Leakey who – besides founding a remarkable family (p. 16) – built the first permanent church, taught and converted the Kikuyu and translated for them both Prayer Book and Bible.

While Lower Kabete was church, Upper Kabete was state. Here in 1892 the Imperial British East Africa Company built **Fort**

Smith. Named after Major Eric S., its designer and first commandant, it was the first of the IBEA's Uganda-route outposts to be constructed of kiln-clay brick. Perhaps because of this, Fort Smith survives as the oldest building up country. Beside the fort (now private) stands the **Tree of Peace**, a giant *mugomo*: by planting it in 1897 Chief Kinanjui and Major Smith's successor, Frank Hall (p. 102), brought to an end seven years of Kikuyu hostilities. Kinanjui is remembered locally for always driving his wood-framed car in second gear; he features movingly in Karen's *Out of Africa*.

Despite stylish developments on the slopes to the left – and the widening of the road since 1975 into an out-of-town freeway – the standards decline as you climb. You finally shake off smart Nairobi and roll across steep red hills of shanties and shambas. Leaving Dagoretti to the left, the highway merges with the 'Old Naivasha Road' and, narrow now, traverses Uthiru. Turnings [18] serve Kiambu (r.)[24 kms] and (l.)[2 kms] the township called **Kikuyu**: 'Saw Millers' and an Ondiri 'hotel' mud-coloured and unwelcoming.

After the Sigona Golf Club and the late (but not lamented) Zambezi Motel – become a Presbyterian Pastoral Institute (l.)[21] – urbanism peters out. The occasional settlements are tin-roofed or thatched, unlovely on the dull mud that dries from russet wet to orange. Woodland, grassland and shambas untidy with banana-plants cover the slopes, which are often too steep for machinery; patches of maize feed posho mills (p. 28), and only the tracts of white-flowered pyrethrum give depth to the somewhat cluttered vistas. This is typical Kikuyu country, by African standards intensely developed. **Pyrethrum** is too: a crop more dependable than coffee or tea, its insecticide qualities were discovered in the 1940s and some Ksh. 84-million worth of extract now goes overseas annually as a healthier alternative to DDT.

After Rironi [28] – and its rather unexpected St Eleftherios Greek Orthodox Church – the roadside business is smaller retail: hides, live rabbits in boxes and colourful arrays of mats, baskets and baubles in beadwork and dyed straw or wool. Their pitches bright with a fence of white sheepskins, the Kikuyu boys' sales techniques range from merely importunate to near-suicidal. They ask twenty shillings for sheepskin hats that make a good buy at seven or eight. (Only farmyard smells spoil their Zhivago air.) Straw table-mats are worth their three-four shillings per half-dozen, and these the Kikuyu women sit making by the second turning to Limuru (r.)[33].

Shambas yield to the Ngubi Forest, and the message on the sign [39½] – 'You are now Entering the Escarpment' – is brought home by the start of the sharp cliff-ledge bends. Here on a clear day the Rift View is superb (p. 7). **Mount Suswa** rises just perceptible from the valley floor, the Masai's *Ol Donyo Onyoke*, Red Mountain. To the north **Mount Longonot** is a higher and broader massif, still active (p. 58). The former is 7660 feet high, the latter 9111, and the communications saucer between them 97. This '**Longonot Satellite Earth Station**', *alias* Mount Margaret, was constructed by Marconi for Ksh. 30 million and opened by the Mzee in November 1970 as East Africa's telephonic link with Europe.

The road that zigzags to the Rift-floor was built by Italian prisoners of war. They followed the track of the railway surveyors, whose path-finders in turn were most probably elephants. Big-game trails up the easiest gradients often helped Africa's road-builders. The Italians then went on, as in Tabora, to build a **Chapel of Thanksgiving**: lying right of the road as you leave Kiambu county [49½], it was dedicated to St Mary of the Angels on Christmas Day 1943.

Halfway downhill the **Rift Valley View Point** is sign-posted 'Forest Reserve Picnic Site' (l.)[45½]. The track, not always open, cuts a half-mile through tight forest to a panoramic promontory of *mutharathari* and *muhuhu*-trees, notice-boards, an incongruous grandstand and decrepit picnic-seats fixed a yard from their table.

The African Inland Church's **Kijabe Mission** is reached by a four-mile murram track (r.)[47½]. Meaning appropriately Wind, Kijabe is important now more as a mission than as a Kikuyu market-station. The former began in 1901: with the help of mainly American missionaries it now comprises churches and clinics, radio station and printing-press, the 1929 Moffat Bible Institute, the Rift Valley Academy and Kijabe High School.

Returning via Limuru, you move from the homely if bitty tracts of small-time cultivation to the other aspect of Kikuyuland: the suave tea-green slopes of the great estates. **Tea** – THEA SINENSIS – was introduced from India and first planted at Limuru in 1903. Needing careful tending and an annual minimum of 60 inches of rain, the 'tea gardens' remained the Europeans' lucrative preserve until the 'Swynnerton Plan to Intensify the Development of African Agriculture'. Nowadays the crop is raised by 100,000 Africans, and one- or two-acre plots make up 60% of the total 138,000 acres of tea gardens, their 'tea roads' one-cart wide between the countless bushes, their pickers colourful with baskets slung papoose-like. Tea shoots are planted out at eighteen months, produce leaves for picking two years later and send, in their sixth and seventh years, up to 5000 lbs of leaf per acre to be processed in the country's 61 tea factories. Which goes towards Kenya's total tea exports – the world's third largest – of Ksh. 186 million per annum.

Coffee betters this with its Ksh. 3844 million. In the 1890s the French Holy Ghost Fathers – and, perhaps, a Scot – pioneered at Kibwezi the first plantings of Mocha from Zanzibar. Brought by the fathers to St Austin's in 1901, with the first beans picked by Father Bernhard at Burnbrae in 1905 (p. 55), coffee was then developed especially north of Nairobi. Until R.J. Swynnerton's reforms of 1954, African farmers were actually forbidden to grow it. Most of Kenya's coffee is of the ARABICA variety (which you smell in German cafés), some ROBUSTA, less EXCELSA. Berries are hand-picked twice annually – 'Fly Crop' and 'Main Crop'; the beans are graded, auctioned and exported, then roasted, ground and blended.

Limuru. We were however at the turn-off (above)[0], where the sign-post to Limuru was recently changed from '4½ miles' to '3 km' and then removed. Old 'Limoru' was, like Kikuyu, rejected in the 1900s as a healthy alternative to Nairobi. As compensation for not becoming capital, it has a fine golf course (Limuru Country Club), a pack of hounds (the Limuru Hunt, p. 27), two *haute cuisine* hotels, the Bata shoe factory and tea, coffee and pyrethrum *passim*. The road crosses the township [3½] and climbs past the Loreto High School (l.), the **Limuru Country Club** (r.) and Brooke Bond Liebig's Mabrookie Estate, the Limuru Cheshire Home (r.) and the 1940 **All Saints' Church** [12](HC 8 or 11.30 a.m. and 'Mattins' 10.30 2nd & 4th Sundays, Evensong 6.30 1st & 3rd Sundays). Here, sign-posted and precisely two kms across the tea fields to the left, General Heath's 1948 farm-house has become the **Farm Hotel**. Though the original *patrons* (who catered impeccably if expensively with the best of French cuisine) are now no more, the present African management strives to uphold the reputation (three rooms; bed & breakfast Ksh. 120/- double, 80/- single; tel. Tigoni 323).

After the YWCA's Vocational Training School and the exemplary **Limuru Boys' Centre** (which welcomes visitors), the **Kentmere Club** (l.)[16] accommodates more spaciously, and quaintly (four double rooms + bath; bed & breakfast Ksh. 203/20 double, 165/10 single; Nairobi POB. 49666, tel. Kiambaa 253). Built as a pub in 1952 and until 1970 the Dinhim Country Club, the Kentmere maintains the cosy mood of log fires, low ceilings and black beams; but what fills the well-run restaurant's 52 seats is the club's first-class food (tel. Nairobi 337496).

Next, the neat green acres of Brooke Bond's Kentmere Estate, the Consolata Sisters' Nazareth Hospital and the long drop of **Banana Hill** (so named because the hamlet halfway down is called Banana). You descend, with the tips of Nairobi's tallest buildings protruding above the trees. The city starts officially just before you merge (l.) with Limuru Road [25½]: the extensive **United Nations UNEP headquarters** and UNICEF regional office (l.)[30½] seem somehow intruders in the discreetly select suburb of **Rosslyn**. You then wind through steep woodland and, at the roundabout [32½], can fork either left on to Muthaiga Road which, gilt-edged with embassy residences, meets

On the edge of the Escarpment – Kikuyu women sell souvenirs

Murang'a Road (p. 60)[35½], or right along Limuru Road which comes into town alongside City Park (p. 54)[36].

Lake Naivasha. If you have not a half but a whole day free, add to the pleasure of the Rift View trip the drive on to the lovely 'Sunshine Lake'. From the foot of the Rift-wall and the Italian chapel (p. 56)[49½] the main road passes (l.) the B 3 [51½] to 'Narok 89 km' and Keekorok, and (r.) the Shell 'fortress' of Maai Mahiu – not a mediaeval relic but a farmer's 1959 pastiche. The temperature rises perceptibly, while the railway descends from its cliff ledge (r.) to cross the road at Longonot (p. 56)[66].

Mount Longonot blocks the view left, its sides lined with lava runnels and its crater rim crumpled. And relatively easily reached. Take the track (l.), inches before the level crossing. The 'Police Warning to Visitors' here has gone, but its message holds good: 'Beware Theft from Motor Vehicles'. The route is passable, despite a high centre ridge then rocks. You fork left after two kms and at six reach the 'roadhead', whence you follow the clear and un-demanding footpath up around the four-km. crater.

Longonot village is wood-slatted shops, a breeze-block Catholic church, a four-shack police post and a 'Longonot Safari Hotel'. The main road thereafter tops the Uplands Road to Nairobi (p. 59)[69] and Lake Naivasha appears, a rippling expanse with a half-farmed hinterland dramatically backed by the Mau Escarpment (but somewhat spoilt by pylons). The fine shady **acacias** around – Yellow-barked or Umbrella thorn, ACACIA XANTHOPHLOEA or ACACIA TORTILIS – were dubbed 'fever trees' because that befell many pioneers who slept under them (the real culprit being the malarial mosquitoes that they harboured). Many acacias have of late been cut for charcoal but, as this has 'created more indignation from the public than any single action in recent years', the World Wildlife Fund, the Kenya government and the National Parks have all responded with saplings, which the 'Men of the Trees' – and the late Mzee – soon set to planting. (Some went also, along with baobabs, to be grown in California by William Holden, who plans to repay Kenya with redwoods and sequoias.)

'Naivasha' is the Masai's *En-aiposha* – The Lake – corrupted for perpetuity by early Europeans who recorded not the locals' place-name but the mispronunciations of their Swahili porters. The German naturalist Gustav Fischer 'discovered' Lake Naivasha on 11 May 1883, but here the Masai discovered him too and his 300-man caravan was halted and had to turn back. The following year Joseph Thomson arrived, gored by a buffalo but 'unpunctured by spears', and in 1888 Count Teleki found the lake 'in not quite the right position' – on the maps, that is. (A modern map, sketched but adequate, is available for 1/- at Fisherman's Camp.) Until the colonial boundary-play of 1902 the province of Naivasha was part of Uganda and in 1904, when the Masai agreed to move to Laikipia, the first governmental farm was started here to experiment with cattle, sheep, pigs and zebras. Captain Macdonald, the railway surveyor, had found the lake 'full of hippo': it next featured in transport history when, for seventeen months from May 1949, the BOAC flying boat splashed down here three times weekly. If Naivasha's islands seem never quite the same it is because they are papyrus-clumps, constantly splitting and drifting. And if reliable guide-books never mention its depth, size or height above sea-level, it is because the lake rises and spreads, or sinks and shrinks, with the rainfall. (In 1917 its waters reached the railway, Naivasha town once lay on the shore and many east-bank farms owe their existence to the shore-line's recession – until 1979.)

Naivasha itself is no metropolis [89]. So unless you want a snack in the roadside Kenchic – the old **New Bell** – **Inn** (r.) or a comfortable night in the **Malaika Hotel** (precisely two kms, and three times r., uphill), turn left before it on to South Lake Road [84]. Tracks (r.) lead to the **Lake Naivasha Hotel** [87½] and – when the water subsides – to **Crescent Island** [90]. Safariland Lodge and the Lake Hotel offer 20/- crossings by boat, while the causeway laid by the KAR theoretically takes this three-km. track through the papyrus to the 1000-acre sanctuary ('Where you can Walk freely with Africa's wildlife' . . . for Ksh. 25/-). On and along its crescent-shaped ridge you may see '340 species' of birds and wander close to '120 dikdik, 300 waterbuck and 500 Thomson's gazelle'. The 100-odd hippo are no danger and predators non-existent. Archaeologists here in 1976 discovered later Stone Age scrapers and burins of obsidian (p. 115).

On shore, after the suave **Safariland Lodge** [93½], Longonot Farm was part-location for *Living Free*. The tarmac ends [95] but is soon

58

revived for an odd half-km. – in order to keep down the dust, they say, for a World War II artillery camp. The YMCA's Naivasha Camp (r.), a colony of rondavels and an obtrusive transformer station are then the improbable harbingers of Hell's Gate [98].

Hell's Gate, to judge by the owners' warnings, must have brought out the devil in people: 'Road open to Visitors unless and until We are Compelled to Close it by their Misconduct/WARNING Be Careful of Thugs/No Camping . . . Or any other Kind of Nuisance'. The track turns sharp right [2 kms] and dramatically before you stands **Fischer's Tower** [3], a volcanic stack where may have been the outlet of the primaeval lake that united Naivasha, Elmentaita and Nakuru. The broad corrie around you now is technically the **Njorowa Gorge** – and spectacular with cliffs eroded, stratified or just precipitously sheer. Continue straight, to rejoin the old route and follow the 'Death Gulch' sign on, veering with the cliffs. The track, an ordeal for exhausts, deteriorates steadily; then the boundary walls fall away and, by the well-head [10½], only a pillar of rock marks the start of Hell's Gate. Of the three forks here the first forms a loop and comes back as the second. So park and take the right-hand track: for a five-minute scramble down a deep eroded fissure in which two rock pinnacles stand sentinel, a minor and a major Cerberus. The gorge then opens out magnificently before you, its rock walls stratified and often streaked mineral red, the vegetation dense and the birdsong incongruous. An easy but lengthy track leads down to the hot springs. Naivasha's 400 species has prompted its being described as a 'bewilderment of birds': at Hell's Gate may be seen the rare lammergeyer, Nyanza swift and Verreaux's eagle.

The lake shore beyond is now almost urban with its rondavels for workers and packing sheds for flowers. Here Brooke Bond's Sulmak Company produces carnations for airfreight to Europe. **Fisherman's Lodge** is an off-shoot of the older **Fisherman's Camp** (r.)[102], which still provides mooring and water/fire-wood for camping (Ksh. 20/- p.p., children 10/-), hires boats (10/- for rowing, 20-60/- per hour's bird-watching) and accommodates in its 'Top' and 'Bottom' camps (Ksh. 46-57/50 p.p.p.n.; bookings and obligatory payment in advance to A.A. Travel, Nairobi POB. 14982, tel. 742926-9).

The narrower, worse track winds and climbs away from the lake, past the late Joy Adamson's 'Elsamere' and an exquisite (but private) moorish villa, the well-named Gin (but really Djinn) Palace. Thereafter over ridges with views of the **Small Lake** (its bar of papyrus being the real Hippo Point) and from open woodland across tighter acacia forest.

Precisely 6½ kms after the South Lake police station (l.)[113], you can turn (r.) through an unmarked ranch-gate, carefully close it again, and climb to the Masai's **'Secret Lake'** (r. at the diagonal crosstracks at 0·7 kms and 1·4 kms up the clear hillside path). From the rocky crater rim a path descends through the acacias to the cold black waters, 'mysterious' but also sufficiently mineral for the locals to bring their ailing cattle here for a purgative cure.

With the main track at its best, you are hub-deep in dust: the only consolation – or justification? – for completing this lap of the lake are the volcanic humps that rise from the stubbly plain, the flower farms' splashes of colour and the road-cutting black with obsidian (l.)[135]. After the turning to Eburu (l.)[137] – known for its china clay pits – you rumble (or slither) on murram to the tarmac of the A 104 [146]. Turn left for Gilgil (p. 114) and Nakuru (p. 117); or right, across miles of the Marula, Morendat and Manera farm-estates, into Naivasha [158].

The **Uplands Road** offers the fastest return to Nairobi. (It also spares you the fumes – and fuming – of the lorry-clogged drag back up the Rift-wall.) Sign-posted as the C 67 near Mount Longonot [177½], this fine highway was constructed in 1973 by the Israeli Solel Boneh company . . . but starts with a Jewish joke: the nine rough kms up from the main road for which the plans – or the funds – must have been mislaid. Viewpoints (r.)[189 & 209] provide a magnificent panorama: over Lake Naivasha and almost into the Longonot crater. There follows a plateau of conifer forest, saw-mills and shambas; turnings serve the Kinangop, Kijabe and 'Escarpment'. After Uplands, the 'Place of Bacon' (l.)[213½], the road is pristine and rejoins my 'Rift View' route at Limuru (p. 56)[220].

Olorgesailie and Magadi. The certainty of fine scenery – and heat – makes up for the long drive beyond the Ngongs. A full tank of petrol and cold drinks are advised. From Olepolos (p. 53)[38] the road, smooth but serpentine, drops steadily to dip across the estuaries and creeks of the Rift Valley's quondam sea. The countryside slowly dries out, too, and the temperature rises with the distance from Nairobi. With the croton scrubland being eaten increasingly bleaker by the Masai herds of goats and donkeys, you pass the last sign of (occasional) life at Oltepesi (r.) and turn by the sign (l.)[67½] to '**Olorgesailie Prehistoric Site**/Museum 1,5 km'.

Before earth movements diverted the Ol Keju Nyiro River, it fed a lake on the site; this attracted game and the game attracted hunters. The bones of their animal meals – antelopes, giant baboons, hippos and horses, soon fossilized – and their tools – hand-axes, cleavers and putative bolas, most from Olorgesailie lava – were slowly buried in both lake silt and volcanic ash. In a geological change of mind, erosion and faulting then removed and exposed these deposits, 90 feet deep. The geologist J.W. Gregory first noticed surface remains in 1919; Dr and Mrs Leakey started systematic excavations in 1942. Their finds were of such abundance and antiquity (4-500,000 years BC?) that this Masai tract was in 1947 declared a national park, 0·08 square miles small. Entrance costs adults Ksh. 5/-, children 2/- (residents 2/-, 1/-). The knowledgeable guides are free and obligatory, Mr Isaac's booklet is worth its 1/50 and the site's birds and mammals are the subject of a cheap *Checklist and Notes*. You can spend the night under canvas for Ksh. 2/- per person or in one of the four self-service bandas for 15/- (reservations Nairobi POB. 40658, tel. 20141). A further banda gives shelter for picnics and another, bigger, is since 1975 the 'museum'. Accompanied by stone-axe specimens, its diagrams and explanations of Olorgesailie's formation and excavation are simple and explicit, but there is scant justification here for Dr Leakey's verdict of 'the richest and most significant (site) in the whole world of Acheulian hand axe culture'.

You move on down the Ol Keju Nyiro valley, very broad, usually dry and its vegetation interspersed with sharp volcanic outcrops. You skirt deep gulches where the cattle wallow for water, cross a stony ridge into an even drier valley and finally drop to **Lake Magadi**. After the cross of Magadi's old Christian cemetery (l.)[113] the road and rail together traverse the lake's rim of mud. The next ridge, where the Magadi Soda Company's scattered settlement starts [116], has a view that makes the long drive worth while. The soda-pans shimmer, some crystalline white, others palely pink. More deeply roseate are the banks of flamingos that often edge the lake. The factory smoke rises whitish-grey, with the far shore a sere and blue-hazed silhouette. You can drive down (r.) across the pans. Their trona – c.f. Lake Na*tron*, sodium sesqui carbonate – renews itself as removed and furnishes some 107,000 tonnes of soda-ash annually. This goes by rail to Kilindini, where the Magadi Soda Company in 1913 built the first deep-water berth. Nowhere over ten feet deep, the lake was 'discovered' by Fischer in 1883 and worked by the Germans before World War I.

Thika, the Fourteen Falls and Ol Donyo Sabuk you can reach more easily. Turn off Moi Avenue by the Isma'ilia Mosque (p. 48) into Murang'a – formerly Fort Hall – Road. Keep straight on despite the Globe Cinema's sloping, far-flung roundabout and turn first right, then left to join Forest Road by the smaller **Isma'ilia Khoja Mosque** (which the Aga Khan founded in November 1957 and opened thirteen months later). Just before it stands the E.A. **Ahmadiyya Muslim Mission**, the mosque of a latter-day 'heretic' sect. To the left now lies City Park (p. 54). Beyond the roundabout [0] Murang'a Road would be an African freeway, rolling fast over hills and valleys, were it not for the never-ending roundabouts. The first [1½] features a memorial to the members of the Muthaiga Country Club fallen in World Wars I and II. On the site of Muthaiga's first 5000-acre estate stands **Gertrude's Garden** (l. in Muthaiga Road). This £30,000 children's hospital was built in 1946 by the 'grand old man' of the Kenya colony, Colonel Ewart Grogan, and perpetuates the name of the wife he won by being the first man to walk the length of Africa (p. 55). Left of the Muthaiga police station ahead, Kiambu Road skirts the **Muthaiga Golf Club** and drops to Peter Greensmith's nursery (p. 42).

Stay with the dual carriage-way (r.), which dips and rises past (l.) the headquarters of the National Youth Service (p. 114) and a Benedictine priory, and (r.) the **Utalii Hotel** [3] and the Fox Drive-in Cinema [4]. A second roundabout [5] is military with the barracks of the Kenya Army's crack General Service Unit. Kikuyu for a 'queue of women', **Ruaraka** then consists of the Kenya Breweries (r.)[5½], beside the Rui Ruaka River, and the **Safari Park Hotel** (l.)[8]. Neighbours of the latter are the Fleetwood Kennels, the Grace Independent Baptist Mission and the Thika Road Baptist Church (Sundays 10.30 a.m. &

6.45 p.m.). Widened in 1972, the road rolls on past a dinky Sunni mosque (l.)[13] and across a plain of piecemeal cultivation. The former Sir Gerald Templer's barracks, the **Kenyatta University College** (also l.)[15½] and Kahawa – Coffee – are the only features amidst the tracts of eucalyptus, acacias, banana-plants and occasional sisal 'sticks'. There are glimpses of the whaleback of Ol Donyo Sabuk (r.) between the cuttings. **Ruiru**, though honoured with a new approach-road (l.)[19½], still passes imperceptibly. A small dam and turbine built here in 1906 supplied Nairobi's first electricity: power cuts were caused by hippos stuck in the flume. Here too was the 20,000-acre Juja Farm, where the McMillans settled in 1905 to entertain famously. After Winston Churchill in 1908 came Theodore Roosevelt, whom the locals nicknamed *Bwana Tumbo*, Portly Master (even though he was no match for his 24-stone host). As the coffee estates start, you traverse Juja itself [29], the police station a well-endowed repository of car carcasses, cross the Komo River [31½] and rise to Thika [38].

Thika. For your en route dosage of local colour here, guide-books prescribe *The Flame Trees of Thika*. Russian schoolteachers, too, take Dickens as Gospel on present-day London. The trip you have just made in under an hour took the authoress Elspeth Huxley two days, and 'the giants who sleep at Thika' do so now to the rumble of factories, textile- and paper-mills, tanneries and canneries. Still in 1971, though, 'Thika – Your Industrial Town' was occasionally 'terrorized' by hippos. A Huxleyan relic is the **Blue Posts Hotel** (r.)[39½]. Attracted perhaps by the nearness of Nairobi – and the hotel bar – the makers of *Tarzan* and others on low budgets have filmed the African Jungles at the **Chania Falls**. This modestly dramatic cascade is – with the inscribed silverware – the hotel's saving grace, making it pleasant for tea on the lawns or a dip, should they refill the pool.

The bridge here, or the previous clover-leaf turning (r.), leads into Thika town. There is little of tourist interest: the Salvation Army School for the Blind and 'Variety Village' for the physically handicapped, the Equator High School and a cross-roads clock-tower 'In Loving Memory of Walter Cox of Leicester & Kalamu'. From the stadium roundabout [0] General Kago Road leaves town via the prison, posted with intriguing lists of 'Prohibited Articles/Trafficking', the

Catholic church, district hospital and **Thika War Cemetery** (r.). Behind its cross of Botticino marble are 130 Commonwealth graves: all of Africans save seven – with four Unknown – and two not military but Kenya Police killed in 1954. In the civilian cemetery (next r.) several of the British and Afrikaaner headstones are similar reminders of the Emergency.

From the cemeteries [½] you turn left [2] across the railway. This 'Old Garissa Road' leaves town through a light industrial limbo, then sporadic sisal fields. Take the marked park track (r.)[20], past the 'Motel Fourteen Falls' (l.), and turn left at the T-junction [21]. Left again by the **'Fourteen Falls'** sign [22] and 0·7 kms through to a clearing where the locals often wait to guard your car (which, but for them, would not need guarding). A path leads through the screen of trees to the foot of the falls, but stop halfway down for the finest view of the 90-foot cliff face of splendid cataracts.

Ol Donyo Sabuk. Crossing the broad Athi River's three bridges [22½], turn right by the sad shanty hamlet [23½]. After two kms of coffee the national park starts with a guard who makes you sign in but not pay. 'Entry by Motor Vehicle Only'; 'Park closes 7 15 pm.' Some say the Masai's *Ol Donyo Sabuk* means Big Mountain, others Sleeping Buffalo: the Swahili *Kilima Mbogo* means Hill of the Buffalo and thus reinforces the warning. Less for its buffalo than for its bird life and forest was the mountain declared a national park in 1969. On the highest point of its whale-shaped back (7041 feet) only the masts of a relay station mar the all-round vista: Mount Kenya magnificent – when its clouds disperse – and the many lakes below, as Novalis says, 'like eyes in the landscape'. One D. Powell-Cotton first made the ascent in 1902, but Sir William Northrup and Lady McMillan are the names the locals know (p. 47).

From the entrance picnic site [25½] the nine-km. track to the summit stumbles up steeply past their graves. They lie on a panoramic bluff to the left [32½], marble plaques on slabs of rock, alongside the smaller tomb of 'My dear old Louise (R. Decker) . . . died 1 December 1938 after 75 years of long & faithful service'. Lady McMillan was English, her husband a wealthy American (the Sir being due to the KCMG awarded for his work in World War I). The coffin-bearers' difficulties with his portly corpse explain why they came to rest not on the mountain top but here only halfway up.

THE COAST

One long tropical fringe, the Coast complements Kenya's attractiveness. It also forms a stark contrast – in climate, scenery, populace and history. Nature, you feel, was right to provide the *nyika* (p. 100): between the Coast and the up-country mountains, plains and game you need this scenic No man's land as an aesthetic respite.

With the nyika a barrier behind, the coastal peoples have for centuries looked east. Skins, slaves and ivory went to Arabia. Arabs came back to trade and breed (p. 9). India and the East Indies, too, were 'Manfasa', 'Mombass' or 'Monbaca's' early trade partners; even Europeans came first from the east to invade, convert and colonize. Traces of all this remain, for besides its beaches and off-shore attractions the Coast boasts most of Kenya's few antiquities.

They add interest to an already lovely country. Along the beaches **palms** are picturesque – coconut-palms, COCOS NUCIFERA, introduced BC from Indonesia, providing *madafu*-milk for cocktails, fermented palm-toddy and/or plasma (p. 27); white copra inside pressed for coconut-oil; coir for matting, fibre for rigging, and leaves for *makuti* roofs, cheap, waterproof and everywhere. More characteristic northward are the **mangrove swamps** – impenetrable, evergreen, off-shore jungles where the hard *boriti* poles are cut for scaffolding and roof-beams, of homes both here and in Arabia. Smallholdings and large estates share the fertile shore. Besides casuarinas, cashew-nut, mango and kapok trees are common: the first bearing most in December; the second supplying wood for *ngalawa*-canoes, and fruit, and the third shedding its hard nuts of soft down that whitens the roadsides and goes to stuff pillows.

Swahili, Giriama, Digo or Bajun, the locals are farmers and fishermen too. The Coast owes its off-shore wealth to the **reef**. Many coral species, long before the tourists, were attracted to these clear warm shallow waters. The dying generations of coral polyps built up a fantastic submarine cliff that now 'protects' almost all of this coast; entwining, poisoning and eating tiny fish, new coral continues to push the 'cliff face' ever further out to sea.

Beyond, in the deep, more sizeable fry fall prey to big-game fishermen. **Fishing** is by line, for the coral shreds nets. Baskets also are set. For big fish you troll, with shiny spoons or live bait while, in 100-yard V-shapes, sapling-traps catch smaller fry in every sandy inlet.

Inside the reef you can walk at low tide: wear rope-soled shoes or 'flipflops' as the bottom is for fakirs. Or you can peer from the glass-bottomed boat that most hotels hire. Alternatively, **goggle**: with a breathing-tube, flippers and tight-fitting mask you will soon be quite literally in another world. The sea-bed is littered – exquisitely with starfish yellow, purple and bright blood-red, grotesquely with sea-urchins, black and shiny-spiked. Fish, coral and underwater flowers . . . in this natural aquarium the colours are ethereal. Man, typically, has plundered and defiled it, using dynamite to kill and catch the fish, trapping rarer species live to market overseas, and gathering the shells en masse to sell as souvenirs. Their removal affects the ecological balance: unchecked by these natural enemies, the 'crown of thorns'-starfish – ACANTHASTER PLANCI – is devouring the polyps that perpetuate the reef. But marine parks now protect the waters off Watamu, Malindi and Shimoni, and here, as you gaze down on the silent wonder, time is easily forgotten.

Which may be why hotels hire boats by the hour. Remember a swim-shirt – the sun can burn your back; rubber gloves, too, if you reckon on exploring down where lobsters nip and the corals sometimes sting. Sharks rarely venture inside the reef and are, so they say, in any case good-natured. (They are caught on lines slung from a palm-tree or buoy, and prized as an Arab delicacy.) Only the experienced should venture over the reef: the pretty coral sea-bed drops suddenly and startlingly into the ocean chasm.

Above all this you can safely sail, in one of the hotels' modern boats, the fishermen's *ngalawa*-canoes or the larger, traditional *jahazi*-dhows that several Coast concerns have purchased and adapted. At sea the breezes moderate the year-round average of 83° and 75% humidity even more than on shore, where they make air conditioning unnecessary. The Coral Coast's two-score hotels now make a nonsense of the 'White Man's Grave' – even for early up-country settlers the Indian Ocean meant 'sea-level and sanity' – and nowadays the 300 miles from Lamu to Shimoni constitute 'one of the world's greatest holiday playgrounds'.

MOMBASA. The coastal capital's original *raison d'être* was a break in the reef: ships could come into Kilindini, Place of Deep Water. In 1971 they changed the city's insignia-slogan to *Mlango wa Kenya* – Gateway of Kenya – thus recognizing that, although perhaps Diogenes' a British naval base, Mombasa owes most to its transit significance. Landlocked like Switzerland, Uganda and Ruanda could scarcely survive without the Rhine-like life-line of the Mombasa Road and the railway. With urbanization otherwise absent, Mombasa became the first protectorate capital by default. And as entrepôt for almost all the region's sea-borne trade, Kenya's second city almost opted out: the coastal strip having been 'leased' by Britain from Zanzibar for £17,000 in 1891, the 'Coastal Strippers' called for autonomy, with Mombasa as a free port, in 1963. John Jewell's *Mombasa the Friendly Town* is a lavishly illustrated, if somewhat unwieldy history-cum-guide written in a style well above the East African average. The inhabitants – of every cross-bred hue, coexisting, mixing in a state of happy languor – were for all that counted in 1979 and pronounced 400,000.

Moi Airport was inaugurated by the same-named president on 28 August 1979. The work of an architect confident of the climate, its design is expansive and strikingly open-plan: few walls, concrete pillars, and canned music wafting everywhere. The plastic seats under the mango trees, the odd guano-mine mural, are now only regulars' memories: already by late 1977 the reconstruction was sufficiently advanced to receive a first 'package' Jumbo. With the start of its scheduled London service direct, Mombasa 'came of age' in mid-1979 as a fully fledged international airport.

By hired car from the Hertz or Avis desk, by Kenatco taxi or the Kenya Airways' bus you leave the airport [0] and drive in through **Port Reitz**. Pronounced 'Reetz', the suburb and nearby bay commemorate Lieutenant James John Reitz. Wishing to fly the Union Jack to discourage attacks from Oman, Mombasa's Mazrui in 1824 agreed to stop slave-trading and accept a 'British presence': this first one-man protectorate ended one year later when Reitz died of malaria, 23 years old. In 1976 a short cut was constructed to bypass the headland of clinics and schools . . . and to put the **Tower Hill Hotel** off on a panoramic limb. By the change of name – from 'Port Reitz', from 'Miramar', from 'Mombasa Airport Hotel' – the owners hope to dispel a reputation that not even the creek view redeemed. Turning right between the BP station and Changamwe Methodist Church, you come in by the flowery hilltop roundabout at the tail-end of the road and rail trip from Nairobi [4].

Ahead, the long dual carriage-way drops with the railway to a picturesque complex of headlands and creeks. Until 1896 Mombasa's 5½ square miles of coral rock could be reached only by ford or ferry. The Uganda Railway necessitated the construction of the Macupa Viaduct, which the iron Salisbury Bridge replaced in 1899. Too vulnerable to Axis bombs, this was in turn replaced by a wider causeway during World War II. A mangrove swamp with a backdrop of palms, and you

climb the cliffs to St Luke's Anglican Church (r.; Sunday HC 7 a.m., Family Service 9.30 or 5 p.m.). By the island's first roundabout [7½] the 'Elim Evangelistic Pentecostal Church' is spireless but with a butterfly roof, and of the two palms planted respectively by Princess Margaret in 1956 and the Queen Mother in 1959, one is now quite sizeable and the other dead and gone.

Alongside the Lutheran Parish Hall (l.), **Tom Mboya Avenue** skirts the city centre: across an unobjectionable residential area, past (r.) the African Inland Church and a convent complex – the 'Little Sisters of the Poor' – and (l.) the Mombasa Gospel Tabernacle, St Austin's Preparatory School and the Tudor House/**Port Tudor Hotel**; along the Port Tudor cliffs, enhanced by gardens, to the Bahai Centre, the 'H.H. Aga Khan Jamat Khana' (r.) and the lavishly arabesque **Mombasa Polytechnic** (l.). The Aga Khan contributed also to this former Mombasa Institute of Muslim Education – along with the Sultan of Zanzibar, the Bohra High Priest and the British Treasury – and the stylish complex was opened by the Sultan in 1951.

Turning right into Swaleh Nguru Road, then right along a path euphemized as Makaburini – Tombs – Road, you reach the Commonwealth War Graves Commission's '**Mombasa (Manyimbo) African War Cemetery** (1939-1945)', small and now almost as neglected as the civilian cemetery beside, the Muslims' headstones inscribed in Arabic and others with '*Soldat mort pour la France*'. Tom Mboya Avenue thereafter has been cut by the approaches to the new Nyali Bridge, so follow Swaleh Nguru Road straight on for the main thoroughfare.

This – predictably **Jomo Kenyatta Avenue** – continues across town from the 'Elim roundabout': the Macupa police station (r.), the Tom Mboya Memorial Hall (l.) and a 'First Baptist Church' (1974) beside (r.) an oblique curio of a mosque (so built because the *mihrab* must face Mecca). Small-time

Swaminarayan Temple, Mombasa

businesses are interrupted by timber yards – charcoal and *boriti* poles piled high. Then comes **Mwembe Tayari** (*tayari* – ready – because the punctilious Mr Ainsworth mustered his porters beneath the trees before setting off on safari, p. 48). The area was known for its Saturday 'band' shows and its stalls of victuals and voodoo ingredients until the covered market was built that cost it its character, and much of its aroma. Left of the **bus station** stands the **War Memorial**, like Nairobi's (p. 47) but two years younger and with four bronze *askaris*. After the spectacle of taxis and Nairobi-bound buses loading noisily outside the Bohra cemetery (l.), Kenyatta Avenue joins Digo Road. Still Salim Road on many a map, this is Main Street Mombasa. To the right, opposite the obtruding Khonzi Mosque, it tops **Haile Selassie Road**.

This former Station Road, exactly one km. long, is first bordered with bars, small businesses and local hotels (the best, by default, being the **Excellent**, r.), then adjoined by a Khoja cemetery and climaxed by the **Shree Cutch Satsang Swaminarayan Temple** (also r.). Its entrance guarded by two blue-coated plaster sahibs and portraying Lord Khrishna's sundry reincarnations, the temple was erected in 1957-60 by volunteer members of the sect (Hindus who are said to be exclusively builders and market-gardeners). After the lesser attraction of the cream-and-olive Shree Swaminarayan Temple (r.; 1955), normality returns with the **Central Railway Station**, resited here in the 'Jubilee Gardens' in 1932.

Digo Road is next distinguished by the £180,000 **post office** (l.), which the Mzee inaugurated on 4 January 1971. Gusii Street (r.) leads to the 1870, £75,000 **Shaikh Jundani Mosque** and to the **Splendid Hotel**. Meru Road (l.) permits a glimpse of the Lord Shiva Temple (below). Clothes and shoe stores yield to curio shops, and to the left of the central, gardened island stand a 'Royal Theatre' (in fact a seedy cinema) and the Huseini Stationery Mart, Mombasa's best bookshop. The roundabout now is Mombasa's city centre, of interest only for one simple, inscribed plinth: 'This commemorates the renaming of Kilindini Road into Moi Avenue . . . on 3rd January, 1979'.

In honour of the second president's first visit to Mombasa, **Moi Avenue** is the long straight dual carriage-way descending (r.) to Kilindini docks. You pick your way between its pavement peddlers only to be confronted by the itinerant. Through the passage (l.) the courtyard Fontanella serves snacks to canned music; Teodim (r.) deals in cut and uncut gemstones and, beside the **taxi stand** (l.), fruiterers sell pineapples and mangoes packed ready for the flight home. On the terrace of the **Castle** (l.) baubles are not all you come by. This popular hotel is pick-up point for most bus-trips into town. 'Sir Ali Street' opposite (formerly honouring Sir Ali bin Salim, p. 70) has been Africanized to Msanifu Kombo Road. The excellent **Home Industries Centre** here was enlarged in 1974; run by the National Christian Council of Kenya, 'Tototo' opens from 8.30 a.m. to 12.30 and 2.30 to 6 p.m., Saturdays 3-6, and its workshop merits a (free) visit in Mariakani Lane.

Beside the **New Carlton**'s garden bar (r.), pink and black soapstone, baskets, drums and sheepskins are hawked on the corner of Chembe Road, along which waft the irresistible aromas of the Anglo-Swiss Bakery (and in which 'David's Mombasa Art Centre' is remarkable less for its wares than its wordy, near-English and pseudo-German shop-front). Opposite is Omee's Supermarket and downhill, in every sense, the Skyway Hotel (r.). The Mombasa Coffee House and Pollman's office (both r.), then much bittier shops and bars. The four giant **Tusks** that arch over the road are Mombasa's hall-mark – but no tusks: rather, hollow sheet metal like an aircraft's fuselage. Beside them (r.) **Uhuru Park** is a shady place of old cannons, benches and bums, with the 1963 **Uhuru Fountain** – a concrete Africa in a blue and usually waterless pool – and implacable curio vendors: 'Take time to look, man'. Backed by the Kenya Red Cross Building (r.), the **Information Bureau** lives admirably up to its name (8-12 and, except Saturdays, 2-4.30; POB. 99596, tel. 24173, 25428). It is run by the **Mombasa & Coast Tourist Association**, a remarkably friendly and rivalry-free body that does much to ensure the Coast's touristic success.

After a Wimpy (l. where the tusks touch down) and Agip's Bella Vista Restaurant, **Kenya Airways**, the **Ministry of Tourism** and UTC/Hertz (all r.), the souvenir shops yield to safari outfits and 'clubs'. The **Hong Kong** was Kenya's first Chinese restaurant (r.; 1958), then the road dips under the 'Kenya & Uganda Railway's' 1927 bridge and sinks to the docks past ship-chandlers and honorary consulates.

East of Digo Road the attractions are far more intense. For this is the Old Town, still very much The Orient. You can take pot-luck down any turning off Digo Road – the **Jain Temple** (1963; in Langoni Road) provides from afar a white sugar-ice guide. Or into Makadara Road by the post office, behind which the previous **Baluchi Mosque**, not the present pink, green and white sight (1964), was founded 'by the Baluchi Ancestors 1875'. Across **Jamhuri Park**, laid out – somewhat sparsely – in 1971, stands the 1952 **Lord Shiva Temple**, its white spire crowned with a crock of gold, its gateway topped by two Disney lions and a small (but elephantine) Ganapati. The wondrous assemblage of animal images – life-sustaining cow, evil-shunning tortoise, simian godhead and actual pigeons everywhere – is the pantheon of principally the Gujerati Brahmin. They hospitably show you every corner . . . but do not enquire about the symbols' significance unless you have an hour or two to spare. Thereafter, again, you are on your own.

So better enter the Old Town by the trippers' front door. Across Digo Road, Moi Avenue becomes **Nkrumah Road**. That the **Holy Ghost Cathedral** occupies the corner is not chance, for the government in 1918 let its builders take coral from a nearby quarry on condition they build the road in between. Having arrived at Mombasa disguised as an Arab, Father le Roy bought the site in 1891

Mombasa's hall-mark, in Moi Avenue

and built the first church. Brother Gustave's replacement, the present edifice, is loosely Romanesque-symmetrical, its roof a facsimile of Westminster Cathedral's. The twin towers went up in lieu of the coral-rock spire that, built too hastily, promptly toppled down; their aesthetic impact has been somewhat diminished by the concrete-box Ambalal House alongside. Inside, some of the stained-glass saints approach Gothic, but most are in 1890s Birmingham style (Sunday mass 6, 7, 8, 9 & 11.15 a.m. & 5.30 p.m.).

Government offices and Asian banks and businesses then border Nkrumah Road. The Palmcourt has become the New Palm Tree Hotel, which is new only in name. The **Mombasa Memorial Cathedral** lies right (Sunday HC 7 a.m., Morning Service 11 and Evensong 6.30). Built by the CMS in 1903-5 as a tribute to Bishop Hannington (p. 100) and restored in 1955, the cruciform, Regency-oriental edifice is topped by two towers and a silver dome, and beautified inside by a fine rose window. British commissioners, officials and bishops are remembered on well-polished plaques – 'Who dies if England lives?' – and the organ itself is a Great War memorial.

Treasury Square (next r.) was the site of Mombasa's first railway station, constructed in 1900 usefully close to the Old Port. And here, amidst the first administration buildings, Sir William Mackinnon long stood suitably in bronze. Alone since independence, a small 1937 bust on a disproportionate plinth commemorates **Allidina Visram**, a 'leading Indian merchant & planter of East Africa . . . Born, 1851, Arrived in East Africa, 1863, died at Kampala in Uganda 30-6-1916'. This worthy Cutch Indian's wealth endowed many East African schools and public works and, in the days when cowrie shells were currency, protectorate officials leaned heavily on his far-flung banking and trading 'empire'. Containing also an arabesque cupola and *saqia* – water trough – Treasury Square retains its colonial-evocative air despite the modernistic block beyond, the *Ofisi Kuu ya Mkoa wa Pwani*, the Coast Provincial Headquarters (1972-74).

Fort Jesus then dominates (r.) downhill, impressive in its sheer mass. The walls, often eight feet thick, rise some 50 feet from a two-acre coral ridge that defied undermining. Storming the walls was suicidal because re-entrant angles meant that almost every facet was covered by cross-fire. From 1593, when Mateus Mendes de Vasconcelos founded 'Jesus of Mombasa', until 1875,

when the British bombed out the *akida*, Portuguese, Omani, Mazrui, British, Baluchi and even Masai forces swapped control with a frequency that altogether nullified the fort's supposed impregnability (p. 18). Completing the construction in 1596, in part to thwart the Muslim Ali Bey (p. 17), the Portuguese were massacred in 1631 by a renegade protégé: though master of Mombasa, this Yusef bin Hassan, *alias* Dom Jeronimo Chingulia, was shunned by his local co-religionists so, having repelled a counter-attack, he set sail voluntarily in 1632 leaving the fort to its builders. Then came the **Great Siege**: from 13 March 1696 a handful of Portuguese and loyal locals from Pate resisted a superior (if somewhat remiss) Omani siege force; reinforcements were stultified by plague, and on 12 December 1698 only nine Portuguese, three Indians, two women and a boy survived, still to fight all night. Though overrun, one of them led the Arabs to 'gold' in the powder-house . . . and there blew up both himself and his escort.

Arab intrigues replaced Portuguese: such was the feuding between the local Mazrui, 'a most avaricious family', and their Bu Saidi rivals from Oman (p. 18) that the Portuguese stepped in and reoccupied Fort Jesus in 1728-29. In 1746 the Omanis established a garrison, which the Mazrui evicted via a hole blown in the walls by an obliging British warship. Captain Owen proclaimed the 'Reitz protectorate' here in 1824 (p. 63) and Sultan Sayyid, sailing for Zanzibar four years later (p. 18), left the fort in the charge of 300 Baluchis, whom the Mazrui promptly starved out. Having ceded the fort by treaty, the Mazrui leaders were in 1837 then seized and removed from the scene. Masai raiding-parties put the sultan's Baluchis to (temporary) flight in 1857, and when in 1875 the akida-commandant of the fort ignored the sultan's recall orders, a two-hour bombard-ment by two British gunboats made him change his mind. The fort thereafter served as a prison until in 1958 the Gulbenkian Found-ation gave £30,000 for its restoration and the creation of a museum. On 29 October 1960 both were opened to the public . . . by a Portuguese government official.

A Portuguese vessel is currently the subject of the **Mombasa Wreck Excavation**. Attempt-ing to relieve the Great Siege, the *Santa Antonio de Tanna* sailed in from Goa on 15 September 1697 but – bombarded by the Arabs, parted from her cables, washed on to the reef and hauled off rudderless – she sank. Amateur divers saw porcelain on the sea-bed

in 1963; **Dr Kirkman** organized a first reconnaissance in 1971, and in 1977 commenced the professional (but seasonal) excavation of the underwater treasure trove thought to be this 42-gun frigate. The American Institute of Nautical Archaeology and the National Museums of Kenya direct; the National Geographic Society and the Gulbenkian Foundation help with funds; the divers come from Britain and the Kenya Navy, Portugal, Australia and the USA. They have to date raised timbers, tools and a bronze cannon complete with breech-block; buckles, buttons, bowls and compass-boxes; a faience plate, square glass bottle and (half-)hour-glass all intact, and what was proclaimed an ink-pot but turns out to be a fire-bomb which, in the words of a 17th-c. writer, 'will much prejudice the Enemy'.

Six 19th-c. cannons – and guns from the *Pegasus* and *Königsberg* (p. 21) – stand outside by the **Great War Column**, in memory of the Muslim Major Wavell and his Arab Rifles. Below them you enter by the ramp and bastion added in the 1630s; 9 a.m.-6 p.m. daily; Ksh. 5/-, under 16s 2/- (residents 2/-, 1/-, on week-ends and 'Puplic Holidays', 1/-, -/50). Notices direct you to the Passage of Arches, the Captain's House, the Hall of the Mazrui and the bastions of Saints 'Filipe, Mateus and Matias'. Clambering to the top of the ramparts, you have excellent views of the old 'Mombasa Harbour'. The **museum** exhibits sketches, maps and sketch-maps of old 'Mombass', plus well-displayed proof of the multi-national influences that Coast households have felt in the last 1000 years. Tanks beside the book-stand preserve relics of the presumed *Santa Antonio* (above). A folder in the shape of the fort summarizes its history nicely and Dr Kirkman's 3/- guide is good.

The Old Town. Below Fort Jesus the walk through the Water Gate is attractive if photographically frustrating. Ahead, it is easy to drop inadvertently in on the **Mombasa Club**, opened as the 'Chini Club' in 1896 and still very British despite multi-racial membership. Temporary membership is possible for tourists – Ksh. 60/- p.m., pool 2/- p.d. – but 'only if they are introduced . . . and we do have a long waiting list'. For the Old Town skirt it (l.) via Mbarak Hinawy Road. Formerly Vasco da Gama Road, the alley commemorates the penultimate *liwali*. The *wali* or *liwali* was the sultan's coastal governor until the office was abolished upon independence. Traditionally he was expected to give

swaddling for every new-born baby, a gown for every bride and a four-fathom sheet to shroud every corpse.

The lanes around were made narrow for defence in the days before machine-guns, but projecting upper storeys – half Elizabethan, half Arab *mashrabia* – protected the Portuguese invaders on occasions from the townspeople's missiles. There are antique carved doors and phoney new features like the 'Arab Coffee Pot'. The **Manadhara/Mandhry Mosque** is conspicuous (l.) with its phallic minaret, and thinks itself the oldest of Mombasa's 49 mosques (c. 1570). Its sect is strict Sunni, so the boys who touted to show you around then presented, ultimatum-like, their 'List of Contributors' have now been suppressed. Round the bend in **Government Square,** Sharif Mohamed Abdulla Shatry, having made way for the spivvier Sanaa Gallery, sells carpets, chests and coffee-pots from a humbler premises now. The **Fish Market** functions, smelly and noisy, each morning. And, beneath the Alfred E. Newman head that adorns the keystone, the Customs let you through to the **Old Port**. This is Mombasa's overrated show-piece: the three-score dhows that the monsoon should blow in are admittedly picturesque and a carpet show on board, plus a cup of bitter coffee, does make an Arabian break. But dhows like donkeys are a waning conveyance – Arabia-to-Africa trips like the Ricciardis' or Marion Kaplan's for the *National Geographic* read like requiems – and even in the 'peak' month of March your view of the Old Port may be oil-drums and empty jetties. Which makes it easy to heed the warning: 'Taking Pictures in the Port is strictly Prohibited'.

Thereafter the Old Town is labyrinthine. Though roads were pushed through in the 1930s, do not try to drive (other than up Thika Street alongside the Sanaa Gallery). Better leave your car outside the port. Those locals not watching whether you lock it will offer a guided tour: you either agree on the price in advance or disagree afterwards. Ahead in Bachuma Road, an enclosure of Bohra Muslim tombs occupies the slope below the **Dawoodi Bohra Mosque** (built in 1902, enlarged in 1974). To see Mombasa's Thirty-nine steps take the first right after the mosque, then second right. Or, from Thika Street, turn right and right again into the first bituminized passage after Mwea Tebere Road. The cliff-top wasteland is then relieved by the steps' arched entrance, via which slaves were 'secretly' brought to blockade-running dhows below. In the waterside cave a remarkable fresh well supplied the slavers. (The historic feature is nowadays filthy with refuse so, unless you feel like slithering through a sewer, negotiate instead the broken stairway outside by the water's edge.) The local misnomer of **Eleven Steps** is not a miscount but a reminder of HMS *Leven*, the flagship of the survey squadron here in 1823-26. The nearby Leven House was supposedly built in 1825 by Midshipman Emery, Owen's successor (p. 66); seat of the short-lived 'protectorate', it was later offered by the sultan to Dr Krapf as his Mombasa pied-à-terre. It served in the 1870s as the 'Mission House' headquarters of the United Methodist Free Churches and subsequently housed the IBEA's first administrators, then the Old Port Customs – the early concentration of offices around accounting for 'Government Square'.

Fort Jesus, Mombasa

From the Catholic Cathedral two headland drives, not walks, follow **Nyerere Avenue** – once Prince Charles Road – out past the **British Council Library** and the **Manor Hotel** (r.) and the pavement of souvenir-peddlers (l.) dislodged from Digo Road. The Mombasa Institute (l.), begun in 1926, replaced the 'Goan Reading Room' the community had founded in 1901. You then cross Dedan Kimathi Avenue (p. 47) – not only formerly Ayub Khan Avenue but also the track of the first railway line to the station in Treasury Square (above).

Kaunda Avenue (l.) leads to the Loreto Convent (1960-61), St Margaret's Presbyterian Church (1956; Sundays 9 a.m.) and the turning (r.) – Mbuyuni Road – which crosses the pleasant garden suburb of Kizingo and stops at the **Oceanic Hotel**. Its architectural style 20th-c. Kuwait, this is Mombasa town's best. In December 1972 the owners of Nairobi's International Casino (p. 50) opened up here: roulette, blackjack and craps, with Italian croupiers, for Ksh. 10/- nightly (free to hotel residents).

From the roundabout above Likoni Ferry you have the choice of two routes back into town. A sign-posted park drive to the right rejoins the Kilindini cliffs near the **Mbaraki Pillar**. Beset by baobabs equally odd-shaped, the Pisa-like structure of coral-rag and limestone plaster rises round and hollow from a square podium, its sides pierced with 'arrow slits'. Distinctly phallic too, it is said to be the scene of secret rituals performed by barren women. All we know of its history, thanks to a map, is that it existed already in

1728. The sign-board, viz. Dr Kirkman, states that the pillar 'Probably marks the tomb of a sheikh of the Changamwe One of the original twelve tribes of Mombasa' – which may bear out the belief that Mbaraki was inhabited early by Arabs and Persians. The drive skirts cliff-top villas and rejoins Mbaraki Road (l.) beside the **cemeteries**: not strictly Christian because Jews share the area with British, French and Dutch, not strictly European because Goans predominate amongst the sundry Orientals. The Great War contributed 52 Commonwealth military graves, the Second World War 146. After the **Little Theatre Club**, Archbishop Makarios Road (also l.) and the Mombasa Sports Club (r.; 1896) Mnazi Mmoja Road meets Moi Avenue below the Castle (p. 64).

Off Archbishop Makarios Road – second left in Tangana Road – notices direct you to the Mombasa Rowing and Yacht clubs and the **Outrigger Hotel**, Italian owned, British managed and base for 'K Boats'. Beside it the **Mombasa Yacht Club** (1910) will make you a member for Ksh. 6/- p.d. or 10/- p.w., plus 40/- p.m. for use of the pool. The secretary arranges sails with members as the club does not own boats. The possibility of sharks is sufficient deterrent to swimming.

Near by – best ask your way – stands the **Kilindini Mosque**. Kilindini, in the mid-17th century, was founded by the 'Three Tribes', Swahili who migrated from the hinterland, and the only relic of their original settlement was the Kilindini or 'Wailing' Mosque. It was an eerie ruin, its walls, pillars and arches in the stranglehold of mighty trunks, until in 1973 they removed it to build the new Kilindini Mosque . . . or rather two new mosques, the first having collapsed upon completion.

To the left of the Likoni roundabout, **Mama Ngina Drive** runs under the Oceanic and around the pleasant headland where Asians stroll at sunset. Benches are everywhere, for you to admire the harbour-entrance view and the scattered vestiges of **Fort St Joseph**. The **Baobab Forest** here may have been the site of Mombasa's first settlement – or the upshot of a Christian cemetery, since baobab fruit were reputedly buried together with Portuguese dead. Far less evident is the entrance to a secret tunnel said to connect with Fort Jesus.

The New Florida's pool and dubious night-club, then the fine nine-hole golf course straddles the road. With the land cleared of bush in 1909, the club established in 1911 and the pavilion added in 1921, the **Mombasa Golf Club** now welcomes visiting players – to 'the coolest place on the island'. Following this former Ras Serani Drive further, you see the lighthouse up a side street (l.), the Kenya Police Coast Headquarters and (also r.) the long wall of **State House**, originally built from railway funds and 'Government House' until independence. You then re-enter town via Treasury Square (p. 66).

Mombasa's safari and car-hire firms seem, to a man, to be in Moi Avenue. In *Kenya's Coast*, Simon Mollison's research on its cafés and restaurants must have meant a gastronomic marathon. 'Just right for a sailor's night out' is the travel brochures' *double entendre* for Mombasa's many 'Day & Night Clubs'. And Edward Rodwell's *Coast Causerie*, which affably chronicles the region's recent past, has been reprinted from *The Standard* in three very readable books.

MOMBASA SOUTH

The **Likoni Ferry** takes four shillings and four minutes . . . for the actual crossing, that is. The often long wait explains the sign 'No "Q" Jumping. All Vehicles to Take their Turn'. Likoni's first ferry here across the Kilindini entrance was a sailing-boat. Two rowing-boats replaced it in 1930, carrying passengers but towing cattle tied astern. The government took over with motors in 1934; a pontoon carried the first cars across in 1935, and pontoons continued in service until the *St Christopher* was commissioned in 1957, preceding the present *Safina*, *Mvita* and *St Michael*.

Atop the far bank (l.) the **Likoni Beach Estate** starts. 'The roads,' a notice used to announce, 'are privately maintained by a few residents. Please do not tear the bottom out.' With the bottom torn out, the Mombasa Municipal Commission finally gave Ksh. 2 million for their replacement in 1977. So the road left from the ferry [0] now runs faster past the CPK Guest House – the late New Sea Breezes Hotel – and the Consolata Sisters' Stella Maris House to the **Shelly Beach Hotel** [2½]. Beside the Consolata Fathers' counterpart you find the **Children's Holiday Resort** [3½](POB. 96048, tel. 451417). This former 'European Children's Resort' was founded for up-country infants during the Depression (but significantly with servants' quarters), and continues to be managed by the original non-profit-making trust. Which explains the tariff: Ksh. 70/- p.d. for two adults and four children, plus 35/- for adults, 10/- for under 18s over the above, and 15/- 'departure cleaning charge'. Low in profile as well as in price, the resort was endowed by Sir Ali bin Salim KBE, CMG, the liwali of the Coast between 1922 and 1931 who, co-operating the most closely with the British government, appears the most frequently in the colonial archives. The final few yards of tarmac beyond serve, not the now-closed camping site, but **Timbwani Beach** and the Rose Beach Cottages (r.).

This coast southwards – Digo country – has several minor Arab ruins and fine beaches *passim*. You can be guided, minutely, by Mollison's *Kenya's Coast* or simply take almost any track left of the road and so 'discover' your own. The reef determines whether you swim, but the shells on shore and the underwater wonder add to the blissfulness of palms, sun and sand.

From the ferry [0] **Likoni** is long drawn-out after its open-air market (r.) – post office, housing estate and a Harambee Maternity Home (*Harambee* meaning 'Let's all pull together'). The Salvation Army's School for the Blind, a police station and 'Filadelfia Pentecostal Church' (l.), then the Kenya Navy's **Mtongwe** headquarters and base (r.)[3].

Banda-hamlets under the palms and farm-plots that vie with the natural luxuriance embellish the littoral south. Waa lies scattered on both sides of the road [13]. Running flat and straight through the palm-plantations, the A 14 passes the turning (r.)[16] to 'Shimba National Reserve 15 m.' (which laters boards shortened to '17·6 km').

Tiwi. Now classified and state-maintained as the E 964, the track sign-posted (l.)[18½] runs smooth to the smarter end of Tiwi Beach: straight on at 2·2 kms to the four **Sand Island Beach Cottages** (POB. 96006; Ksh. 220/- p.n. for six, 180/- for four, 120/- for three, 80/- for two). Or right and one km. further to **El Capricho** (POB. 96093, tel. Tiwi 2Y9): 22 seaside acres, prettily landscaped in 1968, fresh-water pool and ten self-catering cottages (100-320/- p.n.). **Maweni** (next track l.) is fourteen smartly stylish cottages, for couples, foursomes and half-dozens, in well-developed gardens of coral and bougain-villea (POB. 96024, tel. Tiwi 2Y5; 400-1200/- p.w. according to cottage and season). Precisely two kms further, parallel tracks (l.) serve the six **Tiwi Beach Bungalows** (POB. 96008, tel. Tiwi 2Y7; 180/- p.n. for four, 120/- for couples, + 16-18/- p.n. for the compulsory servant) and the 1948 **Twiga Lodge**'s eleven bandas (74/75 p.n. + 5/- p.p. for gas and fridge) and camp site (10/- p.p.p.n.; POB. 96005, tel. Tiwi 2Y2). These, though, are better reached by the three-km. track marked left of the main road [20].

Amidst the bandas of Tiwi itself comes the turning (r.) to Kwale, then a long gentle dip across the Mwachema River.

Where this meets the sea stands **Mwana Mosque**. The state of the track makes its length academic: the mile or so to Kongo means a fifteen-minute drive – best with a guide from the roadside Mnazi Bar (l.)[25]. Kongo's is a surprising ruin, the barrel-vaulted roof of its 15th-c. prayer-room intact and even replastered, the floor swept clean for worship, and the site delightful (but for increasing crime) with gigantic baobabs guarding the sweep of the Tiwi estuary.

Diani. After the village's minaretless mosque (l.)[26] the E 965 to Diani Beach appears in a thicket of sign-boards [27]. One said till recently 'To all Bungalows': the rest could have been economized as 'To all Hotels'. Six of them share this six-mile delight of gardens, palms, white sand and tight forest. At the end of the two-km. link-road, left of the T-junction [0 kms], **Leisurelodge** and **Leopard Beach**, then a footpath to the right of the final roundabout that stops atop the

pretty cliffs [3]. To the right, the Amphibians' airfield and **Trade Winds** [2], the **Two Fishes** [4] and the so-called Cobra's Camp (r.; 1976; a sparse, disappointing assemblage of snakes, plus a glue-and-canvas rhino and buffalo, life-size but far from lifelike; 7 a.m.-6 p.m. daily; Ksh. 3/-, under 16s 1/50). Between the **Jadini** [4½] and **Robinson Baobab** [6], **Nomad's** is boats for tailor-made trips, a seafood restaurant open all day every day and, since December 1978, a camp of eleven tents for couples on the beach (Ukunda POB. 1, tel. 01261 2155/6). After which, both beach and tarmac end by the **White Rose Villas** and **Four Twenty South** [6½]: seven four-bedded cottages, with fridge, electricity and inside loo, for Ksh. 150-170/- (March, June, October, November 120-140/-, May 100-120/-, plus 20/- p.p.p.n.; Nairobi POB. 14681, tel. 60960 or 01261 2034). A half-km. track continues to the twelve **Diani Beachalets**: self-service cottages in blissfully tranquil gardens, each with hot water and large fridge (80-285/- p.n. depending on season, size and air conditioning), and **camp site** (12/- p.p.p.n. in own tent; Ukunda POB. 26, tel. 01261 2180).

All encroach upon **Jadini Forest** (where some dump their garbage too). The nearest nevertheless that most tourists come to jungle, it is happy with butterflies and boasts colobus (p. 38); baboons often lope across your track and the forest's bird life is brilliant. Off shore, the coral **Chale Island** was a popular boat-trip destination until displaced by Wasini (below). If you find it more inviting for being less frequented, Nomad's will take you on a boating barbecue.

The main road runs on flat, bordered by palms, swamp and sugar. Another turning (r.)[36] is another alternative for Shimba Hills [20 kms]. At the village with the good Palestinian name of **Gazi** [46] the Education Department occupies the 1840s house of Shaikh Mbarak bin Rashid, a Mazrui leader (p. 18) who reputedly tortured in one of its rooms, then stifled survivors with the fumes of burning chillies. With the palms around as symmetrical as sisal, the **coconut factory** (r.)[48½] is of aromatic interest, and East Africa's largest. From 3182 acres, with 56 palms per acre, some 3 million nuts yearly are brought in by lorry to be husked. Some are bagged and shipped overseas, but most are shattered – the milk draining to waste – and laid for three days to dry white, as copra, then sold in Mombasa as a source of oil and soap. The hair is treated in the crushing plant adjoining, then baled and freighted to Nairobi to stuff mattresses and make coarse scrubbing brushes. All this, begun in 1951, now occupies here some 300 men.

At **Msambweni** – Place of the Sable Antelope [51] – is both a putative slave-pen and an exquisite beach, which the government's information handbook proclaims as 'almost entirely unknown to visitors'. After the last alternative for Shimba Hills (below) the sugar estates start in earnest. **Ramisi** (off r.)[64] is the Associated Sugar Company's sugar-industrial township. Founded in 1927, now employing some 3000 workers and growing half a dozen varieties over 11,000 acres (1000 by overhead irrigation), it produces annually around 15,000 tons of unrefined 'Plantation White'. Which explains the colour of your hotel sugar-bowl's contents. Crossing the Ramisi River [64½], the road rolls attractively from sugar-cane country into gentle green hills on which doum-palms predominate, then across lusher valleys to the Tanzania border at Lunga Lunga [99].

Shimoni. More interesting is the track marked (l.)[67] to 'Kisite/Mpunguti Marine National Park 15 km'. Sandy between the palms and homesteads, then harder rock and murram, it enters Shimoni by the hulk of the old Police Lines (r.) and the two-storey ruin of the DC's house (ahead)[14½ kms]. Though base for an IBEA agent and perhaps the Coast's first administrative boma, Shimoni declined when the District Commissioner removed to cooler Kwale for the sake of his garden. Its name is Swahili for Place of the Hole viz. the caves of bats and stalactites, by the first of which you fork right. Local slavers are said to have stored their human wares here pending shipment; an army expedition, and subsequently speleologists, followed the subterranean maze for about twelve miles. Till recently only the fishing club, Shimoni's touristic importance has been increased by the creation of the **Kisite Marine National Park**. Tanzanians from Moa Bay, having dynamited dead their own coast's stock of fish and moved northwards to do likewise here, prompted the Kenyan authorities to establish this aquatic sanctuary in October 1973. It has since been reduced from four coral islands to the Mako Kokwe Reef and Kisite Island itself. Being for years the only boating base for miles, the **Pemba Channel Fishing Club** could rightly claim 'to offer an exclusive service from the nearest coastal point'. Best started two hours before low tide, the usually four-hour trips cost Ksh. 100/- p.h. for a maximum eight passengers, with snorkeling gear hired for 5-15/- (plus national park fees of 10/- each for adults, 2/50 for residents, 1/- for children and 25/- for boats).

Thanks however to Kisite Tours, you can now combine the Coast's 'best place for goggling' with a dhow-ride and a visit to **Wasini**. The 'package' is well publicized in the beach hotels (or contact Mombasa POB. 81953, tel. 311970): by road to Shimoni, out in the *Taisiri* (a 'totally non-smelly', refitted Lamu *jahazi*), around the coral gardens (with snorkeling gear for hire) and back for seafood lunch at the **Wasini Island Restaurant**. This was built in 1979 on Ras Mondini, the island's southern tip, and on condition that (hitherto banned) alcohol be served to none other than its customers (and that these be 'sober and decently clothed'). For the rest, the 17½-km² island boasts two Muslim fishing-villages – Wasini itself, *alias* Vumba/Kisiwani, and the larger Kifundi, *alias* Mkwiro – a pillar tomb with porcelain (p. 84) and abundant shells both natural and man-made. The former are now protected and may be neither collected nor sold; the latter remain from the island's use in World War I as a naval-training target.

Shimba Hills. Behind, the turning [53] was your last chance to detour via Shimba Hills. Another victim of East Africa's fickle nomenclature, the 'Kwale' or 'Shimba Hills' or 'Sable Antelope Game Reserve/National Reserve' was clarified into a 74½-square-mile national park in 1974. The last of its former names is explained by its 200 head of rare *palahala*, HIPPOTRAGUS NIGER, and *shambe* in the local dialect. Roan antelope too – *korongo* or HIPPOTRAGUS EQUINUS – were in 1970 evacuated here from the Ithanga Ranch near Thika. They are faring better than their fellows deported to Solio (p. 106) and their breeding to date has brought them to a score or more.

From Likoni or Diani (p. 71) you enter via either the East Entrance at Kivumoni or the Kwale – Spurfowl – Gate. After the tin-roofed African Inland Church of Manyata (1977), 25½ kms up the turning as above, comes the Kidongo Gate, closed like the others at 7.15 p.m. and with the normal national park entrance fees. 'Some of the Animals in this Area are still showing a timid Behaviour' . . . just as they were in 1971 when the warning went up. The track climbs on through tight forest, and for an eerie jungle experience follow the marker-sign (l.) to 'Mwele Mdogo Forest 1 km'. After not one but four kms the difficult track is engulfed: lianas and branches as thick as your arm hang earthwards to hit the car roof, butterflies flutter in the chiaroscuro gloom and the route stops short at a wall of impenetrable undergrowth.

The main track rolls on over lush half-timbered slopes; above the Makadara and Longomwagandi forests ahead, the hills' bald pates break through, topped by the distant wisp of the borassus. (Eagerly eaten by the park's 400 elephants, the fruit of these *mvomo*-palms can ferment in their stomachs . . . and make them belatedly tipsy.) After the 'Welcome to Picnic Site – You are Requested to be Silent', the higher slopes are neatly afforested, with each acre dated and labelled. Here, with lions absent, you may safely walk – or spend the night at the camp site for Ksh. 5/- per person. Marker-posts are plentiful beside the well-kept tracks, guiding you to Giriama Point and the Pengo Hill Look-out, the 'Highest Point of a dissected Plateau measuring 1500 ft a.s.l.'.

NORTH TO NYALI, KILIFI AND WATAMU

Mombasa's **Abdel Nasser Road** runs north from Kenyatta Avenue (p. 63) and the municipal – ex-Mackinnon – **markets** (r.), where the boys tout hash and 'a pound for a pound' (and similar excesses for Swiss francs). Behind, the Tanga Trading Company advertises its 'Spice Market' significantly in German and French. The buses load for Lamu and Malindi by the Sunni sect's **Masjid Nur Mosque** (l.) and the 1940s blocks give way to shanties somehow Central Asian.

The road dissects the 17th-c. *Cidade dos Mouros*, the Portuguese appellation for the Arab town, which (perhaps) occupied Mombasa's first settled site. Beyond a 'Lighthouse for Christ Eye Centre' and behind the Institute of Islamic Culture (r.), the ruined mosque may be a relic, the area around still being known by the name of its founder. The records are not categorical as to whether **Shehe Mvita**, *alias* Shahu bin Misham, was sultan here when the Portuguese arrived, but local veneration appears to confirm that the grave near by is his. Its proximity deterred the sponsors of the **Allidina Visram High School** (next r.): the Swahili *Mizimu* – 'Guardians of the Spirits' – were however placated (with gold, they say, buried in the foundations) and the 'H.H. the Aga Khan Mombasa Boys School' was thus safely established in 1918 and later renamed to honour the merchant prince (p. 66).

The Portuguese in 1505 sacked and burnt the settlement here. With little discovered – or not covered by building since – the plans to extend the **Coast General Hospital** (l.) provided a welcome, once-and-for-all opportunity. Seizing it before the site was 'lost' – and offering to dig trenches that could later be used as foundations – Hamo Sassoon began a 'rescue excavation' in 1976. Massive walls – coral rag with lime-and-sand 'mortar' – suggest a defensible residential quarter; 'Islamic monochrome' – bowls in blue or green – point to the expected culture, while finds of Chinese celadon and blue and white Ming show the occupation to be pre-Portuguese. The site, to judge by its 'Kilwa kitchen ware', may date from as early as 1180; its interest, for research purposes, ended abruptly in 1978 when the hospital contractors moved in. Then the Lady Grigg Maternity Hospital and a stumpy phallic lighthouse below a public loo with a view. Though a much-needed replacement is currently under construction 'up stream', the 1931 **Nyali Bridge** remains the north coast's life-line (Ksh. 1/- per car and 10 mph). Despite 1300 feet of planking and 4000 tons of steel, its 100 pontoons are in places high enough for boats to pass underneath.

On the cliff of Kisauni ahead, Cement Road (r.) serves the **Tamarind Restaurant** (1972; reservations tel. 471747). Its décor is strikingly Moorish, its food good and its terrace view pleasant, but the management's avowed aim of 'relieving the average customer of at least Ksh. 120/-' rather mars the ambiance. 'Cement' because of the prominent silos (r.), the road leads on to **English Point**. This owes its name to the Coast's first colony for liberated slaves – established by 'the English' – and commemorates the Krapfs (p. 19). 'They reached Mombasa May 1844,' the memorial records, 'but in July she died and he by her grave (near this spot) summoned the Church to "attempt the conversion of Africa from its eastern shore".' The tomb, replastered and partly illegible, lies beside that of 'her infant child who died 14th July 1844'. It was erected by the then US consul in Zanzibar, 'so that it might always remind the wandering Swahilis and Nyika that here rested a Christian woman who had left father, mother and home to labour for the salvation of Africa'. Beside the graves the 'Mombasa Swimming Club' of 1910 has been fiercely private since 1975. To the left, **Moi** – the late Princes' – **Park** was bought and named by the Dukes of Windsor and Gloucester, then presented to the city for the annual **Mombasa Show** (which was started and stopped in 1903 and resuscitated only in 1967).

Nyali. The show-grounds encroach on Nyali, Mombasa's highly desirable garden suburb. Its Swahili meaning of 'clearing' remains apt, but the sisal-plantation cleared and pioneered by Smith, Mackenzie & Co in 1908 has become the **Nyali Estate**. Privately owned, expensively developed and best reached straight on from the Tamarind/Total cross-roads, its good roads, villas and sundrenched gardens make for a pleasant if envy-inspiring drive. Public features are few: **St Peter's Church** (1960; Sunday HC 8 and Family Service 9 a.m. 1st & 3rd Sundays); the Nyali Club's pool, eighteen-hole **golf course** and squash and tennis courts (temporary membership Ksh. 250/- p.m.; pool 2/50 p.d.; green fees 60/- with clubs available); the 1946 **Nyali Beach Hotel**, the £315,000 **Mombasa Beach Hotel**, which the Mzee opened in 1970, and the **Silver Beach**, **Bahari Beach** and **Reef** hotels.

Left from the Tamarind/Total cross-roads [0], the main road passes the **Bahari Club** (l.) [1] which, like 'K Boats' at the Outrigger, hires boats, crews and tutors – 'Professional Game Fishermen' (Ksh. 50/- per hour) – for deep-sea fishing (150-300/- p.h., 1300-2200/- p.d.) and inshore fishing, harbour trips and goggling (70-150/- p.h., 600-1200/- p.d. – membership 5/- p.d.; POB. 90413, tel. 471316). You then traverse **Freretown**'s banda

suburb. The first mainland sanctuaries for emancipated slaves were set up during the 'protectorate' (p. 63); Sir Bartle Frere established and gave his name to this haven in 1875. Claiming that it was sheltering runaways, Mombasa's Arabs attacked in 1880 and 1895, and the IBEA, again far more magnanimous than business interests warranted, bought the liberty of 1422 slaves in 1888 (as a plaque in Mombasa Cathedral recalls). Isolated – as though on an inland island – by the new Nyali Bridge road-works, the **Emmanuel Church** (l.)[1½] was built in 1884 and remained the CMS's Kenya headquarters until the move to Limuru in 1930. Its bell was originally rung every hour of the night as a warning when slave-dhows were in sight. The portrait in the vestry depicts Matthew Wellington: an orphaned slave saved by the British and converted in Bombay, he returned to join the African expedition that followed Stanley to Ujiji (p. 20), escorted Dr Livingstone until he died and – despite the African's abhorrence of corpses – carried him, mummified, 1500 miles to Zanzibar.

Kongowea's African Inland Church and the Pwani Bible Institute (r.; 1974), the junction of the new Nyali Bridge approach, the Swalihina Mosque and Muslim school (l.; 1973) and a Christian cemetery (r.)[2] with an overflow of Indians from Mbaraki (p. 69). Then you leave Freretown's forest for Nyali's hinterland of lantana scrub. The well-publicized **Bombolulu Gardens** (l.)[4] are a worthy venture, well worth a visit. Mombasa's Rotary Club helped establish this 'Farm and Training Centre for the Physically Handicapped' in 1975-76, adding a 'Memorial Dormitory' in 1978; your contribution could be to buy – if not eggs and vegetables from the farm (a 'While you Wait . . . and wait . . . Service') – the 'hand crafted jewellery in copper, seed pods, banana fibre and old East African coins'. Made by 25 handicapped craftsmen in the project's Mazeras workshop, this is displayed (and well documented) in the shack-shop run since 1979 by enthusiastic Nordic volunteers (POB. 86097, tel. 471704).

Nyali's Links Road then leads (r.)[6½] to the hotels; the Bamburi Portland Cement Company smokes conspicuously to the left. Its attraction for visitors was until recently an eyesore, for the scar of its workings – not the usual ponds in pits – has been aesthetically healed. Turning left opposite the **Coraldene Beach Hotel** [8], left at the first roundabout and straight on across the second, you drop to the **Bamburi Quarry Farm** (entrance free; 7 a.m.-5 p.m. daily). Here you suddenly find yourself amidst shady woodland, a contrast – yet so close – to the tropical glare of the Coast. The forest is alive with fauna; peacocks preen in the glades; fish teem in the experimental tanks; vines, citrus, bananas and mangoes flourish, while weavers nest in the reeds around still pools. Incredibly, the lofty trees – 20,000 eucalyptus, cónocarpus, palms and casuarinas – were planted only in 1971. Now the 65 afforested acres are home to 60-odd bird species. All this is the agronomist René Haller's reply to the company's query whether grass would grow where, since 1954, their open-cast mining had despoiled some fifteen acres annually. His *Rehabilitation of a Limestone Quarry* (1974) gives a self-effacing, scientific account of this remarkable achievement.

Kipepeo Aquarium is another 'lay-scientific' feature popular with the public, and complements the Quarry Farm delightfully. It is also, for land-lubbers, the next best thing to visiting the actual coral gardens; its seventeen tanks give a colourful glimpse of the shells, corals and kaleidoscopic fish off shore. Sea-slugs and -caterpillars are the classic grotesque element enhancing the submarine beauty; amphibious mud-skippers – PERIOPHTHALMUS KOELREUTERI – thrive in a side-tank as an odd biological anomaly. The tastefulness of the aquatic display is a tribute to its creator: Monsieur Allard now has here some 150 species on show (8 a.m.-6 p.m. daily; entrance Ksh. 10/-, under 5s 5/-; follow the signs down the Coraldene track, as fast as possible past the **'German Beer Garden'**, and turn l. beside the hotel).

From Nyali on, fine beaches stretch beyond Mtwapa Creek. Bamburi, Kenyatta, Shanzu and Kikambala, they are not left unexploited. The 'Coraldene Beach Cottages' and 'Ocean View Cottages' have now become hotels. A track sign-posted (r.) between them – just before the petrol station, 'Deluxe Stores' and Bamburi police station – serves the **Jomo Kenyatta Beach** [8½]. Expressly public and given a municipal £2000 face-lift in 1971, it boasts the late president's beach-home (called 'Thiririka' after a stream on his native Mount Kenya).

Whitesands Hotel follows [10], completely revamped and revitalized, and no longer recognizable as 'The Olde Inn next to the Sea'. (Size, prices and opinions for all the Coast's hotels are given on pp. 136-39.) The 1970 **Bamburi Beach Hotel** is a pleasant and compact establishment, alongside the smarter **Kenya Beach** and the stylish **Severin Sea Lodge** [11½]. Sharing the Severin's approach-road, the cottages of the 'Holiday Inn' (l.) have been replaced by the thirteen split-level, studio-style **Cowrie Shell Apartments** (reservations Nairobi POB. 40224, tel. 27828; Malindi POB. 20, tel. 206; Ksh. 415/- p.n. for 4; 372/- p.n. for over three, and 354/- p.n. for over eleven days' stay). Beside them the nine **Bamburi Chalets**, also with pool and tarmac drive (Ksh. 345/- for 6; December 575/-; April, August and January 460/-; reservations Mombasa POB. 84114, tel. 485570, 485706). And beyond these the **Baharini** Chalet **Hotel**, with its attractive **La Taverne Restaurant**.

Shanzu Beach begins with the **Red Lobster**, the pre-1970s Shanzu Frigate Club, the late Don's Inn and now neither club nor inn but a fair restaurant with three rooms (bed & breakfast Ksh. 160-300/- double, 120-225/- single; POB. 84988, tel. 484221). Next north along the beach, which the high tide squeezes, the cliff-top Casuarina has finally found its feet as the African Safari Club's **Palm Beach Hotel**. Refurbished, renamed and reopened in 1978, it now adjoins delightfully the club's **Coral Beach Hotel** (likewise sign-posted r. of the main road)[12].

Shimo la Tewa. Left of the main road [12], the sign reads 'African Safari Club 2 km Shimo la Tewa Sportscenter'. You should read not two but three kms; straight on past the prison and borstal compounds. As you veer left [2½ kms] the 'Danger' warning ahead survives from Mtwapa Creek's former 'Singing Ferry' (its name from the labourers who tunefully hauled you across). Swahili for Cave of the Cod, *Shimo la Tewa* also means an impressive recreation complex. In November 1976 the African Safari Club finished converting the headland gardens of a colonial villa: into cliff-top swimming-pool and riding stables, volleyball, handball and football pitches, archery and air-rifle ranges, two tennis courts and two Swiss bowling/boccia alleys, ping-pong tables and mini-golf course, a restaurant attractive below the lawns and lily-ponds, a disco and even – for those who overdo it – 90 rooms on the spot in the **Shimo la Tewa Hotel**.

The main road continues past the Shanzu Teachers College and the well-marked turning (r.)[13½] to the **Dolphin** – the former Shanzu Beach Hotel, the £540,000 **Serena Beach Hotel** (r.), and the late Boulevard Beach Hotel, a sister-establishment of Nairobi's Boulevard until in 1975 the African Safari Club took over and renamed it the **Malaika**.

The one-km. track beyond is worth enduring for the club's **Marina** (converted dhows, yachts and the – somewhat Teutonic – 'African Night').

Mtwapa. Marina and sports centre both overlook the mangrove swamps of Mtwapa Creek, Mombasa's municipal boundary [14½]. The old 'Singing Ferry' (above) was replaced by the grey suspension bridge built, below the 'Prison Industries Show Room' (l.), in 1958; and this, wood-slatted and one-way, is now due for replacement by the Sumitomo Construction Company's 208 yards of pre-stressed concrete.

On the far bank (r.)[15], James Adcock (POB. 95693, tel. 471258) and **F.G. Macconnel** (POB. 82849, tel. 485230) hire boats for fishing and skin-diving trips (the latter's equipped with ship-to-shore radio). Kenya Marinas offer similar facilities and, in addition, the **Kenya Marineland & Snake Park**. The 90,000-gallon 'oceanarium' was stocked in September 1974 with sharks, turtles, sting rays, eels and smaller reef fry. These, from an underwater 'observation area', you see hand-fed by a skin-diver at 11 every morning. (The fish have the influx of visitors to thank for a second daily feeding now at 4 p.m.; Ksh. 23/-, under 14s 10/-). First additions to the oceanarium were the neighbouring booths of wood-carvers, a small serpentarium of snakes and crocodiles and – in consequence? – a Samaki Bar with stiff drinks. The last became in 1977 **Le Pichet**, a Belgian-run restaurant that proclaims itself French but sells itself in a boat-trip 'package' (by Ocean Tours' 50-seater *Sea Creek* or on Marijani Tours' 'Seafood Seafari' from the Mombasa Beach, Serena and Whitesands hotels). By car, follow the well-marked, soft-dust track, 1½ kms right of the main road (above)[15].

Jumba la Mtwana. This 'National Monument' is clearly indicated (r.)[16]: 'Open Daily 8 a.m.-6 p.m. 3 km.'. The track passes the sign to the Kanamai Hostel (below) and forks left to the car park ('Are Your Windows and Door Locked') and the ticket office (Ksh. 5/-, under 16s 2/-, residents 2/-, 1/- and, on week-ends and national holidays, 1/-, -/50). The ruins of this 14-15th-c. slave-trading settlement, 'unknown to history', were in 1972 un-earthed, or rather disentangled, and made accessible to the public. Though covering several acres, Jumba la Mtwana – the 'Large house of the young male Slave' – is less spectacular than Gede: four mosques, a cemetery and three (supposed) houses, 'of the Kitchen', 'of the Cylinders' and 'of the Many Doors'. Best preserved is the Great Mosque, on the beach with its *mihrab* intact. By the time you arrive Dr Kirkman's 1/- *Notes* may be out of (roneo-typed) print, Hamo Sassoon's *Guide* still not published, but the sketchy leaflet should still be free.

After a stretch of palm and lush grass 'parkland', the board (l.)[19] just before the *Masjid al-Azhar* – the Illustrious Mosque (1973) – announces the '**Kanamai Conference and Holiday Centre** 3 km. Camping Site' (the National Christian Council of Kenya's; Kikambala POB. 46, tel. 46; one-, two- and three-room cottages Ksh. 45/- p.p.; February, March, May, June, October and November 30/-; residents 30/-, 20/-). For the **Whispering Palms Hotel**, the two-km. track from Kanamai along the coast through the coconut-groves is a tropical experience – and definitely preferable to the three-km. turning right of the main road [21]. This passes en route the Hoares' 'Alzo' camp site and the **Kikambala Beach Cottages** (all l.), and bypasses, on the main road, the '**Porini Village** . . . Traditional Dance and African Dishes' [20].

The reef closes northward with the four-mile **Kikambala Beach**. Being Mombasa's last hotel, the **Sun n' Sand** tries hardest, with quiet rooms and enticing prices. Its two-km. drive (r.)[22½] is shared by the Kikambala Catholic Church, a Baptist guest house and church and the five **Bahari Beach Cottages** (POB. 80455, tel. 25060).

'Poultex' (l.), a Total petrol (r.) and Kijipwa police station (l.), then endless **sisal**. First sown here in 1934 and now grown over 20,000 acres, this crop explains the factories, workers' estates and even narrow-gauge railway of **Vipingo**. The assiduity with which first German, then British planters have crossed and 'back-crossed' sisal since the turn of the century is suggested by the fact that the AGAVE AMANIENSIS developed at Amani and grown at Vipingo is officially 'Hybrid no. 11648'. Production none the less continues to decline: exports from Kenya in 1979 dropped to Ksh. 149 million. Which may explain why the gentle hills combed suavely with well-kempt plants soon give way to the serried 'sticks' of the acres gone to seed. Takaungu lies off right [44]; the track from Mariakani – the Kilifi ferry bypass – enters left (p. 100)[48], and the road rolls on to **Kilifi Creek** [54].

Mnarani. The ferry's two decrepit craft make the four-minute crossing gratis round the clock – so do not hurry to it. First a track indicated right [53], then a second on the cliff top, past a dinky mosque with the usual arches like upturned hearts and its façade. 'completed in 1390' (Islamic for 1970) . . . both leading to the **Mnarani** – Lighthouse – **Hotel**. Overlooking the exquisite creek, with airstrip, pool and boats for hire, this well-run establishment is a scenic holiday centre. Its carmine bee-eaters now seem to have abandoned their nearby nesting site, but ardent ornithologists might well sight up to 60 different species in an afternoon or two. Traditionally and still, though, the place is most famed for its fishing, with the Lady Delamere Cup in February, the Schweppes Competition in March and the Duke of Manchester's Cup in December. If no longer a club, the Mnarani's mood is at such times esoteric.

Mombasa's north coast – two dozen beach-hotels

Also before the ferry, the **Mnarani Serpentarium** lies to the left (daily 8 a.m.-12.15 & 2-6 p.m.; adults Ksh. 5/-, under 14s 1/-). 'You enter . . . at your own Risk' warns the sign, but no risk exists: behind glass and a guard-rail Mr Bramwell's small collection, most from Kakamega, seems safely somnolent – save for the marine monitors that do their press-ups huffing.

The **Mnarani ruins** have exemplary directions: 'Follow the green Posts' behind the serpentarium, 'only three (easy) minutes walk and a short (60-step) climb'. The people of Kilifi were occasional participants in the tussles between Mombasa and Malindi, even following the Zimba against the latter and being likewise worsted by the Segeju (p. 18). Experts conjecture that the inhabitants, stormed by the Galla 'in the second quarter of the seventeenth century', sought final (and futile) refuge in the mosque. This, with its several remnant Arabic inscriptions, and the pillar tombs around – one the Coast's tallest (and thus needing its ugly supports) – may date from the 1590s. Cleared and excavated since 1973, the site was opened to the public in 1977 (7 a.m.-6 p.m. daily; entry Ksh. 2/-).

Kilifi. Where you wait for the ferry, or land on the far bank, coconuts and cashews are cheap in the waterside shacks. The latter risk being under-roasted, but I always take a coconut – if only as sustenance for such times as the ferries break down. The vendor will husk it and slash off the top like a soft-boiled egg:

fresh in its milk, the inside is delicious – meaty-succulent and quite unlike shop-desiccated. That the eating soon cloys, though, may be Nature's safeguard: un-accustomed tummies suffer from a surfeit of coconut 'flesh'.

On the far cliff top (r.) Kilifi starts with a 'Toplife Restaurant', blue with murals and offering 'Boading and Lodging'. The township's centre is bus station, hospital and prison, a Catholic church and a Muslim school. The administrative blocks (further r.) will one day be shaded by the Mzee's contribution to 'National Tree Planting Day 1973'; St Thomas' Anglican Church, of (hopefully) unique design and derelict air, was founded in 1960 and, from the cliff-top beacon beyond, steps descend to the beach and the former (dug-out) ferry. Since 1974 the road continues as a beautiful corniche, past properties mostly European, to end after seven kms in a cove of casuarina.

The main road climbs steeply from the ferry [54], passing the turning to the '**Seahorse** 1½ km' [55] and (also l.)[57] Kilifi's **cashew-nut factory**. Costing Ksh. 50 million, employing 1500 men and capable of processing 60 tons daily – of finished nuts for eating and shell liquid for brake-linings – it was completed in 1975 by a company from Bologna specializing oddly in the construction of cashew-nut factories in Africa. Kilifi's cashews cede to low, tight growth over which the baobabs tower, then to recent afforestation with neatly labelled plots of casuarina, conifer and palm. The tarmac cuts north across the **Arabuko-Sokoke Forest**. Adjoining

Jilore Forest, its 140 square miles were early recognized as being important for both trees and birds, and became first a colonial Crown forest reserve, then in 1977 a 7402-acre Natural Reserve. The Sokoke pipit and Sokoke Scops owl are its exclusive species; mimic butterflies, Ader's duikers and golden-rumped elephant shrews are natural idio-syncrasies found here in particular. The reserve's native wildlife, though, is suffering from the soft-wood afforestation. From charcoal-burners too: with Somalia largely deforested, the Arab states have turned to Kenya and now take annually some 100,000 tons. Charcoal, and mangrove poles, you see stacked by the roadside ready for export. There are snatches of sea through the trees (r.), down tracks that reach to farms and dukas. The Kararacha and Mida outposts watch for fire, but Mida means a creek to Kenyans: the road to it (r.)[98] serves Gede and Watamu too.

Gede or Gedi Ruins/National Monument is/are well sign-posted left then right past Gede village. And, for the same entry fee as Fort Jesus (p. 66), 'Open Daily 7 a.m.-6 p.m.'. After the latter hour few locals deign to stay. Though the daytime flies might make night-fall seem desirable, you will soon see why. The jungle around you broods oppressively: superstitiousness or no, the rustle of unseen snakes and monkeys makes the ghost-town eerie. For centuries the jungle growth in fact concealed this African Angkor Wat. In 1884 Sir John Kirk took the first photographs; in 1927 the government gazetted Gede as a historical monument, but only in 1948 (when it became momentarily a national park) did Dr Kirkman begin his decade of excavation and perpetrate the misspelling *Gedi*).

You can hire a guide for Ksh. 5/- per person, but if you wander alone round the 45 acres, note the sun's whereabouts as you enter: you may need it for orientation later. Otherwise, Dr Kirkman's 5/- booklet guides you to the palace, mosques and walls, and to the fourteen single-storey, coral-rag houses: 'on the Wall', 'of the Chinese Cash', 'of the Venetian Bead', 'of the Ivory Box' . . . each is named from prominent features or con-tents. His, however, is just informed comment on what you can see for yourself. Why Gede was founded, inland and indefensible, or why abandoned can only be conjectured. The Dated Tomb gives the site an *ab quo* of 1399 (though 12th-c. Islamic structures lie beneath). Its 16th-c. *ad quem* is shown by sherds. Chinese celadon and Indian cornelian,

cobalt and red-lacquered glass, eye-pencils and bidets all indicate a prosperous populace of some 2500 souls, yet written history ignores the town entirely (unless Gede – 'Precious' in the Galla language – and not Mambrui is really Kilimani, which was mapped as 'Quelman' in 1639). Another question-mark is its sudden 16th-c. desertion. (Mortaring was left half-finished in the evacuation, and no skeletons survive.) Plague is a possible explanation, or destruction by the Galla or as a Zimba meal (p. 18).

The small museum contains interesting relics but no clue to the mystery. A notice on the ticket office describes another of the site's minor assets: the above-mentioned **golden-rumped elephant shrew** is not a joke but an intriguing natural freak that accounts for the more active scamperings in Gede's under-growth. The RHYNCHOCYON CHRYSOPYGUS – 'Nosed dog with a golden Rump' – eats all day in a 'territory' demarcated by its scent and makes leaf nests by night (unlike its nocturnal neighbour here, the 'knob-bristled forest elephant shrew'). In spite of super-stition an American student spent twenty months here to research the species, unique in Kenya, for the sake of a doctorate and a half-page in the *National Geographic*.

More prosaic, and more prominent, than these 'golden-rumped/knob-bristled' oddities is the 'typical' **Giriama Village** in a clearing behind the museum. A sparse, artificial affair, it does at least give some idea of the Giriama's home and social set-up with its 'Hut of Mzee' (the old man), 'Hut of Mzee's mother', 'of the Big Baby' and 'of the *Barobaro*', Teen-agers.

Watamu. After Gede village's British-red 'phone box, school, football pitch and almost pretty women, the road runs six straight kms between shambas and coral quarries and forks left, 1½ kms to Watamu village: just a clearing with shacks, palms, goats, camels, an ornate mosque, a thatched 'Doorie Cinema' and the **Mushroom Restaurant** and Bar, well stocked for visiting bachelors. The **Watamu Beach Hotel** is panoramic, its 'rock-pool' over-looking a bay of craggy, unnamed islands, but unless you have booked through its (mostly Swiss and German) agents, you may well find it full. The tarmac beyond ends [3 kms] above the coral cliffs of the exquisite **Blue Lagoon**.

In 1972 the tarmac was extended right of the T-junction too. At **Ocean Sports** (l.)[1½ kms] Ian Pritchard GM once landed his 30-foot boat to settle, establish this landscaped sea-centre and win a reputation as a paraplegic painter. **Seafarers**, next door, likewise hires fishing-, sailing-, skiing- and glass-bottomed boats, and also made a virtue of refusing 'package' parties until the change of management in 1977.

Like the 1971 **Turtle Bay Hotel**, imposing on the hilltop beyond, they line the delightful **Turtle Bay**. The area off shore, from the Blue Lagoon to Mida Creek, is since 1968 a **Marine National Park**. The idea of this and Malindi's park, and the adjacent 82-square-mile reserve, is to preserve the coral wealth and stop the depredations of both local anglers and overseas collectors of tropical fish. You, too, are forbidden to take shells or coral, or to sail in without a ticket (Ksh. 10/- p.d. or 40/- per fortnight, residents 2/50, under 12s 1/-, boats 20/-). The park's office (sometimes) provides free *Regulations and Directives* and good 10/- booklets, and permits 'free swimming, water-skiing, walking, basking and picnicking' along the beach. Though open the year round, the park is best visited between October and March, and then at low tide (when the fish 'expect you and crowd the boat'). Whale Island shows itself, most at low tide, opposite the mouth of Mida Creek. To the north, more in shore, buoys mark the **coral gardens**.

Mida Creek, with its winding inlets alive with birds, complements the park's offshore richness in coral and tropical fish. The road continues for five kms of predominantly European villas and ends by the park's staff quarters. From here however there is little to see: better hire a boat from one of the hotels and sail in over the **Tewa Caves**. Those who like game-viewing two fathoms down can skin-dive here to see the groupers when the tide is right. Because the six-foot fish – rock-cod or *tewa* – now number up to a dozen, these are no longer the 'Big Three Caves'. The shore-line above is a tangle of mangroves, broken by clearings where the cooking-fires smoke and the fishing-boats are beached. Drifting through this coastal jungle is especially rewarding from March to May, when the waders are en route.

After the E 899 to Gede and Watamu [98] the Malindi road passes Msabaha's Cotton Research Station [104], the dispensary (off r.) where Kabwere Wanje sold 'Antiwitchcraft Medicines' and potions to cope with his 100 wives, the 'Giriama Dancing Village' (r.)[109] and **Malindi Airport** (1952)[111]: 'Please dim your lights – Aircraft Approaching'. Arrivals by air then share the road into town [113].

MALINDI

Though Milton's 'Melind' and Portugal's long-standing ally, modern Malindi is no more for historians than are Hastings or Hurstmonceux for chauvinistic Frenchmen. Until recently it was home to only Giriama fishermen and farmers, a relaxed place of retirement, too, for expatriates up country. Their properties still stand seedy-luxurious in flamboyant gardens behind the sweep of beach. Hibiscus, frangipani and bougainvillea everywhere are as colourful as the coral in the shallows near by.

All this lured the tourists and, although the town owned only five hotels, its tourism soon became the tail that wagged the dog. The result by the early 1970s was a 'down-market' destination for German 'package' parties – but they and the famous annual fishing competitions still failed to shake Malindi long from its sunny, unsophisticated languor. Of late, however, things have grown slicker: one successful hotel chain has taken on the hapless Sindbad; Lawford's has become the headquarters of another multi-hotel group; a casino has opened, British Airways' flights to Mombasa have led to an increase in the UK 'contingent', and Italian investment has given Malindi three suave new hotels of almost South-Coast class.

The travel agents' potted histories like to identify it with 'Ma-lin' where, a Chinese chronicler wrote in the 9th century, 'the people are black . . . fierce . . . and not ashamed of debauching the wives of their fathers'. A 12th-c. geographer fancied that the Malindians 'hunt tigers . . . exploit iron mines . . . and know the art of enchanting snakes'. Only Arabic records and pottery finds date Malindi reliably to the 13th century.

Its inhabitants thereafter sent a giraffe to China (p. 17); welcomed da Gama regally, in April 1498, and provided the pilot that helped him 'discover' India; struggled long with Mombasa, and were in 1589 almost eaten (p. 18). When the Portuguese withdrew from their Malindi 'factory' in favour of Fort Jesus (p. 18), the town waned. The Omanis in 1662 forced the inhabitants to seek refuge in Mombasa and for the following century

Galla raiders from the north camped in what remained of the sultanate's 16th-c. heyday, the 'houses stately and magnificent'. Captain Owen found them there still in 1823; Dr Krapf in 1845 reported the town derelict and abandoned. The Sultan of Zanzibar sixteen years later re-peopled the region with 1000 slaves and 150 Baluchi slavers for the sake of its grain and citrus estates. Then a short period of prosperous slaving which the IBEA abolished in 1890, thereby ruining the Arab residents. Cotton, introduced in 1889; orchella, producing purple dye; root crops, rice, copra and palm-toddy carried the town's economy – just above subsistence – into the 20th century. A revival, through rubber, in the 1910s did not survive the Slump. In the 1930s hotels presaged a prosperity that the War temporarily postponed: the Italians raided Malindi Airport on 24 October 1940, but most of the fifteen bombs dropped were dud. After the War up-country settlers and overseas visitors looked increasingly to Malindi for retirement and holiday homes: though revenue from palm-toddy *tembo* almost rivals the fishermen's, tourism has since 1965 been the town's mainstay. It provides employment for 45% of the population, has made of Malindi 'the fastest growing' of Kenya's (three) coastal towns, and explains the publication of E.B. Martin's *Malindi*. The digest of a doctoral thesis, it was re-edited in 1973 and much improved with pictures from the archives and Joy Adamson.

After the airport the road enters town between churches (l.) and schools, a mango-packing station and the Harambee KANU office (l.) – one of the few discreet manifestations of this one-party state. A bougainvillea roundabout sees the bypass (r.) off to Silversands and the Marine Park. Forking left after the 'Cleopatra Theatre' (i.e. cinema), it skirts the bus station, the covered market and the open-air *Soko Kubwa* – 'Big Market' viz. cloth, charcoal and dried fish – to pass the New Safari, New Mahrus and New Kenya hotels (all far from new) and narrow through to the Village Green.

The road straight on from the roundabout bends past the turning (l.) to Ganda, Jilore and Tsavo (p. 98) and meets the unassuming main street by the **police station**, the **post office** and a coppice of notice-boards. The roadside cottages opposite – the Malindi Air Services and Bunsons offices, a bank and 'Malindi Boutique' – form the façade of **Lawford's Hotel**. A retired District Officer from Fort Hall, Commander Leo Lawford turned his hand first to sisal near Thika then to a pioneer combination of cattle- and hotel-management. The establishment he started here in 1934 was supplied with dairy produce from his experimental farm.

Turning right, you run the gauntlet of stalls hawking drums, knick-knacks and Akamba carvings (p. 25). The Malindi Ginneries process the cotton from twenty miles around for subsequent export via Mombasa; the Nafisa Store (also r.) is a well-stocked African curio shop, and a neglected Muslim cemetery (l.) has some recent insertions already overgrown. The road opens into the Village Green, now **Uhuru Gardens** – and Malindi's 'town centre' *faute de mieux*. To the left the 'H.B. Fishing Service' became the well-named Shell Shop when H.B. died in 1974, and then – with shopping for shells forbidden – the Curio & Gemstones Co. Next left is the 22-foot **Vasco da Gama Monument** with its stone sail, Cross of the Order of Christ and single surviving medallion behind, an effigy of the explorer. When a Portuguese minister unveiled the memorial in 1960, African nationalists protested: stealing its two brass plaques may thus have been a lucrative political gesture. The **Council Offices** beyond are a fine colonial period piece, completed by the IBEA in 1890, now colourfully fronted by flowers and *msonobari*-flame trees, by a bell and four recarriaged cannon.

The concrete block on the Village Green's lawn is Malindi Sub-district's World War II memorial. The tradesmen behind who nowadays proclaim their wares in German and Italian do not, presumably, appreciate the irony. To the right stands the plain **Bohra Mosque** (1928) and, all around, the **Old Town**: overall atmosphere, not any special 'sights', makes a visit worth while Exiting left, the road dips back to the beach. The Sunni sect's prominent **Juma'a** – Friday – **Mosque** was also the site of the Friday slave market. After 1873, when the shipment of slaves for sale was banned, only local Giriama could be auctioned weekly on this Islamic sabbath. Amongst the oldest of the town's eleven mosques, the edifice is almost Brighton Pavilion with its domes and crenellations, but mosque hangers-on who can neither read the Qoran nor speak the language of the Prophet may – with untypical bigotry – prevent your entering. The ornate, if anonymous, graves alongside are in any case more interesting than the bare, rush-matted prayer-room. So best confine your sightseeing to the ruins of Shaikh Hassan's 15th-c. **Pillar Tomb**. Though its shorter 19th-c. neighbour is unquestionably circumcised, Africans dispute the phallic

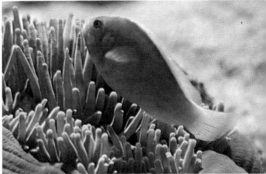

association; but they too are baffled by the origin and function, and these interesting erections remain a mystery – and East Africa's only architectural innovation.

Further right come visibly cheap hotels – Gilani's and the Metro – and the **Malindi Sea Fishing Club**. The jetty, though new, works only part-time, being high and dry at most states of the tide. It does however serve as a guide if you want to wade from it – at very low tide only – past the light-pillar to the coastal steamer wrecked in 1925. In the **Fish Market** (next l.) prices astonish at the daily auctions. Nowadays the waves off shore bob more with motor-boats than with the traditional dug-out *horis*, the larger dhows and *mashuas* or the fewer *ngalawas*.

Thereafter, lowly offices and shacks, dominated by an Isma'ili mosque and a 'Shree Malindi Hindu Union Hindu Temple 1970'. In 1913 Malindi's *Political Records* reported 'a number of plots in town covered with rubbish and bush': this remained the case with the ramshackle African esplanade ahead until its recent, relative embellishment of a broad sea-wall and -walk.

The **Vasco da Gama Church** (r.) dates perhaps from 1541, an unassuming 'first church in East Africa'. 'Part of this building,' according to the board, 'is the Portuguese Chapel near which St. Francis Xavier buried two soldiers during his journey to India in 1542.' On an inside wall, in 1933, plaster was removed to reveal a painting of the Crucifixion complete with Virgin Mary. 'Proper display facilities' not being available, the government ordered that the plaster be replaced. On the mostly colonial graves outside only the inscriptions in concrete or marble have survived. Beyond the link-road to the bypass (r.), Malindi's 1976 **youth hostel** is smart with 36 bunk-beds in cool and usually clean rooms for six (Ksh. 14/50 p.n. + 1/- for non-members; POB. 494, tel. 365).

To reach the **Vasco da Gama Pillar** here, follow the green signs opposite the hospital, left before the 'car park' – 'Please Stay in the Foot Pass' – straight on through a corridor of undergrowth and left along the rocks to the natural coral bridge. The Portuguese explorer erected this *Padrao* cross of Lisbon limestone beside the Shaikh of Malindi's palace in January 1499: the Muslims, unchristianly, tore it down, and the Portuguese settled for this site in the 16th century. The crew of HMS *Briton* saved the column from collapsing in 1873 by enclosing it with the concrete cone; the eroded cliff itself was kept from a similar fate by underpinning in 1938 and 1949.

The tarmac runs on to **Silversands**. Backed by a fine screen of palm and tamarisk, the beach may not always live up to its name: the sea is encroaching at an annual rate of 25 feet, and cost stands between the Council and the sea-wall needed here. This, though, does not affect the pleasant **camp sites**, one run by the Council (Ksh. 5-10/- p.n. per tent/caravan, 1/- for water and loo), the other attached to the 1950s shop and cafeteria (sixteen double or triple bandas, lockable and with electric light, for Ksh. 45-55/- p.n. – 100/- with shower and loo – and two double tents for 35-45/- p.n.; POB. 619, tel. 336).

The road ends as the rocky drive of the **Driftwood Club**, base for the Afro-Sub Scuba Diving School. Rejoining the tarmac bypass (p. 80), you drive south past **Birdland**. Opened in 1971 (and daily 9 a.m.-5.45 p.m. for Ksh. 9/-, under 5s 3/-), the Glovers' ornithological colony is the largest in East Africa. Its $1\frac{1}{2}$ acres of aviaries house about 1000 birds in 226 species both indigenous and imported. Some, such as carmine bee-eaters and crowned hornbills, even breed successfully – despite intruding snakes and small predators that prey on eggs and young – and Oskarini the ostrich has to date laid 40 eggs. Though Vervets, baboons, mongooses and tortoises are on view too, 'the Birds have preference Here', says the sign: the 'Walk In's' many gorgeous varieties fly round you blithely as though well aware of it.

Straight on, the tarmac passes pretty villas and dwindles into tracks. A half-mile before the odd roadhead, the Marine Park turning (l.) also serves the 'private' **snake collection** of 'Mark S. Easterbrook (Snake Catcher)' which, since 1975, 'Visitors are welcome to view . . . 9.30 am. to. 5.30 pm.' (Ksh. 5/-). The reptiles, all caught locally, live not in cages or cases (which shorten lives) but in 'natural' and neatly 'coral-gardened' pits. (This landscaping was an aesthetic necessity: until the enclosures were cement-floored, snakes escaped through the hollow coral.) Besides terrapins, pancake tortoises, lizards and a couple of crocodiles, a score of snake species can be seen. 'But we've no idea of exactly how many, because they not only breed but keep eating each other.'

Malindi Marine Park. The next turning (l.) leads to Casuarina Point, the headquarters and 'entrance' of Malindi's marine park (costs and conditions like Watamu's, p. 79). 'It is an Offence to Enter without a Permit or Ticket, kill, break, disturb all Fish Corals Crustacea and other Marine Life', says one sign; another, above the kiosk, reads: 'Ensure you get a Ticket worth your Money'. Sailing over Barracuda Channel to the North Reef's **coral gardens**, you invariably do. Whether you arrive in a hired hotel boat or haggle with one of the outboard owners here (Ksh. 25-30/- p.p., with equipment), the 'gardens' are the most popular venue for snorkelers and glass-bottomed boaters. And rightly so: the sea-bed's coral-heads and fish-filled hollows, brilliant with colour and at every turn dramatic, make this aquatic wonderland the best and most accessible on the Kenya Coast. The submarine features are more varied here, too, than at Watamu: south-east of the channel the Barracuda Reef, predominantly potato coral but with mushroom and stag-horn, finger and brain corals also; Stork Passage, deeper, for keener divers, with bigger pelagic fish in the coral chasm; Tewa Reef off Leopard Point and Ed's Caves by Sail Rock.

North of Lawford's, in the 'Lamu Road', are the unlikely neighbours of the **Palm Garden** Bar & Restaurant ('Italian food & Specialised in Indian food') and **Malindi Snake Park** (9 a.m.-6 p.m.; Ksh. 5/-, under 7s 1/-, or 10/- for the Friday 5-6 p.m. feeding). This enterprise, African managed and owned, comprises cases of local snakes, cages of monkeys, enclosures of tortoises – one a 200-year-old giant from the Seychelles – and monitor lizards in a cruelly deep pit.

Opposite, the one-time Cooper Motors' workshop now houses Hertz/UTC, Shell, a bank and a 'Delite Cinema'. The old Skyways Bar/Beer Garden (l.) now fares better as the **Number One** Bar and **Restaurant** ('Guests going to Casino Club & Disco will get free transport . . . here from 9. pm onwards'). Amidst grocers and boutiques, the **Coast Air** office (l. – where you book for Baomo, p. 90) faces its **Kenya Airways** counterpart, Pollmans and a 'Medical Store'. The **Blue Marlin** behind them is a much-improved version of the Bradys' 1931 Palm Beach Hotel (where Hemingway & Co once drank late and missed out on the early-morning fishing). Sitawi House (l.) consists of another bank and pharmacy, more grocers and curio stores, Nimmy's Bookshop, Caltex and **Avis**. And – cleanliness being not necessarily next to godliness, the **Habari Night Club** neighbours **St Anthony's Catholic Church** (l.; English Mass 5 p.m. Sundays, 7 a.m. Saturdays and 6.30 a.m. Wednesdays).

The features of interest then alternate left-right along the road. First left a track to the **Lutheran Church** (English service Sundays at 11 a.m.) and first right the **Sindbad**, beautiful with bougainvillea. Left again, **St Andrew's Church** (English service Sundays at 10.30 a.m.), opposite a 'Footpass of Access to Sea', and (next l.) the sign-boards that send you round the houses to the **Malindi Safari Club** – 'Italian Restaurant'. After its **Tropicana Club 28** (r.) the **Eden Roc**, German-owned and -patronized, is a far cry from the pre-War club run on the site by pilot John Carberry (whose landing-strip was the beach alongside). Between tennis courts and the **Marijani Stables** (l.), the **Malindi Chalets** are Jambo Hotels' – and attractive around lawns and pool (prices and bookings like the Cowrie Shell's, p. 75). Where the road veers left to the **Suli Suli Sporting Club**, the track straight on – 'Malindi's worst' – hobbles past the Malindi Bay Flats, the **Number One Casino Club** and the abortive Indian Ocean Hotel (all r.) to the '**Malindi Golf & Country Club** 800 metres'. Built in 1961 and a club since 1962, it welcomes visitors (for Ksh. 3/- daily membership) to its tennis courts (5/-), its Sunday film show (5/-) and its nine-hole golf course (10/-, caddies 4/-, 'No Tips Please').

Malindi's magnificent four miles of beaches monopolize most of your time. A break in the reef lets in rollers for **surfing**, best in July and August. The hotels hire surf-boards, the Marijani Stables **horses** (tel. 174). Riding on the shore, or driving a rented beach-buggy, is ideal for those in a hurry to go nowhere. Malindi is short of taxis – in town they stand by the New Kenya Hotel – but Hertz and Avis rent and the hotels run cars for trips out of town. Besides the sights I mention *per se*, the 'Circular Drive' to Ganda and the Giriama villages is popular. Equally so once were their topless **girl dancers**. But the local Council, who also dislike bikinis and have set their face against European nudity, recently barred bare black bosoms. For a while it was on/off with the Battle of the Bra, but the Council won through and now the girls dress, exceptionally, for the hotels' shows.

Malindi attracts also – like Watamu, Kilifi, Mtwapa, Mombasa and Shimoni – for **deep-sea fishing**. The Indian Ocean is 'the fisherman's dream of the unexpected in unknown waters', according to the blurb. From the end of the monsoon in August/ September until March or April the coast here excels for barracuda, wahoo and tuna – longtail, yellowfin, skipjack and bonito; king-fish and sail-fish; dorado/dolphin and marlin – Pacific Blue, Black and Striped; Tiger, Mako and Hammerhead shark; cobia, caranx and Rainbow runner. Fish caught off Kenya have broken six world records and 36 of the 79 all-Africa records. Whales have merely been seen. High-lights of Malindi's October-February peak are the Henry the Navigator Competition, the Malindi & North Coast Sea-fishing Festival, the Uhuru Competition and Coca-Cola's Bill-fish Competition. *Where to Fish in Kenya* provides general information, the Malindi Sea Fishing Club both local details and the obligatory 40/- licence (POB. 364, tel. 145).

MALINDI NORTH

Between the Suli Suli [0] and the **Palm Tree Club** (r.)[½] Malindi – and the tar macadam – ends. The Kiswani dairy farm (l.) has flourished since Commander Lawford proved that Jerseys and Guernseys could thrive here in the tropics. Only speed-bumps spoil the respite of the surfaced bridge across the broad **Sabaki River** [8]. Until the completion of the K£8-million Chakama Dam up stream, the river's silt will continue on occasions to turn Malindi Bay mud-brown. (It has for centuries stopped coral growing there.) As the river once formed the northern border of Zanzibar's ten-mile coastal strip (p. 63), Malindi's run-away slaves used to settle in safety on the far bank (but found they could survive only by returning to town, and possible re-enslave-ment, in order to market their produce).

Hell's Kitchen. Follow the signs (l.)[8½] to Marafa and Garashi, left then right through Marikebuni [15½] and on through Bomani.

Hell's Kitchen

These sunny villages you usually traverse to a chorus of '*Jambo!*' and '*Wazungu*'. In clearings under the baobab and jack-fruit trees, they are little more than bandas, bare bosoms and bananas. The soft-featured, mild-mannered **Giriama** predominate – a Bantu people whose nine tribes were driven south by the Galla in the 13-15th centuries to settle between Garsen and Kilifi. They are known for their drumming akin to Buganda's, their *kaya*-stockades (where tribal assemblies are held, the chosen few farm and the elders are buried), and for their pretty women (these in turn for their palm-fibre bustles).

Forking right through Marafa village [38½], do not follow the sign 'Chief's Office' but fork right again for a half-kilometre. A gap in the trees (l.) then gives on to Hell's Kitchen: a spectacle of cliffs and pinnacles fantastically – and enigmatically – eroded. Maroon, buff, russet, pink and white, the 100-foot stacks are geologically Pliocene 'demoiselles'. Walking, cautiously, down the steep paths, you can only rarely see how the various strata have resisted rain erosion in differing degrees.

Then best return the way you came. Following straight on past Hell's Kitchen [39½], the longer, little-used track forks slightly right [40½] and sharp right [64½] through Adu. Of unpredictable passability, it finally drops to the main coast track by the 'Public Posho Mill' at Fundisa [88].

Mambrui lies south of the junction above, thirteen kms from Malindi. A sleepy 15th-c. relic, perhaps of the 'Quilimanci/Quelman'

mapped by the Portuguese, it is well worth a visit. The Arabs' erstwhile slave-plantations were still prosperous from cotton in the 1930s: now they are a has-been like the hamlet itself. Opposite the '*Duka la Sigara*', beyond the just-perceptible cemetery (l.), the **pillar tomb** is a modest 'Gazetted Historical Monument'. The topmost of its original 27 feet fell off on 9 June 1934: of its ten inset, late-Ming porcelain bowls, 6½ inexplicably remain. The **Riadha Mosque** (1962) overawes the village from the only elevation, focusing attention with its rococo façade and lime-green dome. Qoranic texts like icing on a cake adorn both it and the *Nur* – Light – School alongside.

Ngomeni, right of the main track north, is sign-posted [17½] '*Centro Ricerche Aerospaziali*'. The original settlement is patently ancient – a curious but unstudied ruin guards the harbour entrance – but why, with its superior anchorage, it never rivalled Malindi or Mombasa is not known. The Bajun inhabitants maintain that God depopulated it with a flood in the 13th century to punish its women for bathing in milk. A historical storm came in 1968 but then the cause, according to the locals, was an Italian satellite which had 'pierced the sky'. The Italians' **Equatorial Rocket Site** was established here in 1966. The track to it, raised along a marshy estuary, skirts salt-pans (l.) and sand-pits (r.) where the cattle are watered and the women wash. After the fishing-village, the Space Research Centre and a desultory huddle of huts, the twelve-km. track ends above the low cliffs of **Formosa Bay**. Now renamed *Ngwana*, it is mangrove islands, sand-banks and two rocket platforms.

Robinson Island shares that view too. Fundi Issa – 'Jesus the Mechanic' – died at Ngomeni and, after the hamlet that honours his name [33], you read 'Robinson Island Turn Right'. Four much-improved kms bring you past the airstrip to the creek: 'Lunch & Crossing 90/- Crossing Only 40/-'. Balancing their calabash of water on their head, Giriama women still wade across breast-deep as they did in Fundi Issa's time. This Swahili shipbuilder, so the story goes, went into seclusion here in the 1920s. He let the local womenfolk draw water from his wells but only on condition they shave off their fancy coiffures. They acquiesced, but named the place *Kinya'ole*, Barber's Island.

David Hurd changed the name and the reputation. Having fished for shark, survived Somali capture, written *Kidnap at Kiunga* and been shipwrecked near by, he settled on this square-mile island in 1964 – to build a boriti, makuti and sackcloth home that Man Friday would have liked, to fish, grow melons and entertain uniquely. Here you can dine on delicious (and original) concoctions of seafood and coconut; a new menu came with a new local manager in 1979. You can fish from the boat his father made, sleep in the bandas built that year too, or simply laze on palliasses, a part-time castaway. Contributions from guests helped pay for an extension to the nearby secondary school . . . and Robinson Island remains the only place to see the local girls dance topless.

The Giriama Village Island must – if imitation is a form of flattery – be something of a compliment to Robinson's. Following the signs (r.) off the main track five kms further, you take a similar drive to a similar creek [2·2 kms]. A likewise serene, fifteen-minute punt-ride – and an equally warm walk – bring you to the makuti-roofed restaurant and bar, all *déjà vu*. Four *nyumba*-huts of shaggy thatch accommodate (Ksh. 130/- p.p. without water), the 40/- lunch includes 'crub' and other crustacea, Giriama dance after the candle-lit dinner and the site, developed in 1978, is locally known as *Mto wa Mawe*, River of Rocks.

LAMU AND THE TANA VALLEY

Lamu means more an experience than a mere excursion, a journey virtually backwards in time. Free of Zanzibar's political tarnish, the island survives mediaevally, a living epitome of most coastal towns throughout the Arab heyday. But, turning its back on the modern Western world, Lamu has perversely attracted its attention. Kenya's tourist authorities – high-lighting a hermit – advertise it widely, jetties and airstrip have been recently improved, a Lamu Society was formed in 1975 and the ratio of guide-books per head of population is here Kenya's highest!

Lamu – Shela mosque and the beach of Manda Island

Communications have so far saved the Lamu archipelago from over-exploitation. Most visitors fly, in aircraft seating only six or seven. From Nairobi, beyond Ol Donyo Sabuk, the flight is somewhat drear – from Mombasa or Malindi, fascinating. You follow the shore, its shoals and shallows in every shade of green. After Gongoni's salt-pans the rivers do not double but treble and quadruple back on themselves; elephants are specks on the marsh and abandoned plantations below, and of the several unexplored lakes one became Lake Kenyatta when that president passed overhead in 1971.

From Malindi the buses of the Tana River, Tawakkul and Malindi Taxi services thunder up the coast, the first's on 'Alternate Days to Lamu'. (I took one on 23 November 1979 . . . so calculate from there on; Ksh. 35/- and 'perhaps half a day', depending on the Tana and the track.) Good sailors can go by dhow – up to 24 hours of pitching and tossing three times weekly from Mombasa's Old Port. Drive if you must: on from the Giriama Village Island (p. 85)[41], past the Tana Salt-pans (r.)[57] and on across acres of flat croton scrub which sudden, lovely pools of lilies here and there enhance. From a final ridge, the broad green Tana Valley spreads before you. The track drops gently to it, past the B 8 to Hola and Baomo Lodge (l.) [106], and, running straight through Garsen, slows into a narrow causeway that stops short at the Tana.

Garsen [110½]. Here the **Galla** replace the Giriama – lithe relief to the otherwise nondescript dukas and usually dry petrol-pumps. Relief you might very well need, for the ferry 'tends to be seasonal'. If the Tana permits, you drive on its cable-raft and are quickly hauled across; but if the river – as often happens – is either too high or too low, your car drive or bus ride stops here. And the boatmen are in business. Nudging their dug-out ngalawas close, they load you, your cases, the locals and their goats and paddle-fight the current to the opposite shore. Where you pay their 1/- fare. And may or may not find a stranded bus waiting for the 19/- ride on to Mokowe.

Witu. After ibis and egrets on the flooded fields, lines of borassus across each horizon, the dyked track runs firmer between the shambas and, 50 minutes from the Tana, enters Witu. The one-horse township was capital of the 'Swahililand' which Ahmad Fumo Loti – in defiance of Zanzibar – declared autonomous in 1862. This Sultan Simba – 'the Lion' – then ceded the state (and its postage stamps) to Germany. Receiving Britain's blessing by the Delimitation Treaty of 1886, she declared a protectorate in 1888 – and established in Witu the first colonial post office – but was obliged to withdraw by the Treaty of Berlin in 1890. Nine Germans however returned to trade, and a murderous fracas with the sultan's guards explains why the first British action in their new protectorate was to send a 950-man force to vindicate their German rivals. (Sultan Sayyid's love-and-war discomfitures in Witu were worsened when his daughter Salma fell in love with one Heinrich Reute, ran away to live with him in Germany and, scandalizing the Bu Saidi, became a minor political pawn in Bismarck's colonial diplomacy.)

All of which is perhaps more interesting than the present-day place: a crude plinth and flagstaff (r.) – 'August 1949' – flanked by two cannon that the British brought from Lamu (one dedicated to the sultan's son Khalifa, the other made in 1852 by 'A. Broome, Cossipore'); the *Masjid an-Nur* – the Mosque of Light (r.), built in the 1900s, renovated in 1968 – and the Masjid Jami Witu Mosque.

The people of Witu are **Orma**, whose territory is interrupted by the oddly 'intertribal' **Lake Kenyatta**. Having overflown and named the place, the president created a settlement here – for Kenyans expelled from Tanzania as a result of the two states' strained relations. Within five years uninhabited jungle has become a self-sufficient township of some 5000 families.

You may have got your vehicle through the Tana's marshes but Lamu has the last laugh: cars like bicycles are blissfully banned – the DC's being the only exception – and, after the 226 kms from Malindi, you must leave yours on the Mokowe shore. From the new jetty here, or the airstrip on Manda, you sail out between the mangrove swamps and across the *mkanda*-channel to the island. Lamuphiles identify their paradise with Diogenes' *Pyralaon*, 'People of Fire' (p. 17). The Swahili *Lamu Chronicle* claims that the town was founded by Arabs in the 7th century. Though 9th-c. finds of Islamic and Chinese ceramics make nearby Manda the oldest site known on the Coast (and though its Pwani Mosque dates from 1370) Lamu was not mentioned by name until 1402. For all its defensive walls, it surrendered without struggle to the Portuguese in 1505. They executed its shaikh for collaboration with Mirale Ali Bey (p. 17) and periodically deposed his recalcitrant successors, but never settled in any number

Lamu Market

(despite a Portuguese chapel which 'fell into the sea . . . near Peponi Hotel in the early years of this century'). Lamu and the islands around benefitted in the 17th century from the Galla's sacking of the settlements on shore, and in the 18th-c. heyday many of the town's better residences were built. **Pate**, the rival island-neighbour, was finally defeated in 1813 (below). Lamu's *Yumbe*-senate was then so afraid of (unlikely) reprisals that it invited Sultan Sayyid's protection, subjected the town to his expeditionary force and so provided his first foothold in East Africa.

The first resident agent in the 19th century was French, with Americans coming later to trade and Carl Peters' associates to colonize (p. 20). But Britons have since contributed most to Lamu's idiosyncratic charm. The Freelanders, en route for Mount Kenya to create a 'socialist Utopia', got no further than Lamu where they 'appalled the local people by their consumption of alcohol and (a far more considerable feat) their morals'. (The subsequent but similar influx of hippies necessitated the quayside warning: 'All Tourists . . . Should Report to Police . . . By Order'.) Charles Whitton – 'Coconut Charlie' – lived here misogynistically, not leaving his house (so they say) for 40 years and bequeathing his art collection to Fort Jesus and £7000 to teach the locals thrift. Percy Petley also first farmed on shore, hunted – with a fist that

felled leopards – and founded the same-named inn. It was taken over in 1957 by Lt. Col. Gerald John Pink RA, CBE, TD, FRGS, MA, sometime HBM's Consul at Harar and Jibuti. He for all that killed chickens in the bath and personally evicted those guests he did not fancy. The rest, it appears, were all Allens. One called sporadically to collect local poetry (Lamu's *Ki-Amu* being the best literary Swahili); another beach-combed in both full view of Peponi's and the altogether; a third hunted elephants, while his brother went laughing round town, repeatedly discovering unsuspected offspring en route.

James de Vere Allen contrasted worthily by collecting and encouraging the local arts and crafts. Lamu's **carved doors** rival Zanzibar's: in wood from the *mbamba-kofi* – the mahogany bean tree, AFZELIA QUAZENSIS – their originally Indian or Bajun motifs even outnumber the latter's. Ebony **thrones** inlaid with bone and ivory are antique marvels, so no longer made. 'Arab' **chests** (from Tanzanian teak) and scale-model dhows are reasonable to buy but tricky to transport, and the few **silver**smiths surviving here and on Siyu produce interesting designs. With the British Navy's help, Lamu invented the *mtepe*, the last sample vanishing in the 1930s: these 40-foot canoes had planks sewn with coir because the sultan responsible mistrusted metal. *Sivas* – great horns of ivory or brass –

were the jealously guarded symbols of king-ship usually blown only on State occasions.

All these and much more you can see in the exemplary **museum**. To the right as you land, it was opened in 1971 and is open 8.30 a.m.-12.30 and 2.30-5 p.m. (Ksh. 5/-, under 16s 2/-, residents 2/-, 1/- and, on week-ends and public holidays, 1/-, -/50). The premises were formerly the DC's house, 'its arches, veran-dahs, courtyard and high wide rooms redolent of imperial days'. Victoria's first vice-consul here was Captain Jack Haggard. Rider Haggard's brother, his other claim to fame was in catching the two dugong, the ten-foot, 500-lb 'mermaids' still on display in London's Natural History Museum.

An ironical façade to the Arab town behind, the fine water-front mansions stand on land reclaimed by garbage: only in the late 19th century had sufficient been dumped to permit building – and to account in part for Sir Frederick Jackson's description of the shore as 'the public, very public latrine'. The only waterside odour now is of mangrove poles, the best in Kenya, which the Bajun load below. In front of the museum, the brass cannon with which the British subdued Witu. On either side, new places of worship: the **Raudha Mosque** (r.) and Mary the Mother of Jesus **Catholic Church** (l.). Lamu's Catholics, mostly visitors, used the Presbyterians' pre-mises until in 1978 the Mzee's support for a new church overcame the local Muslims' opposition. To placate the latter, it was built discreetly back from the street . . . but sounds off boldly every Sunday morning with a drum-and-chant rendering of just-recogniz-able hymns. Alongside (l.) stands **Petley's Inn**. Undaunted (or attracted) by its inhos-pitable ghost, two Texans bought the place in 1971, restored it for £60,000, then fell out with the neighbours and entrusted it to Lawford's. With standards thus assured, it easily outclasses the cheap Shamuty Lodging (further l.). Between the two, a Standard Bank and the booking office for both Coast Air and the 'Orange Nairobi Deluxe' bus services. The front thereafter – since 1976 **Kenyatta Road** – is monopolized by administrative offices and the new Customs compound.

Inland here, there is a market each morning in front of the **Fort**. Begun by the Omanis in 1808 (perhaps), completed around 1820 and repaired in 1857, it now serves as prison – try to photograph and you will see the inside. The 'main street' – the *Usita wa Mui* – has become **Harambee Road**: to the left, the Lamu Castle Lodge and, a half-mile further, **Kandara's Hotel**; to the right, the **New Mahrus Hotel** (which also books for the bus trip back). From this former water-front the alleys run east-west uphill, enabling the town to be drained and cleaned by the monsoon rain running unobstructed down. (Some years' precipitations, however, make this mere theory: District Commissioners in the 1950s reported a town so filled with garbage and vermin that the rats ate the cats.) The museum sells a good 7/- map to guide you through the town behind: white-walled alleys that the push-carts fill; the women all-black in *buibuis*; children peeping cheekily from wood-carved doors, and the sharifs – white *kanzus*, black umbrellas – proffering a hand for lesser men to kiss.

On the upper slopes, the **Riadha Mosque** (1900-1) is doyen of Lamu's two dozen (most 19th-c. Shaaf'i, four Asian). Shaikh Habib Salih came here from the Hadhramaut in the 1880s and, becoming Lamu's patron, made it famous both for a Qoranic college and for *Maulidi*, the Prophet's birthday celebration. Pay a visit on this (moveable) occasion and you will not find accommodation but will enjoy a week of religious festivities, feasting and 'dancing' that draws Muslim pilgrims from even overseas.

Kandara's and the New Mahrus hotels are Muslim and so cater poorly for Europeans ('who like alcohol and pigs'). For lunch or the night, therefore, best take a boat from the Customs jetty: along past the **post office**, the Shia Ithna Asheri Mosque, the boriti-yards, the Fisheries wharf and the *Pamba Nimali*-ginneries, two miles to **Peponi's**. The hamlet of **Shela** behind is a somewhat scruffy ghost of its former self. It dates perhaps from the 16th century when Lamu allowed refugees from Pate to build what became the island's main 18th-c. harbour; the Juma'a Mosque with its stumpy minaret went up in 1829, the first of six constructed during the village's 'golden age'. Shela was the scene of Pate's final defeat: miscalculating the tides, its 'army' was left here high and dry, whereupon the townsmen of Lamu, having received their issue of invulnerability charms, having con-sulted the soothsayers and marched up beating gongs, 'astonished the attackers and trounced them soundly'. Appropriate above the battle-field beach, amidst the thickets on the steep cliff, lie the neglected graves of one Mr Sandys of the IBEA and the egregious Lt. Col. Pink. Climb the 58 steps, each one a different height, of the mosque minaret for the view: the magnificent dunes in which Shela ends are said to cover Hadibu, the 7th-c. site of the island's first Arab settlement.

Manda. The beaches opposite are equally idyllic, and enhanced by an enigmatic emplacement – ruined or never completed ? – for the weather-scarred cannon around. The **Ras Kitau Club** here is a cut above Peponi's. Kitau is a promontory – *ras* – of Manda Island and on the latter lie the 16-17th-c. ruins of **Takwa**. A track links them, theoretically, with the hotel-club, but best take a boat (at high tide only) through the mangrove swamps. The coastal jungle soon closes in;

things are Sanders of the River; the last few yards you may have to wade . . . then walk across baobab parkland to the 'Takwa National Monument'. The 12½ acres of ruins were excavated by Dr Kirkman in 1951, further cleared in 1972 and documented by Thomas Wilson in 1977-79. A tomb lies to the left, dated '1092' (the Islamic 1681-82), complete with corner pinnacles and a 22-foot pillar but no Ming (p. 84). The mosque was obviously impressive: a lofty column – a

Monsoon in Lamu

pillar tomb? – in the centre of the north wall, niches and slots for the roof beams, and a sculpted *mihrab*, restored. Here on the spot, though, best enjoy the birdsong, the baobabs and the 'egg' of coral embedded in the mosque wall, and for site-enlightenment consult Wilson's *Takwa* or Dr Kirkman's texts.

On the same island, Manda 'town' was studied in 1966. For incurable archaeologists James Allen enumerates a further twelve major and fourteen minor sites in the vicinity (Faza, Pate and Siyu – with its fort – in particular). They are accessible only by sea – some in the water-borne bus but most by means of a pricier private hiring – and require a guide. Of the above-mentioned guide-books, the Martins' *Quest for the Past* is well illustrated and better written than their *Malindi*; James Allen's *Lamu Town* is dearer and fuller, with its teeth well into the meat of contemporary research. It has conscientious lists of town-wards, mosques and even carved doors, and the author's account of local handicrafts is elaborated further in his *Lamu*.

For those less keen on reading than on living Lamu's past, eight 18th-c. town-houses have been restored for renting. The initiative was the Lamu Society's, which uses the proceeds for further restoration; the anti-quarian accommodation costs Ksh. 200/- per day, with servant, and is reserved via Thorn Tree Safaris (Nairobi POB. 42475, tel. 25641). Thorn Tree handle also, at the other extreme, bookings for **Kiwayuu Island Camp**. A 30-mile flight north, the camp, developed in 1979, lies off the **Dodori National Reserve** – and the ten beach-tents of the older **Kiwayuu Safari Village**. It sleeps – no more than twelve at a time – in chalets and two six-berth cruisers; for 'all facilities as well as drinks and cigarettes' there is no extra charge, and the charge – plus the charter of a private flight from Lamu – should maintain Kiwayuu's claim to 'exclusive seclusion'.

The Tana River is Kenya's longest, far longer even than its own valley: while the crow flies 600 kms from the headstreams to the sea, the fish has 1012 sinuous kms to swim. Though the river disappointed both Carl Peters and Sir William Mackinnon as a hoped-for route through to Uganda, you might follow from Garsen to Garissa the just-bearable B 8 that short-cuts its convolutions. **Garissa** means for visitors the Consolata Fathers' **Boys' Town**. Brother Mario was the architect of this remarkable project: given 70 desert acres in 1968 – and all too many Somali and Boran boys orphaned by the Shifta (p. 109) – he

begged and borrowed funds to pump water from the Tana, followed David Hurd's lead with melons (p. 85) and so developed a plantation-oasis that now offers even a swimming-pool and guest accommodation. Garissa itself is bustling into the 20th century with tar macadamed roads, piped water, hospital, bank, army camp and twice-daily bus to Nairobi. Between you and the capital, though, lie 380 kms of boring orange dust and croton scrub; the Saabduul and Elephant camps no longer function, and on the 240-km. drive from Garsen to Garissa you will only see the river if it ups and floods your track.

So, to 'do' the Tana, best take the easy option of out to **Baomo** and back. Just south of Garsen (p. 86) the sign-post [0] points the way: 'Tana River Game Reserve Baomo Lodge 49 kils'. A 'high road' and a 'low road' mean a Hobson's choice of track, until old and new merge [34½] and you thankfully turn off right [43½]. When not awash, the eight-km. drive to the riverside lodge is no problem. But the Tana in spate entails a detour, and a probable adventure: left along the clear track [49½] and right at the 'Mchelelo' sign [54] to the warden's huts in the cliff-top clearing. From here a four-wheel driver will (in theory) alert the lodge, and from here – an hour or two later – you should see the lodge launch come battling up stream. Coasting back down in the swirling brown flood is not for the nervy – especially if nightfall is near. Tree-trunks and flotsam bump into the boat (which might – with luck – get charged by or beached on a hippo).

The morning after makes it all worth while. From the stockade (which fails to stop the Tana lopping off land) you sail back out over what was once lodge-lawn. Water-birds – and crocodiles – you photograph point blank. On the far bank the guide, his Pokomo askari and spear escort you on foot through the forest: in the clearings, Lesser kudu and oryx are not rare, the giraffe both Masai and Reticulated, the zebra both Grevy's and Burchell's. Here in the **Tana River Primate Game Reserve** the endangered Crested mangabey and Red colobus are important, the latter being now far more abundant.

Visible, too, in these riverine forests is Hunter's antelope, although this rare hartebeest with lyre-shaped horns is the *raison d'être* of the nearby **Arawale Game Reserve** (up stream, across from Hola). For both reserves there is an entrance charge of Ksh. 20/-. In the case of Arawale the total lack of access tracks makes this wishful think-ing on the part of the Tana River Council.

AMBOSELI, TSAVO AND THE MOMBASA ROAD

Appearances are all against the 300-mile haul from Nairobi to Mombasa: the train gets it over with by night, 'Two-centre Sea and Safari' holiday-operators invariably fly clients and, though the railway surveyors' 1896 track was tar macadamed in 1968 (thus removing an old Kenyan joke), those who motor willy nilly will soon realize that the route is less for tourists than for civil servants and businessmen. The detour via Amboseli is however easily feasible. And, equally accessible from Nairobi and the Coast, Tsavo Park straddles the road.

East from Nairobi (p. 42)[0] Uhuru Highway becomes the **Mombasa Road**, to skirt Kenyatta Airport and keep company with the railway for a while. The scenery is the usual debris of urbanization; a sudden interruption is the odd concentration of lamp-posts and police-men at the 'Public Weighbridge' [17]. Then pylons and telegraph-poles yield to croton and acacia, and the road drops from the Athi Plains to the Athi River's shallow but well-defined valley. Making the same-named cement, the same-named township smokes continually in its hollow. At **Athi River**, too, the Kenya Meat Commission runs its mech-anical butchery; white wives and children were – for their own safety – interned during the Emergency, and there was in the 1900s 'a famous hunting-ground, where many sports-men have slain lions, and some lions have slain sportsmen'.

Turn right [22½] for the Nairobi Park's Cheetah Gate (r.)[2 kms], Namanga and (if the border reopens) Arusha. After the railway bridge, rebuilt in 1969, a dusty track (l.)[24½] leads one km. into the hamlet: a 'Maboko Top Life Butchery' bright with murals, a 'Maele Market' of packing-case stands, and the post office a late-colonial period piece. Opposite, women sell charcoal and six-foot lengths of sugar-cane; the barber sets up shop – viz. a chair and two mirrors – under a tree. Along the sickly river, women wash clothes and half-naked men their cars, while the huddle of acacias broods somehow ghoulishly.

Tar macadamed by Mowlem in 1971-72 and part-financed by US AID, this segment of the **Great North Road** (p. 101) – here the A 104 – rises out of town past the Portland Cement Company and the prison (both r.). Then you sail across the endless **Athi Plains**, a stony expanse with bleak tracts darkened by the shadow of the cumulus. Often the high bright dome of the sky reaches down distantly to touch earth with a black streak of rain. Just clusters of zebra grazing incurious, perhaps a run of wildebeest galloping low-shouldered – reports from the 1900s that 'the quantity of game here . . . is absurd' are again,

with ironical oppositeness, true. The occa-sional Masai abandon their herds to stop you for photographs – usually far from gratis. Their pill-box *manyattas*, of mud-and-dung plaster or corrugated tin, stand abandoned where poor grazing has forced a family on.

The sign-boards amply describe **Isinya** [55]: 'Rural Training Centre, Maasai Anglican Church' and 'Maasai Handicrafts'. The Church Missionary Society and the National Christian Council of Kenya converted this former Mau Mau detention centre in 1961, after 30% of the local Masai and 90% of their herds – 300,000 head – had died in the droughts and floods of 1960. The primary school's pupils are aged from eight to eighteen; range management courses teach the menfolk cattle-husbandry and govern-ment vets provide an after-sales service, visiting the 'graduates' and advising. The 1972 Isinya Tannery sells the leatherware that the Masai make in the workshop adjoining, as well as the beads that their wives are allotted to thread and work at home. Behind the shop, the *Kanisa ol Chekut Supat* is a simple pleasant chapel of grey blocks and timber, consecrated in February 1970.

Kajiado [75] interrupts the vistas of empty plains, stunted acacias and telegraph-poles. The African Inland Church lies left, Snowcem-cream and functional, while opposite the station (l.) a 'Kajiado Lucky Restaurant' boasts murals. If scarcely a metropolis, the township will be remembered for the Kajiado Agreements (below). Or for the fact that its licensing hours are sometimes reduced to two a day.

Kajiado Cemetery is indicated (r.)[78½] after the police station and the Masai Technical School. Turn left on to the track at 0·2 kms and keep straight on at 0·5. Right on the hill at precisely one km., the cemetery contains 24 Great War graves, most the aftermath of Longido (p. 22).

The fast road moves into humpier country, with part-time rivers in the dips, low forest and sisal on the slopes. **Bissel** is just shacks, dukas and odd Masai on each wooded bank of its stream [106]. Higher ridges and gentle valleys then become weaver-bird and termite-mound terrain. Features are few, and now is the time for all good couriers to wile away the miles with the stock safari patter: 'That's a *mukui*-tree over there. This one's a *mvule*-tree. And there's a lavatree'. 'What's a toilet in a Game Park called? Answer Zooloo.'

Thirty minutes of this and you will welcome **Namanga**. A gentle crest gives a distant view of Mount Meru, regular, and Namanga's jaggeder peaks; the riverine forest increases, the acacias thicken and the several signs start that announce the **Namanga River Hotel**. This is no longer reached by the bridge built by Italian prisoners in 1943 but by the marked track (r.)[163]; once pleasant with pool, lawns and aviary, the place began to wane when tarmac to Arusha made a halfway rest unnecessary. Since the closure of the border in 1977 it is not the road to the barriers ahead but the hotel's drive that is lined with hawkers like an African Lourdes.

Amboseli National Park. For Amboseli you turn left, away from all this – only to find more hawkers at the gate. Business is brisk for the park is, after Nairobi's, Kenya's most popular. In this little-frequented corner of the 1899 'Ukamba Game Reserve', then of the 'Southern Masai Reserve', the fauna was such that the government established a national reserve in 1947. This was converted in 1961 to a unique experiment in tribal/wildlife coexistence: the Masai elders of the Kajiado District Council were given the powers (and an £8500 annuity) to run the 'Masai Amboseli Game Reserve'. These **Kajiado Agreements** were not successful overnight – the rhinos' survival means a running war with poachers – but a presidential decree subsequently banned 50 square miles to the Masai and their herds. In 1973 the New York Zoological Society gave £49,000 for the boring of water-holes, enabling the cattle to graze elsewhere, and in November of the following year 150 of the reserve's 1259 square miles were gazetted a national park.

Though the magnificent if unpredictable backdrop of **Kilimanjaro** will – with what little remains of the game – maintain Amboseli's popularity, its picturesqueness may be less. For the **Masai** add colourfully to their terrain. The men's *suka* or *ol karaha* (p. 12) is usually red (which, with bulls and steers their lifelong companions, scarcely squares with the theory that this colour enrages). Longer and often leaving one breast bare, their womenfolk's dress is red too, while the children's short shifts are dull pink, faded orange or buff (and, I suspect, their elders' cast-offs). This distinguishing red – for clothes, ornaments and cosmetics – comes from the ochre present in the Kenya/Tanzania borderlands the Masai now bestride. Boys in a halo-shaped head-dress of canes, the interstices stuffed with feathers, have just undergone circumcision.

Only in guide-books do the Masai live off a curdled milk-and-cows'-blood mixture: in fact this is only for recent mothers, the constipated and adolescents about to take the (officially forbidden) *moran*-test of spearing a lion single-handed. A primitive manyatta is still home for most Masai, their currency still cattle (p. 109) and their social-sexual set-up not wholly orthodox (p. 15). More and more Masai work nowadays in the hotels; they have Technical Schools in Ngong and Kajiado; the latter's MP has again been re-appointed as Minister for Home Affairs; but refusing to pander to the 20th century – few responded to leader Oloitiptip's call for ochre hair-dos to be given to museums – the majority of the 60,000-odd Masai opt out more convincingly than any Western hippy.

By the beaten track the women are not coy but photogenic. Here, too, the *morani* are voracious for money. Some pose for a shilling, but discuss this in advance: if you do not pay enough, spears are brandished – but not thrown (p. 24). This, though, gives a false impression, as does the Masai's bygone reputation for waylaying travellers and annihilating rivals. Most will stand, Nilotic-ally on one leg, and watch you without interest, some even give their big cheery, full-armed salute.

The Namanga Gate [164] is open from 6.30 a.m. to 6 p.m. (prices as in all parks, p. 50). The track beyond turns its back on **Ol Donyo Orok** (the 8200-ft. Black Mountain, 'zoologically unexplored') and skirts the Ilaingarunyeni Hills – at some length. Check first at the gate if you want to fork right for the 'Lake Road to Amboseli' [223]: **Lake Amboseli** is, paradoxically, 'liable to flood'. Usually however this soda expanse is dry, thus causing occasional dust-storms and mirages, attracting fascinating bird life and whitening the Earless Black rhinos. Para-doxically also it was abundant water, not the elephant as usual, that killed off many of the fine acacia-trees: since the 1950s the run-off from Kilimanjaro has repeatedly raised the water-table – and noxious salts to their roots. Destruction of the lesser plant life may well be due to you: one reason for Amboseli's

| Carmine bee-eater | Weaver bird | White-fronted bee-eater |

popularity is that its open parkland tends to go to drivers' heads. Vehicles follow the animals *ad lib*, to give you better viewing but to distract cheetahs from the chase and kill the grasses too. By insisting your driver keep to the tracks you help save the ecosystem.

Firm but corrugated, and with warning signs on many a bend and dip, the main track loops round the lake to Ol Tukai. After the airfield [238½], pioneered by the National Youth Service in 1971 and since surfaced, the Emali track comes in left (p. 94)[239½]. Off right [240], **Kilimanjaro Safari Lodge** is chalet-luxurious on the site, so it claims, of a Hemingway encampment and, as the tarmac starts, **Amboseli Lodge** (r.)[240½] is attractive in Mount Kenya cedar and local stone. **Ol Tukai** itself owes its origin oddly to Hollywood: Paramount Pictures built the first huts as a film-set amenity in 1948 and gave them to the locals when the *Snows of Kilimanjaro* was completed. Now the signs warn, with no small irony, 'Photographing Masais is Prohibited'.

Past the Warden's office – and the drivers' quarters where the ladies of the beer-parlour cater – lies the 'Olkejuado County Council's' **Ol Tukai Lodge**: eleven bandas and a cottage, recently renovated and Ksh. 75/90 p.p.p.n., with a very basic store and petrol whenever the attendant is around ('No hooting please'). In front of the lodge a

barrier of dubious usefulness (open 6.30 a.m.-7 p.m.) marks the track to the **Amboseli Serena Lodge** – past the camp sites [1½ kms] (r.; 5/- p.p.p.n.) then right [2½]. Though it turns its back on Kilimanjaro and overlooks the swampy *Enkongo Narok* – Black Stream – the lodge has a style distinctive and attractive, correctly Masai with its absence of angles and 'ethnic' décor of clay and ochre red.

Superb starlings are everywhere around Ol Tukai, the weaver birds are Amboseli's own 'Taveta Golden' and the park's best game runs centre on the lodges: round the **Engone Naibor** and the **Loginye** Lake/Swamp (the weather decides which) with perhaps a preliminary recce from **Observation Hill**, six kms from the airfield.

Via Emali to Amboseli. Before the tarmac reached Namanga many preferred the route via Emali and, as it is shorter (and due to be surfaced), many still do. After Athi River (p. 91)[25] the Mombasa Road rises towards the escarpment as the land begins to undulate and the acacias to concentrate in every dip and hollow.

Machakos is reached by the turning marked (l.)[46]. After sixteen kms of rolling cattle country the township appears, enclosed in a crescent of well-farmed hills. The clock-tower – its centre and only 'sight' – was erected for 'the Visit of Her Royal Highness the Princess Margaret . . . 22nd October 1956'. Really 'Masaku's', this mainly Akamba market-town became in 1890 the IBEA's first up-country outpost. Its third administrator – *Kithoumi, alias* John Ainsworth (p. 48) – constructed the stockaded fort in 1893. (He was actually ordered not to do so, but had already finished by the time the post got through.) The present jam factories in the nearby Mua Hills look back to the Rev. Stuart Watt, who evangelized here and grew fruit. Having walked up from Mombasa with his wife (who carried him when he went lame), he introduced wattle and eucalyptus too. The CMS added wheat in 1895 and South Africans started an ostrich farm in 1905. Machakos also boasts Kenya's first up-country bazaar, from 1898, and first African Training Centre, which the government took over from the IBEA in 1914. Still in the 1900s though, when old Chief Masaku died, his kinsmen were ritually shunning then spearing some 40 'witches' per annum.

The Mombasa Road runs on through Konza, rarely bending across high bold plains, then between Ulu and Kima through loosely forested hills that are spiked with croton and candelabra cactus. Konza, Ulu and Kima are now little more than railway name-plates: the first has been since 1915 the junction to Kajiado and Magadi (pp. 91, 60), the second was once a tribal reserve on a par with the Kikuyu's, and at the third – which may mean Mincemeat – Charles Ryall was eaten (p. 44). Around **Sultan Hamud** [106] Greater kudu were common in the 1920s; now you see only scattered shacks in the lee of the two gullied peaks – and the C 102 (r.) to Oloitokitok and Ol Tukai. Then plain again, cultivated patchily and ringed by irregular hills. After **Emali** a long bridge stretches over the railway and notices point (r.)[123] to 'Amboseli National Park 95 km/ Kimana Lodge 80 km'. The much-travelled track is clearly marked: over the plains and the thorn-bush tracts, through the *Leme Boti* – Low Table – Gate and so to Ol Tukai [218]. This gate closes at 6 p.m. . . . as the snows of Kilimanjaro ahead turn from white to grey.

East from Amboseli. After Ol Tukai [0] the corrugated track beyond the Serena Lodge runs broad and flat across country almost parkland. To the left the Loginye Swamp is lushly green; giraffe and gazelle, elephant and buffalo roam here in the lee of Mount Kilimanjaro. Now much improved, the track

winds and climbs past **Buffalo Lodge** (1980) and the airstrip (also l.)[33½], dips across the Kimana River [36] and climbs again to the same-named gate [36½](open 6 a.m.-6 p.m.). After curio-hawkers, implacable as ever, the 'main road' ahead is a joke: the directions are painted on oil-drums on this thoroughfare from Emali to Tanzania. **Kimana Lodge** is marked (l.) at the T-junction, a flowery haven after thirteen kms of corrugated murram, rock and dust. For Tsavo turn right instead [37½], into the wheel ruts, then left [41]. You cross a country of sugar-loaf hills, first rolling upland, soon lower plain – called Serengeti but not *the* Serengeti. A belt of green volcanic humps looms nearer, their steep slopes capped in forest and combed by erosion. Hemingway once hunted in these **Chyulu Hills**, 'one of the youngest mountain ranges in the world'. The track skirts their 600 low cones, the chiaroscuro landscape compensating for its roughness. There follows a plain, clearly volcanic, from which the hillocks rise like geological pimples. A board [91] marks the start of Tsavo West: straightway the track is curvaceous and yellow-grey dust. Suddenly appears a startling stretch of blackness: like a sea of shrapnel the **Shitani Flow** engulfs the terrain. The volcanic cone Shitani – Devil – spewed these eight kms of lava 'in the last few hundred years'. But if you alight and climb its 400-foot peak you will, so the locals say, never be seen again. The very rough track follows then crosses the main raised flow [104-6], stunted trees grow on islands of soil and, edging across this expanse of natural coke, you may possibly spot klipspringer. Turnings (l.)[107] lead to Emali, Shitani itself and the 'Chyulu Hills Circuit/Lava Nature Trail'; the main track ahead, very orange, rises to the Chyulu Gate [109½]. This is closed from 7.15 p.m. to 6 a.m. but 'Entry will not be allowed after 6.pm Thank You'. Because you may not travel by night.

Tsavo West National Park. Tsavo is Kenya's largest national park – 8069 square miles of primitive wilderness. North of the Galana River (which was the Athi and becomes the Sabaki), Tsavo East is in fact kept deliberately pristine, open only to parties the Warden permits, while Tsavo West is popularized by lava flows, fine plains and valleys, and the famed Mzima Springs.

Tsavo is reckoned to contain 60 mammal, 400 bird and 1000 plant species. The Mombasa Road, a loose Akamba-Taita tribal boundary, is also a fortuitous wildlife frontier: southward the flora and fauna are 'Masai', in the drier north 'Somali'. The ostrich (p. 40) is an obvious epitome, but specialists will discern many other climatic/ecological distinctions. **Elephants** disregard them, and devastate widely. They may have accounted for the region's change from dense COMMIPHORA woodland to scrubbier grassland during the last three decades. A century ago they were, it seems, far less; Krapf, Rebmann and Thomson did not report them obtrusive and even at the turn of the century man-eating lions, not elephants, were the bane of the railwaymen's lives. Proliferating since, Tsavo's elephants have been forced into an ever-smaller area by human settlement around. For their only natural enemy, apart from ants, is man. African ivory is harder and better for carving than Indian and the **poachers** have increased to meet world demand. Often encouraged by influential backers and risking only mild sentences if caught, they shoot, trap or poison widely, leaving their prey to die slowly. But some authorities – not all – are at last taking action: sentences are being stiffened and conniving officials exposed; the Wildlife Department is receiving increased allocations and overseas bodies are beginning to assist, while local artists are auctioning paintings and Wildlife Clubs raising funds in an unprecedented 'war effort'. A far cry from the romantic *Daktari* image, rangers are being trained as game-park guerrillas, their anti-poaching units liaising by radio, tracking the foe by 'plane, Land-Rover or even camel, and often finally shooting it out with large armed gangs. For the elephants, at least, they are winning through at last. Ivory smuggling from Tsavo had become a virtual industry and was causing world-wide alarm; of the 20,000 total in the early 1970s, only 8000 elephant survived by 1978; yet by 1979 better protection, and breeding, had halted the slaughter and reversed the decline.

No such hope is yet in sight for the rhino. Tsavo's 6-8000 – all Black – were thought to form the largest concentration in the world: now their numbers are put optimistically as 100 in each part of the park. Poachers are mostly responsible for this massacre, but the droughts of the 1960s and early 70s took their toll. Fire is a further hazard, sometimes spontaneous in hot dry vegetation, sometimes spread by the honey-hunters, who follow the Greater honey-guide bird to the hive and smoke out the bees from the trunk. Fire-breaks account for 120 of the park's 2000 kms of track. The network is almost everywhere good and the marker-post system

frequent and usually accurate (despite distances sometimes quite Irish). Seventeen airstrips serve Tsavo West, ten Tsavo East. The older Caltex maps have been well replaced by the Survey of Kenya's (available usually at the gates) and the excellent *Tsavo National Park* has even been done into German.

Six kms separate the Chyulu Gate from **Kilaguni**, Kenya's first park lodge. Opened by the Duke of Gloucester in 1962, it is now a favourite both with visitors and with almost 'resident' game on the water-holes below (one natural, the others dug for the lodge's pool and laundry spill – which the elephants relish). Cheeky hornbills and superb starlings pester at the tables on the long bar-restaurant terrace; the lawns outside scamper with mongooses, lizards and almost tame ground squirrels. To relieve the constant transit bustle – the price it paid for being so popular – Kilaguni was extended in 1974 with a Chyulu Restaurant and conference centre. In the latter the National Parks maintain a sparse **Information Centre**: mineral specimens – quartz, tourmaline and ruby – plans, plaster landscapes and photographic displays.

Around Kilaguni the game runs and views make a day's stay inadequate. The main track northward crosses the **Mungai Plains** – low trees, high grass and the game hard to see; past the park's Kamboyo headquarters and the **camp site** (a pleasant clearing with water, fire-wood and WC for Ksh. 5/- p.n., under 16s 1/-) to the Mtito Andei Gate (p. 99) [29 kms].

East of Kilaguni's airstrip the signs take you across the plain and up to **Roaring Rocks** [7 kms]. Though these hum with cicada rather than roar (and sometimes whistle if the wind is right), both the view from the shelter on the sheer 300-foot scarp and the butterflies, birds and lizards all around make the walk up the basalt steps worth while. **Poacher's Look-out** is another well-marked vantage point, overlooking Ol Turesh with the occasional bonus of a Kilimanjaro view. Until it was thieved (like the public telescope), a plaque reported that the hilltop shelter was 'In Memory of Jack Hilton for many years Deputy Director of the Royal National Parks of Kenya'.

Most however make straight for **Mzima Springs** [10 kms]. Here, sometimes at sunset, the wildlife spectacle can be amazingly rich: elephants soak, half immersed; hippopotami break the surface, to yawn with incredible jaws; gazelles and zebras crowd the slopes and giraffes lope gently between the acacias.

But if at other times, with animals absent, the encircling greenery and trickling falls seem only ordinarily pretty, remember that this is a natural wonder: astonishingly from this arid lava plain 50 million gallons of water gush daily, filtered for 25 miles underground from the Chyulu Hills, to nourish this oasis, supply Mombasa since 1966 with Kenya's purest water and sometimes vanish again subterraneously. (They resurface soon after as the Mzima River and flow seven kms further to the Tsavo River.) There are toilets now and well-trodden paths to the 'Rest Area', 'Rapids' and 'Lower Pool'; baboons, Vervets and Sykes frequent the observation platform and the bridge to the sunken viewing tank (p. 36), and – 'Umbrella Tree', 'Tooth-brush Bush', 'Fever Tree', 'Dogbane' and 'Elephant Salad' – the trunks around are tamely labelled. None the less, be on your guard. Elephants are numerous enough to have stripped most trunks and boughs despite wire netting; 'Beware of Crocodile', signboards warn, and 'You are Likely to meet Dangerous Wild Animals on This Trail . . . The National Park are not Responsible for any Eventuality'.

The signs beyond Mzima [0] are good: past the turnings to Poacher's Look-out, to the Campi ya Simba, Campi ya Faru and Campi ya Mwarabu circuits and on to Kitani Lodge & Shelter Camp [10](1954; six original double bandas and six constructed in 1978 – eight with bath and four with shower for Ksh. 46/- p.n., under 16s 23/- – and a shelter for six – 80/- p.n. - with gas cookers, fridges and lamps, bed-rolls and kitchen help for hire and food for sale; bookings through A.A. Travel, Nairobi POB. 14982, tel. 742926-9). For the park's southern gate on the Voi-Taveta track you can safely follow the signs. But not the Shell map to 'Murka Lodge' for the night: it opened and closed in the early 1960s. The disused mine near the Murka sub-headquarters produced kyanite, an aluminium silicate discovered here in 1946, bought and stockpiled by the US government during the Korea War and later used for insulating spark-plugs. In the First World War Mzima was 'protected' by a British-built fort; a camp to the south, in 1936, housed 10,000 refugees from the Italian *Anschluss* of Abyssinia; gun emplacements facing Kilaguni, redoubts at Kichwa Tembo and the significant place-name 'Rhodesian Hill' are the park's reminders of World War II.

Though a 'main road' runs from Kilaguni to Ngulia [30 kms], the detour is delightful via Rhino Valley. The track, itself soon lava, rises to the **Chaimu** (or Chiemu)(or Chimu) **Flow**. Like Shitani it is stark black coke, but a patina of lichen makes the effect less grotesque, more antique. The notice dates it nevertheless to the last few hundred years and directs your attention to the 'lava fountains', split cone, blow-hole and sulphur deposits. The track drops beside the petrified torrent then, rocky and loose, hairpins steeply down to **Rhino Valley**. Bearing left, with the valley well defined but the 'Rhino' a misnomer, you continue (r.) past **Ngulia Safari Camp** (six double/triple bandas with shower, loo and kitchen; prices and bookings as at Kitani but without the bedding and the shop). It occupies the site of the Old Ngulia Camp . . . abandoned because it was haunted? (A builder was killed here in 1950, and Europeans make sworn reports of ghosts.)

Climbing through the forest of the Ndawe Escarpment you reach **Ngulia Safari Lodge**. This, split-level, open-plan and very well appointed, was built in 1969, its back to the 3000-foot Ngulia Peak and the Kalanga Valley ahead. Floodlit below the veranda, big game is unusually near; you are called if any species you have 'ordered' appears in the night. (As undue noise may make it disappear again, warnings in English, French, German and Italian request what one manager called a 'multilingual silence'.) Leopards in particular are nocturnally around, offspring of those imported into Tsavo in 1961. By day the agamas bask and scuttle round the pool's rock-garden and the weaver birds nest blithely by the door. Situated in a migration corridor, Ngulia is ornithologically important. Rare species, attracted by the only light for miles, have been caught for ringing in the nets set by researchers once the hotel guests retire. Display-cases – and David Pearson's paintings – document the project well.

From the lodge [0] you can return to Mtito Andei by an adequate track through tight but low undergrowth, diverting perhaps for the 'Ndawe Airfield' or 'Mganga Water Hole' circuits, and so to the main track near Kamboyo (p. 95)[39½]. Or, more attractively, continue east along the **Tsavo River**: crocodiles and hippos you may or may not see; certain is a pretty riverside drive with the greenery all doum-palm and 'waitabit' bush. The **Tsavo camp site** (Ksh. 5/- p.n.; no water or loo) lies one km. before the Tsavo Gate (open 6 a.m.-7 p.m.)[53].

Alternatively, for the Taita Hiltons, take the **Maktau track** on from Mzima [0]. At first idyllic, it escorts the springs' lower pool then, rocky and more functional, the telegraph-poles of the 'Mombasa Pipe-line Road' until the two part company [18½]. The track rises across grassland, much improved, but its endlessness is depressingly evident as it stretches across three broad valleys and three ranges of hills. Open from 6 a.m. to 7.15 p.m., the Maktau Gate [57] was added in late 1973 to serve Tsavo's Central and Northern Areas. Across the railway line and the track – the Voi-Taveta 'highway' – an identical gate serves the Southern Areas.

Of the three features indicated – 'Lake Jipe, Kamshari and Kavuma' – the first is popular with bird-watchers and fishermen, a 30-square-mile stretch of water 48 kms from Maktau. It lies in the lee of the North Pare Mountains and was a feature on the route of early westbound travellers wary of crossing the Masai lands further north. The Grevy's zebra seen, unexpected, nowadays were evacuated in 1977 from the Northern Frontier District. The National Parks' other contributions are the self-help bandas and the nine- and ten-seater boats, bookable through the Taita Hiltons.

One km. left of the Maktau Gate, the CWG **Maktau Cemetery** (r.) contains the Indian victims of the First World War campaign (p. 22). The track then runs hard and fast, crossing and recrossing the railway, to Bura. Sign-posted (r.)[77½] are the unlikely delights of two Hiltons. **Taita Hills Lodge** tops the gentle hill, 3200 feet above sea-level. Flowers cascading down its façade, lawns and lily-ponds serene beside the pool, the hotel is film-set resplendent (and served in fact as James Stewart's base for *A Tale of Africa* in 1979). A 28,000-acre game sanctuary shares the estate ('Casual Visitors' Ksh. 20/-) and there, four miles on from the hotel, stands **Salt Lick Lodge**. Both were opened in March 1973, but while the former is customarily stately the latter is safari-architecturally unique (p. 142). The vicinity has recently been opened up with 'Inner River', 'Outer River' and 'Bura River' circuits and a track to Lion Rock.

If **Bura** [86] seems little more than a station and a 'Teenagers Ice Bar & Restaurant', it enjoyed an instant of historical significance in World War I when Lettow-Vorbeck, advancing on Voi, was held and rebuffed by the British near by (p. 22). Its mission, dating from 1892, was the first to be built in the Taita Hills; being run by the Holy Ghost Fathers, from Alsace, and the German 'Precious Blood Sisters', its fortunes fluc-

tuated during World War I. Tarmac then recommences [92] and, for the Hiltons' antithesis in bush accommodation, take the turning (l.)[93] to the Mwasungia Scenery Guest House.

The Taita Hills form a sudden dramatic contrast to the countryside around. As with Uganda's Kigezi and Tanzania's Usambara Mountains, they are for most writers of guide-books an 'African Switzerland'. In fact they constitute a cool and exuberantly green refuge for those fleeing the heat of the Coast. Precipitous shambas clothe the slopes, for population pressures force the Taita to cultivate ever higher – and their womenfolk are such that Taita men work hard. Their forefathers devoted this vigour more to warfare, foraying from their mountain fastnesses to raid the plains around, until in the 1880s they were decimated by drought. Thereafter, like many an invalid today, they turned to Christianity, assisting the Methodist and CMS missionaries. It was from the Taita peak of Vuria that the first CMS missionary, Johann Rebmann, first sighted Kilimanjaro.

The road zigzags scenically into a region of hairpin bends, waterfalls and low gears, to pass **Wundanyi**, a compact hill-metropolis [15 kms], and to drop, as cliff-ledge murram, to the said establishment [17]. Though its views over the juvenile Voi River are superb, the only remarkable thing about Mwasungia is its direction-signs up – and its Taita meaning: 'You are looking at it'.

Taita shepherds, with calabashes and/or bows and arrows, are sometimes seen standing beside the main road as it proceeds across miles of sisal and in long gentle inclines comes up to the Mombasa Road [117½].

Voi. Cotton grew wild here long before the railway brought planters to develop both this crop and sisal. Early missionaries found the local Taveta and Taita welcoming, and World War I made Voi an important junction, the branch-line to Taveta being built to move troops.

Over the main road, the turning between the Caltex station and café and the Voi Sisal Estates' factory loops through town: six railway lines, a Jama'a Mosque (r.) like a green cardboard cut-out, a district hospital (l.), a market place/bus station with cafés but otherwise free of amenities, a post office, Catholic church, police headquarters and African Inland church. Between the last two (l.) lies the CWG **Voi Cemetery**, 'Set aside for

Elephant, contented, at Kilaguni

the Burial of Men who Died during the 1914-1918 War. The Burial of Civilians . . . cannot be Permitted'. The park track is marked (l.) just before the factory where, annually since 1969, some 30 locals have been producing (and since 1980 refining) 900 tons of edible oil from cotton-seeds, sunflower-seeds and soya beans.

Tsavo East National Park. The East/Voi Gate here is open from 6 a.m. to 7 p.m. (prices as usual – p. 50 – and the Survey of Kenya's map good). A half-km. right, just inside, the **'camping ground'** is shaded by name-labelled trees and equipped with three unfurnished, self-help bandas, communal shower/WC, water and fire-wood (Ksh. 5/- p.n., children 1/-). Left of the gate, the **Education Centre** has dormitories, toilets (and a dung-beetle display), cases of Tsavo insects, a nearby 'Nyika Trail' and a copy of the Mzee's *Nairobi Manifesto*, Kenya's response to Nyerere's at Arusha (p. 33).

'Father' of Tsavo for over 25 years was the late David Sheldrick, doyen of Kenya's wardens (and *Saa Nane* to his men – because he insisted they always work until this '2 p.m.'). The park's development is readably narrated in *The Tsavo Story*, written by his wife, and the 200-strong staff he trained continue both to wage a running war with poachers (p. 95) and to keep the tracks in good shape. That to the left climbs five kms to **Voi Safari Lodge,** an architecturally splendid edifice that spreads along and blends with the

locals' Worsessa Look-out. The good game-viewing on the three floodlit water-holes below has been made even better by the building of a 'Photo hide' and bunkered 'Buffalo Bar'. Since 1974 they bring up to 50 guests at a time within ten yards of the animals (and one yard below them, since the concrete roof can take even an elephant's weight).

North from the lodge [0] a track runs parallel to the (unseen) Mombasa Road and railway, past the **Irima Water-hole** [7] to the rock called **Mudanda**, Strips of drying meat [24]. Below this mile-long whale-shape of stratified slabs the animals gather at a natural dam (when water elsewhere is scarce, that is; in wet weather the climb can be a waste of time). Then back and along the **Buffalo Wallows**, winding with the water-course, and left [50] down to the **Galana River.**

Lugard's Falls are unmistakable four kms down stream. Lugard, Captain F.D. and later Lord, led the IBEA's convoy through here in 1891, en route for Buganda where he played a major rôle. The falls he 'discovered' are not lofty, but impress: a small plateau of pinkish-buff-grey rock, fantastically contorted and pierced by a fissure of seething water. You can, the guide-books say, stand astride it, but do not be tempted: tourists have fatally misjudged their stride. The **Crocodile Point** below the falls reinforces the warning. A track then winds with the plateau and the river on via Sobo to the Sala Gate [133](open 6 a.m.-7 p.m. – no entry after 5.30 p.m.).

This is the exit for those driving **to Malindi.** To spend the night here first you have the easy choice between the Sala Camp (devoid of amenities and requiring the Malindi Game Warden's permission) and, four kms further, the unique **Crocodile Camp.** Started in 1974 and completed with a swimming-pool in 1975, the well-equipped riverside site is advertised as the only place in Kenya where you can (should you want to) call the crocodiles by name. From Sala [0] the track has been re-graded and re-dyked: very straight over heaving hills and down through a region of tight undergrowth and less game; stony, and with a high centre ridge, through the Jilore Forest to Kakuyuni [97]; then, appalling between the palms, to the tarmac of Malindi (l.)[110].

To spare both your vehicle and your nerves, better return to the Mombasa Road – at the Buchuma Gate if you cross the Ndara Plains

Young impala in Tsavo National Park

or at **Voi** if you pass by **Aruba**. After 40 miles of elephantine devastation the lake here makes a welcome change. Some 50 mammal species find so too (though fish are no longer sufficient to attract anglers). Flowing on to the sea at Kilifi, the Voi River was dammed in 1952 to form this lake of (usually) 211 acres. (It vanished altogether in the 1961 drought.) In the same year the National Parks built **Aruba Safari Lodge** (occasional petrol, airstrip and six breezy double bandas; bookings, prices and facilities as at Kitani – p. 96 – but without refrigerators, and the shop a misnomer). Camping on the lawns costs Ksh. 5/-.

The Mombasa Road. Those who press on oblivious to Amboseli and Tsavo will find the road's relieving features few and far between. In 1904, Sir Charles Eliot wrote, you could 'make the journey from Tsavo to Nairobi without seeing a village or a single native'. There is scarcely 70 years' worth of difference now.

The Amboseli alternative left us at Emali (p. 94)[123]. Straight on, **Simba** means Lion and **Kiboko** Hippopotamus/Hippo-hide whip . . . and **Hunter's Lodge** [156]. Started by a hunter called Hunter, this is a good place for the (almost) halfway break, on lawns beside a lake where birds occur in some 280 species. The roadside baobabs and sisal are then dwarfed by the splendiferous Sikh temple of **Makindu**, Palm-trees [170]. Sikh temples traditionally offer free food and lodging to travellers – whence the hippies' infatuation with India – and here the only modification is that you stay one night only and make a donation if your means permit. After

Makindu the baobabs alternate with more tangled forest; a stretch of black lava flow escorts the road as the hills around grow starker. At **Kibwezi** [193] a government outpost, a CMS mission and a German sisal factory had by 1900 been started – and stopped by the tsetse-fly.

Bushwhackers – *alias* Masalani Camp [25 kms] – is reached by here taking the turn-off (l.) to 'Kitui 137', crossing the Kibwezi Forest and following the signs (r. at 10½ kms then l. at 16½ kms) across the sisal-plantations. The camp, not ultramodern, has as its 'beach' the Athi's picturesque flat-rock banks (self-service bandas Ksh. 30/- p.n. with bath, 25/- with shower, under 11s half price; camping 17/- p.n., plus 15% tax on everything).

Mtito Andei [232], on the Tsavo Park boundary, offers a further choice of halfway halts. It is not the Great War's German airstrip here that accounts for the **Tsavo Inn**'s usual clientele: this former Mac's Inn was taken over in 1973 by the African Safari Club. Attractively 'Spanish' beside the road, its only fault is the entrance-hall grille: *Mtito Andei* means Forest of Vultures, not Forest of Eagles. All three have in any case long since disappeared. In their place, a motorists' oasis: Total and Agip, 'Esso Autoport', Caltex **AA post** and a 'Divo Crafts & Curios Shop' beside the Main Gate to Tsavo West (r.; p. 95).

'**Tsavo Safari Camp** 16 miles' says the sign (l.)[231½]. The track bends across the railway to the park boundary, open 6 a.m.-7 p.m. but 'Entry Prohibited without

Authority' i.e. a pre-booking voucher from the Tsavo Inn (above) or from the African Safari Club, Mombasa (POB. 81443, tel. 471603). You traverse parkland and dense scrub, the Mtito Andei River and the herds on an enclave of farmland, then leave your car beside the Athi, which you cross by dinghy or Land-Rover. Delightful against the Yatta Plateau, the camp is blessed with hot showers in all 21 tents – and generators switched off at night. Rudi the Rhino was a patron until, intruding too frequently in the ladies' loo, it had to be deported to Solio (p. 106). Plentiful game, and 258 sighted bird species, remain in compensation. To play the old hand you call it **Cottars' Camp**: grandfather, father and son hunted here till the site 'went public' in 1966 and was taken over in 1974 by the African Safari Club.

The Mombasa Road runs on to dissect Tsavo. The miles of *nyika* are relieved only by the **Yatta Plateau**, an odd geological feature almost geometrically level along the northern horizon. Only two kms wide, it runs for some 300 kms and is consequently claimed by Kenyans to be the world's longest lava flow. For the rest the scenery is telegraph wires, railway gang-camps and baobabs, massively gouged by elephants. This **nyika** – commiphora-acacia woodland – was the pioneers' 'uninhabited, totally unproductive jungle' (p. 7). It is still a bore if no longer a hazard to cross (though bus- and taxi-drivers now sometimes seem as homicidal as formerly the Masai).

From unassuming hills you drop to cross the Tsavo River [282], where the Athi becomes the Galana. The **Tsavo Bridge** was an obvious German objective in World War I (the British garrison on one occasion fleeing in a night raid by 'one female rhinoceros and her calf'). The never-finished Man-Eaters Motel (r.) is a reminder of its grislier past: in 1898 two lions, by eating 28 coolies, stopped work for nine months on the Uganda Railway here, until Colonel Patterson killed them and immortalized them in his book. Though safely stuffed in Chicago's Field Museum since, they inspired such long-lived dread that wardens still banned camping here in the 1950s.

A half-km. before the bridge is the Tsavo River Gate to Tsavo West (r.; p. 96), ten kms later the Manyani Entrance to Tsavo East (l.). At Mbololo Hills Prison (r.)[293½] you are 'Welcome to Prison Industries Show Room'. The road thereafter sinks steadily, closes with the Taita Hills (r.) and arrives at Voi (p. 97)[330]. The hills soon sink into the distance behind, shambas and scrubland take over. **Mackinnon Road** [399] commemorates Sir William (p. 21), the British India Steamship Company chairman who in 1892 had this stretch of road built at his own expense. A War-time Allied base and PoW camp, it is now shacks, a railroad halt and a dinky mosque (in which one Sayyed Baghali Shah lies entombed in a green box decked in silk beneath the silver dome). Next Taru [413] (whence this **Taru Plain**), Samburu [428½] (unrelated to p. 109) and Mariakani [456½] (where the C 107 cuts across to Kilifi, p. 76).

Rabai. At Mazeras' row of shanty-shops [472], Rabai and Ribe are sign-posted (l.) – along the Kaloleni turning which, until its surfacing in 1976, was enough to try the patience of a saint. In a sense it may have done so because Dr Krapf, having moved inland from Mombasa after the death of his wife and child (p. 19), established Kenya's first church and permanent mission at Rabai in 1846. Beyond the village's scattered shacks (r.)[4½ kms], **St Paul's** dominates the 'village green'; having been built in 1887, it is, to the best of my knowledge, Kenya's oldest still-used church. Notices in the long, steep-roofed interior record the mission's first troubled years. From here Bishop Hannington set off in 1885 to meet his death in Uganda. The cottage nearest the church's porch was Rebmann's original home.

Krapf went on to help the British Methodists found **Ribe** in 1862: from the Methodist school's hilltop complex (r.)[13] you will need a guide and a great deal of stamina for the sweltering trek through the hilly jungle to the first mission's ruins and the missionaries' graves.

Just below the Rabai junction, right of the main road, a modern Methodist venture is the **Mazeras Craft Training Centre**: in the 'Workshop for the Handicapped' you can see made the jewellery sold at Bombolulu (p. 74). Opposite, Mombasa's **Mazeras Nurseries/ Botanic Gardens** are lily-ponds crossed by willow-pattern bridges and coarse lawns planted with bamboo and palms – a cool green place for a picnic away from the humid heat. The gardens are open 6 a.m.-12 and 2-6 p.m. daily, but there is neither gate nor guardian to stop you elsewhen. Temperature and humidity then rise as you drop between the shambas, palms and mangoes to Mombasa.

AROUND MOUNT KENYA AND THE ABERDARES

However superior flying may be for speed and convenience, the sights en route are inevitably distant. The centres described in the following sections are those generally visited both overland and by air, but my account of the sights between these centres can be of use only to car or train travellers. For the travelogue by air you should ask the pilot: he will know what is down below. Or not let on that he doesn't.

From the Thika turning (p. 61)[39½] the single-lane tarmac continues north. It here forms part of the **Great North Road**, a largely farcical trans-continental track that armchair geographers like to think 'links Cairo with the Cape'. Sisal, then coffee, clothes the slopes, papyrus fills the dips, and the road is lined with the wigwams of reeds that Kikuyu sell for matting. Straight on across the T-junction [51½], the A 2 was immaculately surfaced in 1977, making it the smoothest route to Nyeri and Nanyuki. Bypassing Murang'a, it swings fast over ridges and valleys, crosses the Tana with its power station (l.)[80] and, with the B 6 to Embu (r.)[84], becomes the 'ring road' that encompasses Mount Kenya.

Mount Kenya. There is often more cloud than mountain ahead, but a clear day provides a magnificent view. Mount Kenya's statistics – **Batian** 17,058 feet, **Nelion** 17,022, **Lenana** 16,355 – mask its true self: not three simple peaks but 'the world's most perfect model of an equatorial mountain'. Two hundred and fifty miles in circumference, it rises from farmland and prairie to dense forest and bamboo jungle; then through a zone of valleys and moors, with the Afro-Alpine giant heather, and groundsel sixteen feet high, and finally to its 32 lakes and tarns, fifteen glaciers and three snow-capped peaks.

These are the remnants of volcanic 'plugs' exposed by erosion of the crater rim around. Since time (for them) immemorial the Kikuyu have revered *Kilinyaa* or *Kirinyaga* – meaning White Mountain (or 'It is Glorious'?) – as home of their God *Mwene-Nyaga*, the Possessor of Mystery (or Whiteness). As God provided supernatural transport, Gikuyu (p. 102) must be disqualified as the first to ascend Mount Kenya. Dr Krapf (p. 19) reported seeing 'two large horns or pillars . . . covered with a white substance' on 3 December 1849. This, his second sighting of snow in Africa, was derided even by Livingstone until Joseph Thomson confirmed it in 1883. Count Teleki reached the snow-line in 1887, Captain Dundas' expedition followed two years later and in 1899, at his fourth attempt, Sir Halford Mackinder conquered Batian. Only when the slopes were largely settled and farmed did Nelion 'fall' – to P. Wyn Harris and Eric Shipton in 1929. Closed to climbers during the Emergency, Mount Kenya was conquered by an African, Kisoi Munyao, in 1959. And again in 1963 when he raised Kenya's flag on the summit.

The area above the 10,500-foot contour, plus two lower salients at Sirimon and Naro Moru, was in December 1949 gazetted a 227-square-mile **National Park**, famed for its forest and bird life. All the park rules apply and you must in addition sign in at the gates. (Search-parties set off if you have not signed out within eighteen hours.) Though the bamboo forests defeated Captain Dundas, a drive up through them to the open moors is now easily feasible at Sirimon (p. 108). For a pukka jungle experience try a night at Secret Valley (p. 108). The mountain's 'nursery slopes' are Point Lenana, but its nickname of the 'Tourist Peak' can be misleading: the view from the top, higher than Mont Blanc, is not always worth the long scree-scramble – in bad weather, on poor trails – and the peak should in any case be treated with respect – best under the aegis of the Naro Moru River Lodge (p. 106). If you are one of the odd 400 annually who must see the view from Nelion or Batian, you should first consult the Mountain Club of Kenya (Nairobi POB. 45741) or at least its *Guide to Mount Kenya*. The club's huts (Ksh. 10/- p.n.) facilitate the four-five day ascent, but this requires alpine Grade V-VI ability and a fair resistance to acute mountain sickness, pulmonary oedema and snow-blindness. Its first-hand advice on routes, seasons and problems is the redeeming feature of Phil Snyder's *Safari Guide to Mount. Kenya National Park* (Ksh. 10/- at the gates). Casualties – and fatalities – have been less since 1970 when the Austrian government began training rangers into an admirable mountain-rescue team.

Murang'a – the late Fort Hall – lies on the old Great North Road, the C 71 (l.)[51½] at the A 2 T-junction (above). It crosses tight hills of close-knit cultivation, often winding with the railway. By Maragua's Seventh-day Adventist Church (l.)[67] the picturesque Maragua River's falls are best seen as you drive past in the opposite direction. As the hills, more expansive, then start to roll, you descend a lush valley into Murang'a [81].

Above the bustling hillside centre of gaudy shanty-shops (l.) stand the post office, the hospital and the **Memorial Cathedral Church of St James and All Martyrs**. Founded by the Archbishop of Canterbury on 18 May 1955 and hallowed on 4 February 1961, its attraction is the 'colour reversal' mural by the Chagga artist Elimo Njau: the Nativity negroid in a Kikuyu manger, the shepherds black and the womenfolk bearing their gifts, the Last Supper in a banda with giraffe and acacia beside, and Kikuyu villages on Golgotha's slopes. In the neglected cemetery behind the church repose several victims of the Emergency, one Commonwealth soldier and 'F.G. Hall . . . 1901'. Frank Hall founded and gave his name to this early British government 'station'; at another, Machakos, his contemporary John Ainsworth worked likewise to wean the Kikuyu, Masai and Akamba from waylaying caravans, cattle-raiding and internecine fighting (pp. 48, 94). For the rest Murang'a boasts a fine town hall, pink and white on the hilltop, the Murang'a College of Technology and 'Njau's Night Club – 24 hours Service'.

The Great North Road zigzags out of town. Candelabra cactus – EUPHORBIA CANDELA-BRUM – rise spikey from the red-earth cuttings and wild flowers abound. First the Mathioya Bridge, then another built in 1940 see you over the arms of the Tana, the Kikuyu's Thagana. After **Sagana**'s colourful market and 'fish culture farm' (l.), you turn left on to the Mount Kenya 'ring road' [93½] and roll on through Kirinyaga District: donkey-carts and six-span ox-carts, schoolchildren in bright tunics and bare feet, Kikuyu women with shaven heads and exaggerated earrings, bent beneath precious loads of fire-wood that a strap round their forehead supports. The terrain becomes the humpy hills of a German romantic painting as you enter Nyeri District and climb to **Karatina** [120]: petrol stations, schools and a 'self-help hospital', Karatina Holiday Lodge and the Elephant Castle Hotel. The A 2 thereafter winds steeply, tops the Kiriaini route from Murang'a (l.; below) and drops to a T-junction [132]: straight on to Nyeri, Nakuru and Nyahururu, right – via the **Nyeri War Cemetery** [140](r.; 380 graves, all from Nyeri's three War-time hospitals) – to Nanyuki, Meru and Marsabit.

Mukurwe wa Gathanga. The above-mentioned Mathioya Bridge, however, sometimes succumbs to floods. Though it is usually soon bypassed by a cross-country detour, a tarmac alternative for Nyeri is the newer D 430 north-west from Murang'a [81](marked 'Kiriaini' r. beside the post office). Though more scenic, it is longer and makes for harder driving, tight-roping high along ridges and saddles, switch-backing over precipitous hills and levelling through the rust-coloured cuttings. This route at least makes it easier to reach, if not to find, the sacred *mukurwe*. 'Historical Site', the roadside signs in Murang'a used to proclaim: 'Mukurwe wa Gathanga is the Garden of Eden of the Kikuyu.' They then left you to it . . . and recently even the signs have disappeared. For this 'sight' you have in fact to follow the D 430 for 11·5 kms, take the E 554 (l.) marked 'Gakuyu 6 km' and stop a half-km. beyond that hamlet's church, school and shops. 'And just how do people ever find this?' I asked the watchman. 'Yes I see,' he replied: 'They find it a very nice and interesting place.'

Though the boma-stockade and two 'typical' huts give little hint of it, the site is all-important. **Gikuyu** and **Mumbi**, Kikuyu believe, were their Agikuyu ancestors who, sent by God to live on this hill, bore nine daughters. As directed by God – *Mwene-Nyaga* or *Ngai* – Gikuyu sacrificed a lamb here, whereupon nine youths appeared and helped his daughters found the nine Kikuyu clans. They lived in an 'extended family' homestead, around 1650 to judge by the generations. Today, with family and clan ties still strong, their 2 million descendants are East Africa's most numerous and influential group. And Jomo Kenyatta their most distinguished son. The Mzee's *Facing Mount Kenya* is an authoritative classic.

For 5/- the watchman – found at home below – will unlock the barbed-wire gate. There is nothing of vulgar interest to distract the pious pilgrim. The original museum has been removed, and Gikuyu's original mukurwe – fig-tree – long since felled by lightning. So, as with the Iraqis' actual 'Tree of Knowledge', another has been planted.

Dipping through Kiriaini [114], with its picturesque hill-market on Mondays and Fridays, and just tipping Othaya (l.)[122], the spectacular big dipper of a road veers right at the T-junction [134½] and meets the main B 5/A 2 [140] into Nyeri (l.).

Hibiscus   *Convolvulacea*   *Thunbergia*

Nyeri. 'The nearer to Nyeri the nearer to bliss', quipped Lord Baden-Powell, and if the Kikuyu's unofficial capital is only ordinarily pleasant, The Ark and Treetops near by must be most wildlife-lovers' idea of near-bliss.

You enter town by a jacaranda-avenue. The **Our Lady of Consolata Cathedral** (l.) was built in 1957-58, grey-stone and with an unusual nave that slopes cinema-like to increase the impression of height. Then the **police station** (r.), the Nyeri Library (l.) and the town hall (r.). 'Downtown' hotels are the now very local **White Rhino** (further l.; the hotel which 'charges on sight') and **Green Hills** (exactly one well-marked km. down the track l.). The main street (parallel r.) is tidy with, halfway up, a simple stone cenotaph 'To the Memory of the Members of the Kikuyu Tribe who Died in the Fight for Freedom 1951-1957' and, at the top, a defunct clock and a waterless fountain 'Erected by the People of Kenya in Memory of His Majesty George V'. Here by the boma the two streets converge to meet Baden Powell Road. When in 1902 a Kikuyu clan called the Tetu massacred an Indian caravan, the colonial authorities sent an expeditionary force and its OC, Colonel Meinertzhagen, established his camp on a site that soon became this administrative centre.

To the right stands first St Cuthbert's Presbyterian Church (built 1926 and now disused) then, beyond the T-junction (r.), the **Anglican Church**, 'consecrated to St Peter on 21 July 1962' (Sunday English service 8.30 a.m.). The sign at the junction indicates (r.) the 'Last Resting Place of **Lord Baden Powell**' (1857-1941). Amidst British civilian and military graves, every one facing Mount

Kenya, lies the Chief Scout of the World. Here in August 1977 Lady Baden-Powell was laid to rest beside him. The circle-and-dot sign inscribed on his tomb is the Boy Scouts' 'Gone Home'.

Along from the boma's 'sign-post tree' stands the **Outspan** where, in perhaps the loveliest corner of the hotel's beautiful grounds, **Paxtu** 'was built for Lord Baden-Powell of Gilwell O.M., G.C.M.G., G.C.V.O., K.C.B., Founder of the Boy Scout Movement who lived here from October 1938 until his death on 8th January 1941'. The seat on the veranda was 'Given by Kenya Scouts & Guides in Memory'. The Walkers' first Outspan was opened on New Year's Day 1927. Rebuilt in 1946, this splendid hotel doubles as a well-appointed terminal. But then somewhere you had to change for Treetops. For there – as at The Ark and Secret Valley – you cannot simply drop in. You need to book, often far in advance, then meet, eat lunch and leave large cases at the 'parent' hotel.

Treetops. For the 'Most Famous Hotel in the World' you are at 2.30 p.m. driven up from the Outspan (having lunched there at 12.30), to alight by the 'Treetops' sign (where sticklers can check their altitude, latitude and longitude). The ex-professional hunter cocks his rifle and gives his pep talk, or rather de-pep talk, with a warning to stay in a tight, quiet group and watch out: whereupon the party splits up and chatters. The protective hides on either side are none the less for real. Wooden steps help you up the cedar-wood stilts into the huge Cape Chestnuts. A hunter-host then does the honours (no longer with an African hostess); baboons pilfer and pester, very much at home (so close your windows); Mount Kenya (behind you) sometimes appears and, floodlit on the natural water-hole below, any number of Treetops' four-legged regulars give the all-night show you have waited and paid for.

Treetops was the brain child of Eric Sherbrooke Walker: the answer, he wrote, for tubby City stockbrokers whom he inched through the undergrowth stalking rhinoceros and who then stood up beside the beast, ticked 'Rhino' off their list and said 'Now show me an elephant'. E.S. Walker's very enjoyable *Treetops Hotel* has been paraphrased by Jan Hemsing as *Treetops Outspan Paxtu*. The original, built in 1932, was burnt down by Mau Mau in 1954, to be rebuilt three-storied in 1957 and extended in 1964 and 1969. Of the two Treetops' several royal visits, a plaque on the veranda commemorates the greatest: 'In this Mgumu Tree Her Royal Highness the Princess Elizabeth . . . Succeeded to the Throne through the Death of her father King George the Sixth'. Although she did not yet know it (p. 106).

The Ark. While Treetops is a fine institution, The Ark is luxury. Without a night at one of them, or Mountain Lodge, your Kenyan holiday will scarcely be complete.

Left from the Anglican church T-junction [0] you drop to bridge the Chania River and turn left [1½]; past Nyeri's Masonic Temple, the Highlands Mineral Water Company and the turning to the Italian Memorial Church (l.; below); down to the 'Muringato Bridge 1950' and up out of this second valley, verdant with coffee. Tarmac now, this B 5 to Nyahururu continues past Nyeri's 'airport' [5], the Mountain National Parks' headquarters (also r.) and Mweiga airfield (l.)[12½] to the two-km. track marked (r.)[14]: '**Aberdare Country Club**/The Ark'. The former is delightful in its own right: a converted farm-house – the 1937 'Steep' – manorial with log fires and immaculate grounds, a well-stocked shop, Rena Fennessy's fine-art birds around the lounge and their real-life counterparts in aviaries below. Most, though, see it in transit. With gear-crashing bus and gun-bearing host you climb – 1200 feet in eleven miles – from the slopes of slackening cultivation through the Ark Gate to the Aberdare Forest. On either side stand trees where the ants build high and elephants rub the trunks brown below. A wooden catwalk, or rather jetty, brings you to Graham McCullough's fine Bible replica.

Hot showers, good food and a tasteful décor make for comfort; panorama windows and a ground-level pill-box – the 'Dungeon' – please photographers; a sedgy pool attracts abundant birds and deposits of salt, an animal delicacy, bring bongo and other game here to (*Maji*) *Ya Mthabara*, the (Water-hole) Of the Leeches.

Begun in February 1969, work on the £160,000 project proceeded so fast that the first guests were received in November. (The official opening was to follow, on 25 November 1970.) The guest-list since is impressive: from the Danish royal family and Prince Bernhard to President Tito; from James Stewart to Geraldine Chaplin; from Peter Scott to that other bird-fancier, Hugh Hefner ('Game seen: eight Bunnies'). In view, perhaps, of such a clientele an 'A Deck' of first-class cabins-cum-suites has been added. A somewhat lesser innovation is the Ark moth collection, started in May 1974 and already possessing 30 species 'new to science'.

The Aberdares. These hotels are not on Mount Kenya but the Aberdares. Joseph Thomson first recorded this compact volcanic range on his wandering *Through Masailand* in 1883. He gave it the name of the Royal Geographical Society's then president. The Kikuyu inhabitants prefer **Nyandarua**, Drying Hide (which, with imagination, the skyline can resemble). The name, say some, should strictly be used for the **Kinangop** alone: although Ol Donyo Satima – the Mountain of the Young Bull – is the higher peak (13,104 feet), the former (12,816 feet) is better farmland and better known. 'Kinangop' may derive from the low German *Königskopp* – King's Peak – but the similar sound of (Sir William Mac)kinnon (p. 21) may also have muddled settlers' minds and caused the linguistic corruption. The Masai's paternity bid of *Ilkinopop* – the Owners of the Land – seems even farther-fetched.

Steeper, starker and with denser rain-forest, the Aberdares (save for the North and South Kinangop) were less settled and farmed than Mount Kenya. For this reason, too, they sheltered Mau Mau strongholds, kept flora and fauna intact despite the consequent military ops, and so warranted preclusion as a 228-square-mile **National Park** in May 1950. To the west the steep Rift-wall deters game, and this is better viewed (by Treetops' guests only) around the eastern **Treetops Salient**. Besides Golden cat, bongo and Giant forest hog, the Aberdares' rarities are Black leopard, Black serval and Black genet (try The Ark).

For the altitude apparently induces melanism. The degree of blackness in the forest's hogs has even prompted speculation on a separate species, the 'sunu'. 'Spotted lions' remain unquestionably a legend.

Rainfall – 80 inches p.a. – makes the steep tracks often impassable: to save (perhaps) a wasted trip 'phone the park headquarters (Mweiga 24) or check the 'Park open/closed' boards in the AA office at Westlands, Nyeri's Outspan and the Naro Moru Lodge. These, however, are not always changed with the weather. If an 'Open' sign tempts you up on false pretences, or if rain or mist waylays you en route, do not despair: the 'black cotton' may spin your car uncontrollably but is seldom deep. So rather than dodge the wheel-ruts as you would in mud elsewhere, grit your teeth and stay in them, hard in second gear. They will keep you moving roughly front-wards and, even when waterlogged, should not bog you down.

Until the park's sign-posts improve, you may or may not find the gate. Best make for Rohuruini, twenty kms from Nyeri [0] via the Ihururu track. This – the D 435 – branches off from the B 5 by the Masonic Temple (p. 104)[1½]. Coffee fields yield to the alley of cypress that front, sombre-funereal, the **Italian Memorial Church** (r.)[4]. The campanile stands detached and very Latin (albeit in hewn Kenyan rock); a monument (l.) honours African troops in Italian, Arabic and Amharic (with reliefs of St George and the Dragon). But most impressive is the interior, a red vastness of tiled floors and windows crossed in red and, between the mural Stations of the Cross, the 126 recessed plaques inscribed to Italy's dead. A bust depicts the **Duke d'Aosta**, who commanded these, 'my soldiers and comrades' in the Abyssinian Campaign (p. 22).

The D 435 is surfaced, past the Consolata Fathers' **Mathari Mission** (r.)[5], as far as Ihururu [8½]. Just before this hamlet's sign, turn right to the 'Kabage Forest Station 10.2 k.m.'. Ignoring the barrier to the forest reserve [14], you climb to the park gate by the Kinaini Bridge [20]. Above Rohuruini – 7000 feet a.s.l. – the forest thickens; the 10,000-foot contour can be seen from the change in the bamboo-species, from low-level BAMBUSA VULGARIS to the park's ARUNDI-NARIA ALPINA. The track remains reasonably maintained (many of its 25 miles having been cut in anti-Mau Mau operations and opened – like the park itself officially – by the Queen Mother in 1959). You finally shake off the forest [37] and rise to the moors: the views are impressive, but those writers who enthuse over the 'fantastic growths of moss and giant vegetation' prove only that they work on hearsay. The giant groundsel and lobelia require patience, and a botanical eye, to find. Stone marker-posts direct you to impressive waterfalls, 'discovered' by the road-builders. At the junction you then follow the signs either back to Nyeri or on to Naivasha.

For the former, fork left to the Kiandon-goro Gate, '10,000 ft.' a.s.l. [58], descend through the forest reserve, past the school-village and Tetu Catholic church (r.) and so re-enter Nyeri by Baden Powell Road [88].

'Naivasha 74 km' says the marker-post inside the Kiandongoro Gate [30 kms from Nyeri]. Broad enough for cars to skid full-circle, the track passes the 'Kiandongoro Fishing Camp 1 km' [32] and the 'Cave Waterfall' (also l.)[34½] and leaves the park at Mutubio [48½]. Merely 10,500 feet a.s.l. – and meaning 'Fast Man' (a reference to the long drop ahead) – this gate has replaced Fort Jerusalem as the park's West Entrance (the 'Fort' in turn having replaced Queen's Gate in 1973 and become an overnight shelter-site). Welcome tarmac then snakes down the Rift-wall escarpment which, when wet, would be murderous without it. After the forest reserve below, the only signs on the murram farm-tracks all seem to point back to the Aberdares Park. So best ask your way either (generally r.) to Gilgil or (loosely l.) to the tarmac at Naivasha.

From the turning to The Ark (p. 104)[1½] the tarmac continues past Nyeri's prison (r.) [2½] and the Kenya Police College/Physical Training Centre (l.). Otherwise known as Valley Camp (where Kenya's athletes trained for high-altitude Olympics), it borders the T-junction of **Kiganjo** [10½](Catholic church and Kenya Co-operative Creameries). Turning on to the Mount Kenya ring road (l.), you soon see, amidst many others, the sign-boards (r.) to 'Sagana State Lodge' and 'The Mountain Lodge 28 km'.

Mountain Lodge. The forest closes in on the valley slopes as the track climbs first to **Thego Fishing Camp** [7 kms](the Fisheries Department's two rondavels – beds and wood-fire kitchens for Ksh. 5/- p.n. – and AT&Hs' open-air lunch-stop, built in 1979 to keep Mountain Lodge guests eating while the staff prepared the rooms). Follow the lodge sign (r.)[9½], past the trout-farms on the menthol-fresh Sagana River, to **Sagana State Lodge**

(l.)[12]. From their visit to Treetops on 5-6 February 1952 Elizabeth and Philip came here. And here, whilst his wife was fishing, Prince Philip broke the news of her father's death. The lodge had been their wedding-gift from Kenya.

Beyond the lodge's beautiful gardens, its trees donated from all parts of Kenya and two podocarpus planted by the royal couple, the track climbs on well marked to Mountain Lodge [27](where 'visitors are not usually permitted . . . without a valid voucher')(which they should have obtained in Nairobi, from African Tours & Hotels, p. 41). This altogether plusher 'Treetops' was completed in late 1970, at a cost of £90,000 and at 7200 feet above sea-level.

Naro Moru. From Kiganjo [10½] the main road rolls north with the railway, across waterless ranchland redeemed by the rise of the Aberdares off left and Mount Kenya to the right. The road is escorted by the 7000-acre (and private) **Solio Game Park**, by means of which the millionaire landlord of Solio Ranch has tried since 1971 to keep tick-bearing game from his herds. Roan antelope (p. 72) were moved here from Ithanga, but died; Rudi the Rhino survives (p. 100). Signs [35] announce 'Naromoro Township You Must Slow Down' and '**Naro Moru River Lodge** 1·5 km Alt . . . 6505 ft'. Though the **Naro Moru Route** is served by outfits like the 'Mount Kenya Tourist Escorts', the River Lodge is for most the usual stepping-stone to Mount Kenya. After a 20/- night at its Climbers Bunk-house, the nearby camp site (5/-) or its cosier cedar-log chalets, you set off early – and equipped, if need be, from the store – with a porter-guide (45/- p.d.) or (very) simple porters (35/-). From the main road, the first 26 kms are by car, forking left at six kms and leaving to the left [8½] the **Mount Kenya Youth Hostel** (a farm-house converted in 1978, with 22 beds, kitchen facilities and blankets for hire; members Ksh. 15/- p.n., + 10/- for non-members). The forest reserve suddenly starts [11½] and, by the airstrip (l.), the park itself [15½]: 'Speed Limit 32 km.'. The Naro Moru Gate [16] – '8100 feet' – is very visibly the mountain park's control post with its Warden's offices, ranger settlement and stern interdictions: 'Unaccompanied Walkers will not be Allowed Entry/Overnight Visitors must possess Booking Vouchers or Tentage'. The forest zone thereafter is steep hairpin bends and quagmires of black cotton, the price to be paid for the **camp site** [26](Ksh. 5/- p.n., children

and porters 1/-). While the 'meteorological station' adjacent is now only two rain-gauges, accommodation here has been upgraded with three 10-bed **bandas** (Ksh. 20/-, under 12s 10/-, with gas but no bedding). Drivers might – in hired cars – reach the moorland, which otherwise means a further hour on foot. Climbers then persevere up the 'Vertical Bog' to spend the night at Mackinder's Camp (13,650 feet a.s.l.). The second day sees them up Point Lenana and all the way down. The Mountain Club of Kenya's guide-book is invaluable (p. 27) and the Survey of Kenya's map excellent in English, French and German.

From Naro Moru [35] the ring road moves on from the 'Cole's Plains' of yore into the prettier **Burguret Forest**: rocky outcrops and candelabra cactus, a dip across the Burguret River, St Philip's Church, engulfed in forest (r.)[36], and the warning 'Caution Game'. Embassy Cigarettes then welcome you to Nanyuki [54], Laikipia District starts and the **Equator** is distinguished, at 6389 feet, by a crescent of souvenir stalls.

Nanyuki grew rapidly after World War I, largely as a result of the Soldiers' Settlement Scheme, and warranted township status in 1920 and a rail link with Nairobi ten years later. Railhead for the Allies' advance during the Abyssinian Campaign (p. 22), it is now predominantly a farming (and safari) centre.

There are few Masai north of Nairobi nowadays but Masai place-names like Nanyuki and Laikipia, Nelion, Batian and Lenana are relics of the sway they once held. Under Batian (the *laibon*-chief Mbatiani), Nelion (his brother Neilieng) and Lenana (his son Olonana) they were sovereign from Lake Rudolf to Dodoma. In 1860 Dr Krapf reported them 'dreaded as warriors, laying all waste with fire and sword'. But already Mbatiani had foreseen in a dream that an 'iron snake' would one day divide his land and, their territory split by the Uganda Railway, the Masai had been forced into their present confines by 1909. The Silverbeck claims the site of a manyatta from the 1900s and one mile up the Nanyuki River, between the hotel and Raymond Hook's, the Masai made sacrifice at a sacred fig-tree, as did the Kikuyu at Murang'a (p. 102).

The **Silverbeck Hotel** (r.)[55] stands not only on the town boundary but also on the Equator; in its 'World-famous Equator Line Bar' you could drink with a foot in each hemisphere . . . until in June 1974 the problem of its much-needed redecoration was solved by its being burnt down. After the town centre's Jamhuri clock-tower [0] St George's Road (also r.) runs out past the **Sportsman's Arms** to **St George's Church** (also l.)[1½]; it was consecrated in September 1957 with a fine stained-glass window, an unusual font and moveable services. The civilian cemetery, with an overflow of military from the Emergency, then precedes the **Nanyuki War Cemetery** (l.)[3½]. Started by the army in the 1940 putsch (p. 22), its 199 graves lie on the Equator in a garden of jacaranda, kei-apple and Kaffir boom, the 'Bottle-brush Tree'.

Mount Kenya Safari Club lies, as the crow flies, four kms straight on, but barracks in between make this technically 'No Entry'. Rather than ignoring the warnings and furtively shifting the road-blocks, turn off before, by the Silverbeck, into Haile Selassie Road: past the turnings serving the 'Game Warden Nanyuki' and the 'Benedictine Monastery Our Lady of Mount Kenya' (r.) and five kms further up a much-improved track. In 1958 an oilman, a film star and a banker clubbed together to convert the

Mawingo Hotel. Much as you might convert an old Ford Eight into a Rolls. The 'Charter Members' of the touristic paragon they created read like an omnibus excerpt from *Who's Who*, Debrett and the Oscar prize-winners' list. Bought in 1977 by an Anglo-Arab/Franco-American consortium, the club impresses accordingly, a serene and delightful 100 acres of well-appointed restaurants, bars, suites and cottages; rose-garden, and rock-gardens on a sweep of immaculate lawn; a heated pool with viewing room below and birds strutting gorgeously around; airstrip and tennis courts, bowling and putting greens; a nine-hole golf course upgraded to par three and complete with pavilion; conference facilities for 100 and, if you are a star on a busman's holiday, even a film studio (built by former owner William Holden for the shooting of *The Lion*). All this in grounds overlooked by Mount Kenya and, except on national holidays, open to you. Daily membership is, since 1962, available for Ksh. 65/-; the Nairobi Hilton, since 1977, houses a Members' Lounge, and the latest innovation is a full **safari service**. The club being

Mount Kenya, with its triple peaks and Afro-Alpine vegetation

'Kenya's geographical centre', its furthest point less than two hours' flying time, the programme's 50 options range from Indian Ocean fishing to bird-watching on Mount Elgon.

Gazelle, oryx, eland and Grevy's zebra graze beside the drive up from the gate-house, for the 1216 acres around the club form the Mount Kenya Game Ranch. Largely financed by William Holden and run by Don Hunt, it helps not only with the training of national park rangers and wildlife teaching in schools, but also with trapping and trans-porting game: the Grevy's zebra removed to Tsavo West (p. 97) and the 'Noah's Ark' airlift of Kenyan wildlife as the groundstock of Nigeria's and Ghana's national parks.

Secret Valley. Treetops and The Ark you may not approach alone: Secret Valley you could not. Having hit upon the high, tight-jungle glade of Ondari whilst tracking Mau Mau, Colonel Rose-Smith then spent months trying to find it again. Your landmark is the Sportsman's Arms. The ex-army bus leaves daily at 4.15 p.m. for the 30-minute drive: as you climb and climb, the less steel-nerved duck when bamboos strike the roof. The lodge stands on stilts at a chill 8300 feet and here, so close to the suave Safari Club, is unmitigated Africa. As night falls round the creaking tree-house, sunbirds and humming birds vanish; the jungle resounds eerily near, screeching, rasping, barking and roaring. Elephant and antelope gather at the water-hole but **leopards** are the stars. You are woken the moment one shows. (Though should the baited platforms stay empty all night, your money is no longer refunded. 'Not because of any lack of leopards,' the proprietor adds hastily, 'but because the accountants objected.')

NORTH TO SAMBURU

Behind the Sportsman's Arms, Nanyuki ends with Christ the King's Catholic Church (1960) and the 'Mary Immaculate Dispensary and Dentists' [0]. The road passes from Laikipia to Meru districts and crosses gentle ranch country, dipping over streams Mount Kenya sheds.

The **Sirimon Route** (r.)[14] takes you up the mountain, nine rough kms through the forest reserve to the National Park gate at 8650 feet. Here you sign in and out and pay the usual (p. 50), plus Ksh. 5/- for your horse, donkey, mule, zebra or zebroid. The track climbs into a forest hoary with Old Man's Beard; the Sirimon Valley is deep-cleft to the left; slowly the forest and bamboo fall back from the steep stony track. This persists nine kms further up to the moorland, where mountain safaris meet their beasts of burden and where, by the roadhead, you may camp (Ksh. 5/- p.n., under 12s 1/-).

The Sirimon Bridge takes the main A 2 on across the same-named river [14½]. After Timau [21] and the **Kentrout Grill** (r.) the forest falls back from the rolling hills; wheatfields and sheep take over. A turn in the road [45] and suddenly off left – if the clouds *below* you clear – is an unexpected wonder: the semi-desert of the **Northern Frontier District** is there like the view from a low-flying 'plane. From Mount Kenya's green slopes the country seems simply to drop a half-mile and start again – as the warm, arid plains and hills that cover half of Kenya. The explorer Chandler first crossed them in 1892 and by this route, in 1897, Lord Delamere came to Kenya (p. 115).

Today the tarmac winds down round the hillocks and bears left [52] for Isiolo. Marker-posts (l.)[56] lead you left-right along the farm-tracks to the **Wilderness Trails Camp**. (But – as though the owners were loath to see you go – they do not lead you back, and trying to find the road again may mean a familiarization tour around the **Lewa Downs**.) For 'camp' you should read 'camps' because the fifteen double tents rotate – 'as the spirit moves us' – across the Lewa Downs Ranch. (A proudly boasted feature being the 'long-drop' loos, the sites vacated since 1973 must have left a Cornish tin-mine profusion of unsuspected pits.) The ranch-house provides a pool, and included in the tariff (Ksh. 910/- double, 600/- single) are horses and game-run guides for the elephant, buffalo and both types of zebra, antelopes from eland to dikdik, Reticulated giraffe and even breeding cheetah that share the ranch with 4000 head of cattle – and a hand-ax site (reservations via East African Wildlife Safaris, Nairobi POB. 43747, tel. 331228).

The main road levels to the plain, where scattered shacks intersperse the cactus and acacia: the Ntumbu Methodist church [62], the Anti-Poaching Mobile Force HQ (l.; p. 95)[70] and the 'Excellent Lodge' (r.)[70½].

The tarmac stops two kms from Isiolo [80]. Here until 1970 tourists stopped too, for the desolate terrain and Kenya's frontier dispute with Somalia and its *Shifta* made special permits necessary. The road barrier is a relic, the sign 'Ethiopia/Somalia/Adisababa 1010' a reminder that the corrugated tracks ahead constitute the would-be 'Ethiopian Highway'.

If **Isiolo** is no more than tin-roofed shacks and a market topped with an odd iron honeycomb, a Craft Training Centre, Sacred Heart of Jesus Church, Saudi-built mosque and Barclays Bank in a pink Beau Geste fort . . . the **Turkana** compensate. From here north to Rudolf these nomadic Nilo-Hamites roam, with the lake now even renamed in their honour. The first British officials knew nothing of the Turkana save that they were 'reputed to be of gigantic stature and extremely fierce'. And counted only up to five (thereafter saying 'five plus one' etc.). We later learned that in the 1850s they had routed and ousted the Masai, were often raided and enslaved by Abyssinians and in 1914 unwittingly aided the Germans by engaging the Kenya African Rifles more needed further south. If not gigantic, they are tall, lean and striking, with high cheek bones, aquiline noses and rather un-negro thin lips. Ostrich-feather head-dress and leopard-skin capes are reserved for cere-monials, but everyday wear is the aluminium or ivory lip-plug they slide in and out of a hole below the mouth. Few tourists ascertain that the Turkana do not circumcise, rather rest content with the news that, as in all East Africa, the cowrie shells their women wear symbolize vaginas.

Beside the Turkana, as you take the broad track north, you will see both lithe Somali and Samburu shepherds. Like the Turkana chokered with beads and with metal bands as biceps bracelets, the **Samburu** are nevertheless peaceable relatives of the Masai. They speak the same language – *Maa* – and their *morani*-warriors likewise plaster hair, face and torso ochre-red. Their *soko*-wraps are also often red, but worn more discreetly. An attractive accessory with both Samburu sexes is the metal triangle that rings of beads round the often shaved scalp support on the forehead.

Common to all three tribes is their covet-ousness of cattle. The Turkana, in a near-Hindu parallel, see their scrawny kine as links with their ancestors' souls: the chosen are sung to and told the daily news. For the Masai and Samburu they just represent wealth: though it could often improve the stock, they would no more cull their herds than you would take three clean pounds for a dirty fiver.

Samburu/Isiolo Game Reserves. *Samburu* is a corruption of the Masai's 'butterfly', perhaps referring to their desert restlessness in search of pasture and water. It is also the name of a magnificent 40-square-mile game reserve. A ten-mile stretch of the Uaso Nyiro River divides it from its 75-square-mile 'Isiolo' neighbour. In both, the marker-posts are generally good enough to make the Survey of Kenya's map dispensable.

Invariably warm, and wetter of late, the reserves are delightful with doum-palms and riverine scenery, all in the lee of Ol Olokwe. Dikdiks scuttle across your track; gerenuks stretch, two-legged, to feed; elephants roam, red with dust, and bathe in the picturesque Uaso Nyiro River. This for attractiveness is matched by **Samburu Game Lodge** (which occupies the site of Arthur Newman's camp, an old-time elephant-hunter called locally *Nyama Yango*, My Meat). The lodge – or the twelve-tent annex opened down stream in 1980 – is the place to see many of the reserves' 300 (supposedly) sighted bird species, and especially Layard's Black-headed weavers. You are requested 'Not to feed the Monkeys as they bite Unexpectedly', while signs by the riverside bar warn 'Danger Crocodile' (and, for the crocs, 'Danger People'). Neither, hopefully, has any connection with the mass now held on Sundays at 11.15 a.m.

From Isiolo [80] follow the stony 'Lake Rudolf' track and turn at the first signs (l.)[100]. Ahead, the Ngare Mara Gate to the **Buffalo Springs-Isiolo Game Reserve** is open from 6 a.m. to 6.30 p.m. (Ksh. 20/-, under 16s 1/-, cars 20/-). Beyond the gate [102½] marker-posts point (r.)[104½] to the four **camp sites** (Ksh. 5/- p.p.p.n.) – 'Beware of Crocodiles' – then [107½] to '**Buffalo Springs Tented Lodge**' and 'Buffalo Springs/Chokaa Gate'. Three kms distant, past the 'Isiolo River Circuit' (l.), the lodge replaced the self-help bandas in 1979. And five kms further across the plain of termite-mounds, the **Buffalo Springs** were reportedly caused in World War II by an Italian bomb that, aimed at Isiolo, went astray. The pools of remark-ably cool clear water, now with ugly walls and cemented 'banks', lie one km. before the Buffalo Springs Gate. The markers are likewise good to the Kubi Panya Look-out and **Special Camp Site** (Ksh. 30/- p.p. for your own exclusive use), the West Gate on the Old Wamba Road, Neill's Crossing and the airstrips. The 'Lower' and 'Upper River' circuits are particularly splendid late afternoon, before you take the new bridge across the Uaso Nyiro River [122½] and drive through natural parkland to the lodge [124].

Or you can keep to the Ethiopian Highway, past the Buffalo Springs/Chokaa Gate (l.) [112½] and the Shaba turning (r.; below) [113½], and over the Uaso Nyiro [116]. Here the *morani* pose against a backdrop of doum-palms, the unadorned sell mica and quartz and the cattle wallow below. **Archer's Post** – just Samburu, Turkana, camels, goats, shacks and a Catholic mission – is a questionable tribute (1910) to its administrator-founder Sir Geoffrey. Follow the sign (l.)[117] – preferably straight past the locals dressed to kill, touristically speaking. Beside the Archer's Entrance [122] is a board 'In Memory of Elsa who helped safeguard this Game Reserve'. Admission to the **Samburu Game Reserve** here is like Isiolo's (above); 'No Movement is Allowed between 6.30 p.m. & 6.00 a.m.' and the track, part sand, part corrugation, sees you on to the lodge [137].

Pronounced 'Wusho Nero' and meaning River of Brown Water, the **Uaso Nyiro** epitomizes Kenya's stark contrasts: well watered from the Aberdares, its headstreams cross the Laikipia Plains and, at Naro Moru, even touch Mount Kenya; then drop to the deserts as a long curling artery that vanishes remotely in the Lorian Swamp.

Shaba National Reserve. The Uaso Nyiro forms Shaba's northern border, twenty of the reserve's 250 kms of track being a riverside drive. The riverine scenery overall, though, is diversified by hills (which, wrongly thought to contain ore, explain the name of *Shaba*, Copper). Their precipitations, the river and four springs make Shaba better watered than Samburu/Isiolo, and the denser vegetation makes for more prolific game. For increased killing too: this 'popular' hunting block of the

1960s became the scene of wanton poaching after being declared, in 1974, a 140-square-mile reserve.

Another death, **Joy Adamson**'s, has brought Shaba tragic fame. Ironically, it was the remoteness and lack of 'tourist traffic' that persuaded her to settle here with **Penny**. This female leopard had been 'loaned' to her for a rehabilitation scheme that might have rivalled Elsa's. Having raised the cub (found orphaned near Nakuru) at her Lake Naivasha home, she had almost completely weaned it for life in the bush; *Penny – Queen of Shaba* had recently been published; *Pasha of Shaba* was to tell the Elsa-parallel of Penny's mating wild and giving birth to Piti and Pasha – but 'on Thursday, 3rd January 1980, Joy Adamson went out for her customary evening stroll . . . On this occasion she never returned'.

Her home had been a 'mud and thatch hut surrounded by a game-proof wire fence'. Near by, in January 1978, the public **Shaba Camp** was built rather less austere: bar, restaurant and fifteen double tents occupy a clearing of the wooded river-bank; a waterfall below the bar is a pretty focal centre; the side-stream 'Shaba Wallow' is a natural swimming-pool (bookings Nairobi POB. 20106, tel. 25255). From the main-track turning (above)[113½] the sign-posted approach runs six kms over lava flows and (hopefully dry) river-beds to the Natorbe Gate (open 6.30 a.m.-6.30 p.m.; same fees as Samburu, plus 'Vehicles & Aircrafts 20/-'). The three-km. track (l.) past the airstrip to the lodge deteriorates from lava to all-pervading dust.

Dust (or mud) predominates, too, on the main track straight on from the gate [119½]. The terrain rougher and slightly more dramatic, you veer right [132½] to a trickier track. Things are no better beyond the Shaba Gate [139½]. Nor on the 'main' C 81 [155], where you turn right, to confront the black cotton of the Shaba Dogo Swamp with its dangerous bridge – 'You Must Slow Down' – and thankfully reach tarmac and the Isiolo barrier (p. 109)[191].

ROUND THE MOUNTAIN

Mount Kenya's 'ring road' east provides an alternative way home, but murram runs from Meru to Embu and the sights per mile are fewer.

Meru. Signing out at Isiolo [0], follow the tarmac back up the Timau Escarpment and left [28] to Meru. Farmland reoccupies the

slopes, rolling up to the bald green domes, then yielding to shrub and tight forest. Meru starts with timber yards – Meru oak being a by-word – and a spread of public buildings [51]. The 'Meru Coffee Building' indicates a second local product; others are tea, pyrethrum, cotton, tobacco, bananas and *miraa*, a stimulant which not only the Wameru chew.

Doum-palms beside the Uaso Nyiro

Below the post office, halfway downhill (r.), **Meru Museum** houses an interesting, mini-comprehensive collection (9 a.m.-6 p.m., Sundays and public holidays 11 a.m.-5 p.m.; Ksh. 5/-, residents 2/50, children 2/-, -/50). Started in 1974, it was opened to the public in May 1976 – and in the former DC's office, Meru's first stone building (1917). The first room's display of local woods and rocks, antelope trophies and volcano 'diorama' compensates for its case of horribly stuffed birds. The main hall is prehistory, tribal life and apiculture: cleavers and hand-axes from the Lewa Downs are as intelligently captioned as the more piquant exhibits: 'The Meru Family', 'Boy to Man' and 'Girl to Woman'. Panels and cases on bee-keeping are oddly predominant. Outside there are actual Meru huts, one for the husband, another for the wife and children and a third for the eldest, single, circumcised daughter. The remarkably 'actual', all-round exhibition is completed by beds of local crops and herbs (plus the MIMOSA PUDICA which shuts when touched), by an open-air theatre for Wameru dances and plays, a curio shop, fish-pond and local birds and animals.

Beyond the museum, St Paul Road continues uphill (r. then l.) to the same-named, interdenominational church: tiled witch's-hat spire, modernistic 'Nordic' design and plain-glass window-cross in the altar wall. Opposite the museum, Hospital Road and the murram Cathedral Road (straight on) climb one km. to the imposing **St Joseph's** – very 1930s *Art Déco* (but built by Italian Consolata Fathers in 1957-60). On the main Kenyatta Highway, the Meru Safari Hotel (l.) has become the Meru Co-operative Union Hotel but not otherwise improved. Further down, the **Pig & Whistle** (r.) survives from 1924.

Meru National Park. As you enter town, opposite the new Milimani and Meru 'hotels', signs (l.) announce the preferable Leopard Rock and Meru Mulika lodges, and these enterprising ventures are a token of the park's 'opening up'. The first game reserve to be taken over (in 1959) by an African District Council, Meru was ten years later still difficult of access and terrain. It was reckoned to be 'some 700 square miles' in area, and from Nairobi or Nanyuki was best reached by air. Travel agents had to have seen to surface transport or arranged a foot-safari in the well-named 'Wilderness Area'. Writers confused it with Tanzania's Meru – thus showing their ignorance of **Elsa**. For here George and Joy Adamson lived famously with their lions. George Adamson then went on to work in Kora: his 'big cat programme' for rehabilitating lions being recently completed, the 500 tsetse-ridden square miles were declared the

Kora Game Reserve in 1976. The Tana River divides it from Meru and the 50-foot cascades at the Rojewero confluence, surrounded 'surrealistically' by cairns and quartzite cliffs, have been named the **Adamsons' Falls**.

Rehabilitation was also Meru's main *raison d'être*. Its game had been decimated by hunting when the Adamsons started the lion project that Elsa made famous. Pippa – the *Spotted Sphinx* – publicized their later work on cheetah. To date (1980) 112 leopards have been brought here from Laikipia and so stopped from raiding ranches at Naivasha and Ngobit, Nanyuki and Nyahururu. Beside the Elsa pilgrimage the park's exclusive attraction is **White rhino**: six were drugged, freighted and rehabilitated here as a gift from Natal's Umfolozi Game Reserve. Fossils show the species once inhabited the area: though three of those imported died, the remainder is breeding – and thus reviving the prehistoric presence. Such, however, is the menace of poaching – three already have been slaughtered – that armed rangers 'shepherd' the rhinos by day and pen them into paddocks overnight.

Rainfall – often Kenya's highest – feeds the park's fifteen full-time streams (in which crocodiles should discourage swimmers). It also necessitates malaria prophylactics and mosquito-nets for campers. The park map is unusually accurate, having been produced while most tracks were being made. These are for the most part well graded and maintained, and the thoroughfare to Embu and Nairobi even better than many a 'main road' elsewhere. That from Meru is tarmac on and off: from the main road [0], past the teachers college, girls school and Methodist centre of Kaaga and via Kianjai and Tigania into the Nyambeni Hills. The volcanic peaks are thick on the plains below, as murram takes you down to the Murera Entrance, 'Closed from Dark to Dawn' [78½].

Beyond **Meru Mulika Lodge** [83] the tracks and marker-signs are good to **Leopard Rock Safari Lodge** [88]. Prettily sited on the Murera River and blessed with a generator switched off at night, the six self-service double bandas from 1972 were increased to ten in 1975 (Ksh. 70/- p.n., under 16s 30/-, gas 2/-, fridge 5/- p.n.; bookings through A.A. Travel, Nairobi POB. 14982, tel. 742926-9). The main track runs on to ford the Mulika River [96], skirts the **camp sites** [97](Ksh. 5/- p.n.) and the park headquarters – 'White Rhino' (also r.)[3 kms] – and continues, flat, to Pippa's Camp [101½]. This is now no more than a 'Marker-post 13', so stay with the track across bridges and fords – and, alarm-

ingly, plumb across the airstrip – to the Ura River Entrance [135](290 kms from Nairobi, 160 from Embu and closing '5.45 p.m. sharp'). The track, excellently graded but in places corrugated, crosses innumerable rivers – and Gathu [158] – to meet the T-junction of the Embu-Meru track [195](below).

A Meru friend in Nairobi said that his country 'used to be far away but then they built a road'. More correctly, they half-built two roads. The shorter, from Meru to Embu via Chogoria, takes longer; it winds over the higher slopes, picturesque but steep and often very slippery, this being Mount Kenya's wetter side. After Meru [0] and the **Equator** [6½] the tarmac stops at Nkubu [14]. The inviting sign here – 'Embu B 6' – was a blatant deception: this 'main B road' is soon climbing, appalling, its loose dust and murram alternating with bare bed-rock. It curves round the rim of magnificent chasms, but the steep wooded slopes and trickling rills are no solace for the driver (who may, however, be gratified to know that this is a regular sector of the Safari Rally). Hill settlements occur: Kanyakine [25] with a stylish Catholic mission (l.), Igoji [37] and **Chogoria** [51], long drawn-out with hospitals and schools, and base – with the Warden's permission – for the east-side ascent of Mount Kenya. As you hairpin across the 'Thughi Bridge 1939' and climb through the forest, longed-for tarmac recommences [99], topping the C 92 [111½], the trunk track (l.) to Meru.

This, though a 'C road', is far less painful. Branching (l.) off the B 6 below the Pig & Whistle [0], it crosses the **Equator** [10] at 4225 feet above sea-level. Forest alternates with farmland: tea, coffee, cotton, bananas and the ubiquitous maize. The E 788 to 'Meru Park' is marked (l.)[30], then the 'B.A.T. (tobacco) Leaf Centre' at Mitunguu [34]. The sharp steep peaks keep their distance around until the climb begins. The Mutonga, Nithi and Ruguti rivers are all rocky-attractive with the thickets pressing close. With the countryside drier and the vegetation less, you cross the Meru-Embu District boundary [72], pass the breeze-block and tin-roof Ishiara Mission (r.)[85] and rise over hillsides of increasing cultivation to the main road [114] into Embu (l.)[130].

Embu, like Meru, denotes both the town and the tribe that inhabits its vicinity. Claiming kinship with the Kikuyu, the Wa-Embu farm

Mount Kenya's foot-hills. Their 'capital' is correspondingly market-town functional. An avenue of jacaranda beautifies the road in, between the Institute of Agriculture and **Izaak Walton Inn** (r.) and the district hospital and Catholic Church of St Mary Assumption (1959). St Paul's 'Pro-cathedral' Church (also l.) is more modernistic (1960-64; English service Sundays 9-10 a.m.). The main road drops between Embu's State House (r.) and the police and Eastern Province headquarters, in front of which the flat-topped pyramid, complete with bas-reliefs, is the town's **Uhuru Monument**; past Embu town hall (r.) – this in letters two feet tall – and down between dukas and banks to Moi Stadium, half-lapped by a crescent of garages, shops and cafés.

From here [0] the B 6 ring road takes you back fast to Nairobi: over the Rupingasi River, from the Eastern to the Central Province and from Embu to Kirinyaga District [2½]; past the C 73 short cut to Sagana (r.)[13½], from hills well cambered to rice-fields and dips of black cotton, and so to the A 2 (p. 101)[43½]: left to Nairobi.

If time allows, make a sortie to **Mwea**. The several sign-boards (l.) explain why: 'Rice Mill Factory/Irrigation Settlement Headquarters'. Watered by the Tana and financed by Germany to the tune of Ksh. 40 million, the 14,000-acre Rice Irrigation Scheme has since 1973 occupied some 3000 tenants, each on a four-acre holding, and in 1977 produced a record K£2-million harvest, 70% of Kenya's rice consumption.

NAKURU AND NYAHURURU

Returning from western Mount Kenya to Nairobi, the Nyahururu route has a higher sight value than the Meru-Embu tracks and makes possible the sortie to Nakuru.

From Nyeri to Nyahururu [101 kms] the B 5 short cuts across the **Laikipia Plains**: on from the turning to The Ark (p. 104)[14] and through the hamlet of Mweiga [16]. The stony D 440 (r.)[25] to 'Naro Moru 19 km' skirts Carissa Farm (l.)[14 kms], location for the opening of *Born Free*. The main B 5 then divides [28]: left via tarmac to 'Nyahururu 73 km', right via Ngobit to the Nanyuki route (below). The latter rises prettily into shrubby hills; after Ngobit's hamlet [53] the country is cleft with lowly ravines. Crossing the **Ngobit River** [55] – the Masai's 'Twisting like a Piece of Rope' – do not follow other guides to Ngobit Fishing Lodge . . . it is now a very private 'Quality Trout Farm'.

From Nanyuki's Jamhuri clock-tower (p. 107) [0] the sign-post used to point (l.) to 'Thomson's Falls 60 mi.'. Not only have they Africanized the name – to *Nyahururu, Where deep Water runs* – but also made a false economy on the metric distance: '84 km' says the new sign. You leave town via the old and new 'town market', a Sunni mosque (also l.), the district hospital (r.) and a red-brick and plaster 'Full Gospel Church'. Tarmac gives way to grey gravel and murram [3], running straight and hard across the fenced ranching country of the northern Laikipia Plains. Vultures glout in the low acacias; giraffe and gazelle are not rare. A sliver of

tarmac honours 'Hulme's Bridge 1957' [25], now known as 'Ngare Ngiro'; the Ngobit track (above) comes in left [53] and, after the 'National Boran Stud' (r.)[55], you veer off from the route to 'Rumuruti 15 miles'. With the ranchland cut by streams in low gulches, this might be Montana. Forest stations are marked . . . and often needed: the bush fire that raged here in March 1971 destroyed £590,000 of timber, engulfed 20,000 acres and took some 1000 men to extinguish. You rise through grassy downland, with cows on the slopes and the shacks increasing. Then the welcome tarmac of the B 5 from Nyeri (above)[82] and you enter 'Thomson's Falls' (r.)[96] aptly by the cataract that first gave it its name.

Nyahururu. 'These Falls were Named in 1883 by the Explorer Joseph Thomson of Dumfries, Scotland.' Though Kenya's third highest, the 243-foot, ex-Thomson's Falls – and the gazelle – are scarcely adequate namesake tribute to the Scot who at 22 years had explored much of southern Tanganyika and who returned in 1883, now all of 25, to walk from Mombasa to Mount Elgon (and, by removing his false teeth and mixing up fruit salts, to win a Masai reputation as a wizard). At **Thomson's Falls Lodge** – once Barry's Hotel – you can and must listen to the all-night roar of the nearby falls: 200,000 gallons of the Ngare Naru River every minute. From the lodge, too, you can climb down for the worm's-eye view, but 'Beware of Un-official Guides/Descend to the Falls at your own Risk'. Up top, the savvy curio-hawkers occupy the finest vantage-points. Right of the hill from the falls up into town, the Church of Our Lady of the Immaculate Conception (1959) is cruciform and most remarkable for its steep-peaked roof and likewise Scandinavian-slim spire.

Railhead since 1930, 'T. Falls' is now Kikuyu-agricultural with few reminders of its recent white-settler importance. In 1968, and at 7800 feet a.s.l., it acquired new significance as Kenya's high altitude training camp for the Olympic Games. Their athletic, if not sporting rivals complained that the African champions had an unfair advantage with such Mexico-like heights at home. Until Keino and his team-mates descended to Munich and beat them there too.

The Subukia Valley. From Nyahururu the Subukia track makes a scenic and convenient short cut to Nakuru. Out of town [0] between the hospital and prison, past the 'Nyahururu Country Lodge' (r.)[7], then round a rocky bend [12½] and down a ledge which landslides sometimes block but the view always redeems: a verdant and well-cultivated valley backed by the Marmanet Escarpment and stretching to either horizon. The Masai inhabitants called it *Ol Momoi Sidai*, the Beautiful Place (until they were moved in 1911 to the Southern Masai Reserve). Crossing this expansive farmland, you follow the 'Nakuru' sign (l.)[21] on past **St Peter's Church** (r.)[27½]. It stands almost idyllically English amidst lawns, Africa being only the flowers around and the Negroes uniform in school yellow and blue. Wooded clefts close the valley's southern taper as the track curves down to the cones of the volcanic plain. Kabazi, Berea and Bahati are canning factories, farms and forest, with avenues of conifer giving dignity to the acres of pyrethrum, coffee and maize. Tarmac recommences [50]; the green slopes are scattered garishly with the blocks of the Ngwataniro Secondary School, and you fork left [51½] past the **Rift Valley Motor Club** [56]. Off right, the escarpments form an amphitheatre. You top a final ridge of this cattle, maize and wheat country to overlook Lake Nakuru [59] and to drop beside the quarry to Hyrax Hill (p. 116)[64½].

Via Gilgil and the Uganda Road. Leaving Nyahururu [0], the Gilgil Road has little of interest save the **Equator** [4](7747 feet a.s.l.) and fine panoramas of farmland and Lake Ol Bolossat (l.). Israeli road-builders surfaced this often treacherous track in 1971-72. **Ol Kalau**/Kalou [36] offers an alternative route (r.) through the Dundori Forest to Nakuru (p. 117), the 'Province of Kenya' St Peter's Church (l.) and numerous Acheulian hand-axes now housed at Hyrax Hill (p. 116). You then wind across farmland and drop from the plateau, past Kenyatta Barracks (l.) to the **Gilgil War Cemetery** (r.)[66]. Four cactus stand sentinel at the gate and the usual Kei-apple encloses 225 Commonwealth graves.

The cemetery register remarks on this 'somewhat treeless and wind-swept valley, very cold at night' and perhaps Gilgil became the site of the colony's main barracks because it is, like Caterick, regulation bleak. The scattered installations are now used by the Kenya Army, the Posts & Telecommunications and the Salvation Army . . . all unlikely successors to the 'Happy Valley Crowd' of the 1930s that made this 'swinging Gilgil'.

Turn right at the township's T-junction [0]. Or, coming **from Nairobi**, keep 27 kms straight on from Naivasha (p. 58). Gilgil ends aptly with more barracks (l.) and the **National Youth Service** School (r.)[2½]. Many airstrips, bore-holes and remote makeshift 'roads' are the work of its two-year, often teenage volunteers, provided only with transport, tools, food, uniforms and ex-US army tents for themselves and their womenfolk. The tarmac follows a ledge down to a plain picturesque with volcanic humps – and the pink-rimmed **Lake Elmentaita**. Like Lake Nakuru it is famed for its flamingos – PHOENICOPTERUS RUBER – and one of the greater variety's favourite African haunts. Pelicans breed on the rocky islands also (and at any time of year); Elmentaita being alkaline and fishless, they fetch food by daily commuting to Nakuru. Like Naivasha's the name is a Swahili corruption, of the Masai's *Il-muteita*. Its shores today are mainly farmed, with ploughshares unearthing prehistoric artefacts at Oleolondo, Prospect Farm and **Gambles Cave**. At the last, which you may visit from Lake Nakuru Lodge, Dr Leakey in 1928 discovered a prehistoric puzzle: four skeletons, contracted as at Hyrax Hill, but with Caucasian, not Negro characteristics.

Modern farm-fences keep you at a distance (but not hippos off the crops); though the D 321 brings you no nearer than does the main road, it enables you to say you drove around the lake at least. Indicated 'Elementaita' (l.)[5], it also brings you faster to Lake Nakuru Lodge [25 kms], the park's Nderit Gate [27 kms] and the main Nakuru-Narok route (p. 119). The track drops across cattle country, running at the **Mau Escarpment**. With 'Mau Narok' straight on, you turn right [17], cross the Delamere Estates, leave the Nderit and Lanet gates off left and rejoin the main road near Lanet [38].

Kariandusi. Below the turn-off stands the Scottish Protestant Church of Goodwill (r.), built as Lady Cole's thanksgiving when her sons returned safe from World War II. And beyond this (l.)[7½] the 'Kariandusi Prehistoric Site Open Daily from 8 am to 6 pm'. Until recently a diminutive national park, Kariandusi was discovered in 1928 by Dr Leakey's second East Africa Expedition, to be excavated by the Leakeys in 1929-31 and 1946-47 (entry Ksh. 5/-, children 2/-, residents 2/-, 1/-, under 3s free). The site's latest acquisition comes first: behind the car park (l.) an embryonic museum-shed (1977) containing to date only pictures, maps and hand-axes, but astounding with its announcement that 'The Spot where you now stand was at one time' – 9500 years ago – 'under some 200 ft of water'. Exhibited below – 'Visitors should not go down . . . without a guide' – are hand-

axes and cleavers of obsidian (a black volcanic glass, p. 59) plus a molar of ELEPHAS ANTI-QUUS, the straight-tusked, extinct jumbo that once roamed Europe and even England. From here wooden steps descend through a pretty defile – where Rock hyrax scamper and sandmartins sometimes nest – to the shallow trenches dug in 1973-75. For the layman the pits of the diatomite works adjoining are rather more striking than this 'Lower Site'.

The high-grade **diatomite** mined beside the main road [8] is an 'accumulation of skeletons of microscopic algae' used industrially in paints and insulating products and tribally to whiten Masai faces. Rolling acacia and cattle-ranch country follows. The 'Delamere Estates Soysambu' (l.) survive as a monument to Hugh Cholmondely, 3rd **Baron Delamere.** Hunting south from Somalia in 1897, he had been so struck with central Kenya that he settled for good in 1903: to rent this 100,000-acre tract for an 'excessive' £190 annually, to exhaust his personal fortune in attracting and bettering white-settler development and, though paralyzed, to galvanize and publicize

Hippos grazing – unusually by day – on the Lake Nakuru shore

the farmers' aspirations in their three-cornered tussle with the Africans and HMG. Had Jewry in 1905 not rejected the White Highlands as a proposed National Home, the further complications would have been unthinkable.

The road runs straight at Menengai, regular and flat-topped like an upturned bowl; between the turnings (l.)[32] to the Lanet Gate, Lion Hill Camp and Lake Nakuru Lodge and (r.)[32½] to 'Thomsons Falls Lodge 65 km/Maralal Safari Lodge 217 km'; past the Hyrax Inn (l.), 'Nakuru Blankets' and (also r.) State House [39].

Hyrax Hill. A last-minute stay to the 'Rift Capital' however is this prehistoric site. Sign-posted right [38] then immediately right again, it is open from 8 a.m. to 6 p.m. (prices as at Kariandusi). A farm-house converted in 1965 contains a small but illustrative display of pottery, pestles, hand-axes, beads, and tools of obsidian and flint, while a 'museum on the spot' consists of an Iron Age settlement and hill fort, a Neolithic cemetery and a 'village' of thirteen pit-dwellings. Here the parallel rows of holes carved symmetrically in the rock show that the game of *Bau* was played in prehistoric times as it is today in East Africa and Arabia. Though one caged skeleton 500 yards downhill is the only present exhibit, the cemetery offered food for thought: females were buried with their chattels (pestles, dishes and platters), males *tels quels*. Most skeletons lay contracted, some inhumed with relative finesse, others left pell-mell. Experts no better than laymen can conjecture what social system or beyond-the-grave beliefs this represents. For advanced beginners the *Visitor's Guide* is a good 1/- crib. Whilst investigating the **Nakuru Burial Site** in 1926, Dr Leakey 'noticed' Hyrax Hill; Mrs Leakey started digging in 1937 and excavations, repeated in 1938 and 1965, were recently resumed.

Menengai. The next sign by the main road [40] read 'Menengai Picnic Site 10 kms'. Removed perhaps because it was wrong (the distance being only eight kms), it sent you off right to Menengai Drive (2nd r.) and (4th l.) up Crater Climb: via maize and murram past the Voice of Kenya transmitter and satellite [2 kms] to the Menengai Forest Camp Picnic Site [5](also l.; **camping** Ksh. 3/- p.n., children 1/50), thereafter alongside fresh afforestation to the crater rim, 7466 feet above sea-level. The view now is sublime. Somewhat ridiculous is the Rotary Club's sign with the distance and direction of sundry local and overseas cities: 'London 6924 kms/ New York 12560'. The far slopes, seven miles away, are often lost in haze. On the 35-square-mile crater floor, 1425 feet below, lie the *morani* victims of a famous battle wherein, most probably in 1854, the Naivasha Masai finally defeated the Laikipia Masai by forcing them over these cliffs. (*Menengai* is Masai for Place of Corpses and the site, one local said, is 'popular for suicides'.)

Topping Menengai Drive, Showground Road serves St Christopher's Church (HC 7.30 a.m. 2nd & 4th Sundays, services 9.30 & 6.30 p.m.) and the **Nakuru North Cemetery**. The Commonwealth War Graves here – 26 from the Great War, 45 from World War II – are in a Kipling-esque corner at the back: 'Ye who pass by tell England that we who died serving her rest here content'. In the last War Nakuru was the site of an RAF flying training school. Showground Road continues past the Rift Valley General Hospital and Medical School (r.), the Nakuru show-ground (l.)[1½ kms] and the **Nakuru Golf Club**'s eighteen-hole course (off r.). It then becomes the route to Bogoria and Baringo.

Lake Nakuru. The crater view at Menengai is rivalled by that of the Solai Valley and Lake Nakuru. 'This is the finest bird lake I have seen,' said Peter Scott. 'Unquestionably the greatest' (or 'most fabulous')(or 'finest') ornithological spectacle on earth', is Roger Tory Peterson's much-misquoted endorsement. 'Well worth making a national park,' the authorities thought, and turned this into a 14,540-acre reality in 1961. Count Teleki had reported the 'little bitter water lake' of 'Nakuro Sekelai' in 1888.

It was because the lake had been further embittered – by pollution from Nakuru and the farmland around – that the park was in 1974 increased to 50,500 acres. Until rainfall raised the lake in 1979, dispersing the plankton and with it the Lesser **flamingos**, Nakuru possessed the world's largest con-centration, sometimes as many as 2 million, and the 750,000 gallons of sewage that poured into it daily were presumed (wrongly) to threaten their existence. Calls for action, not only from Prince Philip and Prince Bernhard of the Netherlands, were so vociferous and so effective that the Kenya government in 1974 urgently requested the help of the World Wildlife Fund. It responded promptly: with £132,000 for a larger park – lakeside farms like John Hopcraft's 'Baharini' being bought up and old west-bank land ceded in exchange for an eastern 'sanitary cordon'; with £40,000 for 44 miles of (never completed) perimeter fence, and with further funds for the **Nakuru Wildlife Trust** – the late Baharini Wildlife Sanctuary – to convert six rondavels from 1916 and install a Wildlife Clubs Hostel in 1977. A President's Pavilion and the luxurious Lion Hill Camp have been built, the Nderit farm-premises developed as Lake Nakuru Lodge and new tracks cut, bringing the park's network to 110 kms. Though the lake's 400-odd bird species upstage for many the hinterland's mammals, the ecological gerrymandering has brought the latter's species over 50: Bohor reedbuck and Defassa waterbuck, zebra, Grant's gazelle and leopards with baboons to feed them, buffaloes, rhinos and some 30 hippopotami, spotted hyaenas and now Rothschild's giraffe, 'transplanted' from Soy in 1977.

From the Menengai turning take the main road into town and follow the signs (l.) over the roundabout [0]: down Bondeni Road past the Sunni mosque built in '1352' (the Muslims' 1934) and the Seventh-day Adventist, Presbyterian and Pentecostal churches. A 'Florida Day & Night Club' lies cheek by jowl beside the new park fence, and the park gate [4] a half-km. beyond the memento of this extension: 'Inaugurated . . . on . . . World Environment Day June 5th 1974'.

Until the waters beyond the gate subside, you pay the usual fees (p. 50) and turn back to the east-lake track. It leads (l.) past the 'Hippo Point N° 1' and 'N° 2' (both r.), the former neighboured by the **Wildlife Clubs Hostel** (l.)[5½], the latter (when not flooded) by the Observation Hide (r.)[7]. After the Lanet Exit (l.)[2 kms], the Observation Tower (r.)[9] – with its plan of the lake's localities and sundry denizens – is for the time being an inaccessible island. On this northern shore are the fresh springs that supplement the lake's inflow from three seasonal rivers. Migrants congregate here during Europe's winter, and the pelicans often stop by to wash off soda. The lake is drained not by any outlet but by evaporation alone, which maintains its alkalinity and accounts for the 'simple but delicately balanced ecosystem'. **Lion Hill Camp** enhances the hillside (l.)[11½], the well-marked track continues south through Kenya's finest **euphorbia forest** and indicated (r.)[20½] is **Lake Nakuru Lodge**. The more open southern shore is crossed by the Nderit and Makalia rivers– the latter with a **camp site** by the falls [33] – and backed by the Rift's western wall.

Straight on from the gate [4] the track is bordered by a useful sketch-plan (l.), the Njoro **camp site** [5](r.; 'Only . . . with valid Tickets') and the 'Shoreline Drive' (l.)[6½]. High water means a detour to the President's Pavilion, 'Baboon Cliff Lookout' and Colobus Forest ahead and, even when low, the lake is best reached by the track (l.)[5] marked 'Home of the Cormorants and Mouth of Njoro River'. From the forest of tight acacia and abundant monkeys you emerge through sedge to the primaeval shore, the drowned trees eerie skeletons and the mud strangely spongy, soda-white. The myriad flamingos – more Lesser than Greater – feed head upside-down, their tongue pumping water that the bill then filters for its blue-green algae. In horseshoe flotillas the pelicans dive as one, their ungainly pouch an effective dip-net. They number about 9000 but, like the flamingos, breed elsewhere. Lines of spoonbills comb the shallows, driving the shoals like Kerkenna fishermen. The flamingos were reckoned to remove 150 tons of lake algae each day; fish-eaters share some fifteen tons.

Nakuru – 'Place of the Waterbuck'? – began with a shop in 1900 when the railwaymen paused before the climb to Londiani. (The railway station – l. as you enter – is still Kenya's smartest.) The oldest town up country, with settlers from 1903, Nakuru is now the country's fourth largest. An enterprising American missionary started a cottage industry of **flamingo-feather** 'flower arrangements' (now made by a score of crippled boys, based at the Bethany Bookshop and sold widely); the Nakuru Tanners make good sheepskin coats, but pyrethrum does most for Nakuru's prosperity.

From the first roundabout, the main Kenyatta Avenue cuts across town. Its centre is recognizable only by an old gas-lamp (given by the City of London as thanks for Nakuru's contribution to a Spitfire in World War II). It illuminates Club Road (l.), in which the **Rift Valley Sports Club** reciprocates with several Kenyan and London clubs, sports a 'Mens Bar, Ladies not allowed' and has private swimming, squash, tennis, billiard and cricket facilities which the secretary may or may not let you use. In the main road the **Stag's Head Hotel** (l.) is one storey higher but hardly smarter than the **Midland Hotel** (r.; formerly the 'Railway' and initially – in 1906 – the Nakuru Hotel). Beyond them both, the late Arboretum (l.; 1927) is now *choos*, benches and bums.

THE NORTH AND WEST EXTREMITIES

THE MASAI MARA

Time was when, in German tourist parlance, the Mara formed part of the Classic *Ostafrika-safari*. Couriers called it on the other hand the 'Milk Run' . . . until Tanzania closed its border and – without the Serengeti, Ngorongoro and Olduvai – the Kenyan sector became a cul-de-sac. The hunting ban contributed to its come-back: while some redundant, ex-professional hunters turned to hosting photo-tours, others run tented camps. As a result accommodation in the Mara – two lodges and one Governor's Camp in 1976 – multiplied threefold in the following three years.

The Mara merits such attention and investment. With wildlife increasingly poached out elsewhere, it is fast becoming known as 'the best game country remaining in Kenya today'. Unique amongst the country's reserves in not confining drivers to the tracks, it is also the best for game-viewing. Lions, leopards, cheetahs and rhinos are seen; hippos inhabit the Talek and Mara rivers; on the plains zebra, wildebeest, some 4000 topi and even Roan antelope overflow from the Serengeti next door. Visit the Mara during the annual, month-long Migrations and the wildlife spectacle is both certain and astonishing: the dry-grass plains and gentle hills are close-speckled black with antelope; the tracks become congested not with cars but herds, and the gnus, when 'spooked', stampede away in one unending corrida of flying hooves and dust.

Fabulous game-viewing, but infuriating tracks . . . and of late ruinous 'human erosion'. The 700 square miles of this former national reserve were, like Amboseli's (p. 92), entrusted in March 1961 to the local African District Council. They however got an early start on their Kajiado colleagues by straight-way giving national park status to a 200-square-mile Inner Reserve. Their beau idéal has unfortunately lapsed in the course of twenty years. The Masai since, caring less for game than cattle, have increasingly reclaimed larger areas of land. Already a quarter of the Inner Reserve has been lost; authorities connive at the shrinking boundaries, while the locals and their cattle continue to encroach.

Given which, the Narok County Council could scarcely be expected to pay for tourist routes. With those in the west extended if not improved, the Masai Mara is now *per se* a circuit (which Naivasha, close to the route from Nairobi, and Nakuru, one step beyond, complement). Developments have outdated every map – especially, thank goodness, the pirated Ines May reprint – and the price of *A Field Guide to Masai Mara Reserve* should guarantee it an exclusive readership.

If motoring in the Mara is rough, **ballooning** is smooth. Putting an idea of Jules Verne's to the test, Anthony Smith and Douglas Botting made a gas-fired flight from Zanzibar in 1962. (They described their mishaps in *Throw Out Two Hands*, these being not the crewmen but the handfuls of ballast discarded to gain height.) Their passenger, Alan Root, saw the scope for wildlife photography offered by such silent and low-flying craft – others the tourist potential. Promoted by Root's film *Safari by Balloon*, Keekorok Lodge in 1976 introduced 'the world's first and only scheduled passenger service'. The passengers number five, plus pilot; as with Air Libre at the Serena and Governor's Camp, the schedule starts daily at 7 a.m. In fifteen minutes the ten-storey-high Montgolfier is filled

Balloon safari over the Mara

with 4000 hot cubic metres of air; you squeeze into the basket below and take off – to drift serenely with the wind in what Spike Milligan called a 'transport of delight'. A chase vehicle follows, within radio contact and sight; you float at a maximum fifteen mph and ideally treetop height, but 'could without difficulty go up to 15,000 feet'. Were, perhaps, the champagne breakfast before and not after the flight.

From Nairobi follow the Naivasha route (pp. 56, 58) and on to the B 3, the New Narok Road (l.)[51½]. Far more imposing than Mount Margaret (p. 56), **Mount Suswa** rises to the left, but the driver will not like it if you ask him to reconnoitre the track to the crater rim, or stop and take a Masai guide to its 24 rambling and guano-floored **Bat Caves**. After rolling grass plains and the Ngong track (l.; p. 53)[82], the road is a reassuring ribbon of black across the tip of the escarpment ahead. Mile after undulating mile, then a dip across the pretty Seyabei River [134]

and, from the drier plateau, a long drop into **Narok** [144]: police, petrol and a swinging Narok Inn with loud music, murals and cheap accommodation.

From Nakuru to Narok runs a route proclaimed by Nairobi travel agents as 'opening up a new safari circuit': the few who have tried it quietly drop it from their tours. The westbound Uganda Road on from Nakuru [0] leaves town via the Pivot Hotel (l.) and forks left to Njoro by 'Njoro Valley Cheeses' [5](r.; many well-publicized makes but few ever available). From the Njoro T-junction [6½] the C 56 (r.) leads to Molo and Kericho (p. 120). The C 57 (l.) climbs smooth from rich farmland and ranchland to forest reserve and a Kentish country of farmed rolling downs. Across the Nderit River [46] the district of **Mau Narok** (r.) [50½] was developed as a result of the European Settlement Scheme of the early 1950s. The D 320 (l.)[51] is the short cut to Elmentaita (p. 114), Mathera [55] a very

English church and the start of dire African murram. Then down, bone-shaken, to the green and hazy plains, on to a caricature of tarmac and, via the hospital you feel you need by then, into Narok [118].

Turn left at the Narok T-junction [0]. The jacaranda, acacia and Masai are picturesque compensation for the track as you cross the Narok River, rise past St Peter's and St Mary's schools and the Narok Club (also r.) – 'Welcome Drink' – and check in at the **Mara Game Sanctuary** barrier [16]: 'To all Vistors . . . all Check post (points) Close at 7 p.m. and Open every Morning at 6-30 a.m.'. Exit right [17] the B 3 to Kericho and the west-side camps, left the C 12 and the turning to 'Cottars' Mara Camp 75 k.m.'. The track becomes a motorist's nightmare, all rock and gravel with a high centre ridge. It then improves marginally as, crossing the Loita Plains, you ignore the 'Masai Mara' signs (l.) [53½], leave **Cottars' Camp** eight kms off left [84] and reach the Olemelepo Gate [96] (vehicle and driver Ksh. 20/-, each passenger 15/-, under 16s 7/50; open 6.30 a.m.-7 p.m.; 'Camping is strictry Prohibited'). Thereafter the tracks are such that both UTC and Block Hotels keep *fundis* at **Keekorok Lodge** [107]. With an annual £8000 for the running of the reserve, the Kenya government in 1961 allotted £25,000 for the lodge's construction. It was money well spent: the restaurant, cottages, lawns and pool are an aesthetic amenity (which the elephant and buffalo appear to appreciate too). A petrol station, the resident mechanics, the balloon base and an airstrip adjoining make Keekorok also a traveller's oasis.

Ten kms southward, the Tanzania border is the Olngayanet – Sand – River. Until and unless politics permit you across and into the Serengeti, the onward journey is through the Mara 'Triangle'. On tracks clearly marked beyond Keekorok [0], the Mara New Bridge [30] takes you over the same-named river. Here, by the map, is 'Hippo Pool', but

marabous and vultures are more likely sights, feeding on the animals that failed, leming-like, to make the crossing. To the right of the T-junction [52½] lies **Mara Serena Lodge** [56], scenic atop Ol Donyo Oseyia and splendidly 'ethnic'. Prince Charles spent a tented holiday here in 1971 and you can do so, almost as royally, at any of the vicinity's camps. **Fig Tree** is indicated equally well from the northern Narok-Ngorengore track as from the reserve's Talek Gate [19 rough kms from Keekorok]: 'Keep Silence when Approaching all game Animals . . . Any noises made will make your Revelations Uninteresting'.

Turning left at the Serena junction instead [52½ from Keekorok] and right one km. beyond the Olololo Gate [75½], you soon have an *embarras de choix*. Down in the forest (r.) [78½], **Kichwa Tembo** – Elephant's Head – was sited here by Abercrombie and Kent in May 1978. One km. straight on before the Mara River bridge [82½], **Mara Sara** occupies a clearing, scenic (and sonorous) with rapids alongside. Cross the bridge and persevere two kms more: **Mara River Camp** (l.) is an ill-equipped, riverside glade 1½ kms downhill (bookings through Nairobi POB. 45456, tel. 21992-4). With communal loo and mess tent, and tents without water or light, it contrasts sadly with the suave **Governor's Camp** (r.)[85]. Taking pot-luck on the twelve-km. maze of unmarked tyre-ruts to it – the longest distance between two points – you appreciate why most clients fly.

The next overnight stop – and the last for many a mile – is then **Mara Buffalo Camp**, beside the river down the six-km. track (l.)[94]. The enterprising management in 1979 had the inmates counted in a wallow two miles off: a total of 120 is the basis of their claim to the 'best-stocked **Hippo Pool** in Kenya'. The main track continues, shattering: over hillier parkland and slopes of acacia and cattle, past Lemek [127½] and down to the plain and the 'main' B 3: right to Narok [200], left to Kericho and points west.

KERICHO, KISUMU, KISII AND KAKAMEGA

Those motoring through western Kenya were, until recent years, usually in transit to Uganda. But off the main road, itself an attraction, lie Kericho and the tea country, Kisumu on the shores of Lake Victoria, Kisii, Kakamega and the Lambwe Valley, and Kitale with two national parks near by. Splendid roads through scenic hills, plus fine

hotels at Kericho, Kisumu and Homa Bay, make this a suave and relaxed exception to the new 'safari circuits'.

From Nakuru (p. 117)[0] the main A 104 crosses open country of first corn, then acacia, candelabra and cattle. Turnings are sign-posted (l.; p. 119) to Njoro and Mau Narok, (r.)[16] to Eldama Ravine and (misleadingly) Marigat and Kabarnet. **Njoro** – Spring – was originally planned as the capital of 'British East Africa'. **'Ravine'**, now agricultural, was significantly administrative in the late 1890s, when Sir Frederick Jackson commanded its fortified government outpost. **Rongai**, which you bypass [28], was important for maize in the 1900s and the crop still grows in clearings of the **Londiani Forest** ahead. Atop Mount Londiani's escarpment, roads (l.) are marked [43] to **Molo** and [52] to Kericho. The former is known for its lamb and its **Highlands Hotel**; the latter starts, above the West Mau forests, with model workers' villages on the green tea slopes [106].

From the Mara the faint-hearted should return to Narok and, via Mau Narok and Njoro (p. 119), rejoin my Kericho route west of Nakuru (above). (Milksops who sneak back on the hardtop through Naivasha will regret it: much of the main road on to Nakuru is a poor imitation of a tarmac cart-track.) Bolder spirits brave the B 3 (p. 120), west from Ngorengore through Bomet. For the absolutely dauntless is the **Ololoolo Escarpment**: even without 'the Rains' I have slithered here 60 miles in second gear. And when your vehicle advances mostly sideways, much of the scenery tends to be missed. From Serena Lodge continue, or from the Mara River camps drive back, to the T-junction [0] outside the Ololoolo Gate. Assuming you succeed the ascent, turn right at Lolgorien [27] and cross the Maghor River [36]. Then start looking for locals to ask the way on through Kilgoris [58] and finally up to tarmac [115½]: left to Sotik and right to Kericho [169].

Kericho. The point of all this is the big tea country. Kericho (pronounced 'Kereeecho', not like Jericho) is Kenya's tea capital (pp. 29, 56), its first bush planted in 1906 and its first large commercial estate started in 1924. On the fragrantly lovely hills around, tea-lovers can learn how their beverage originates: daily except Sunday the well-run **Tea Hotel** organizes free, three-hour tours of the nurseries, the green-leaf and Instant Tea factories and (sometimes) the Tea Research Institute. Brooke Bond Liebig run the hospital and aerodrome and cater for conferences in their training centre; the town centre is Chai – Tea – Square. That a Kericho & Sotik Fishing Association is active speaks for itself: anglers are well guided by the river map on display in the hotel foyer. The estates' smart young planters long enjoyed an eligible reputation

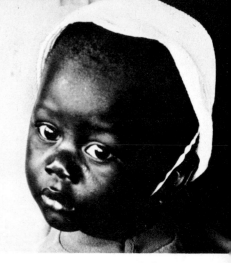

Ja-Luo jnr

with snobbier up-country daughters. Now the town is Kipsigis African. The **Church of the Holy Trinity** (English service Sundays 9.30 a.m.) has nevertheless a tower wistfully overgrown with ivy and, also on the village green, a War Memorial of unhewn rock reads '*Kibwate Ijeget*', 'We Will Remember Them'.

Though the 80-km. B 1 from Kericho to Kisumu was surfaced in 1971, a short cut from the Uganda Road is the murram track marked at Londiani (above)[66 kms from Nakuru]. At **Fort Ternan** [112], built by Major Trevor T. in 1897, Dr Leakey in 1961 excavated what he described as 'Africa's richest known source for animal life 14 million years ago'. After the sugar township of Muhoroni, where Lord Kitchener of Khartoum retired to farm in 1910, you rejoin the Kisumu road [144]. Oddly, it was not the steep climb to Fort Ternan but the easy terrain to the lake that troubled the railwaymen. Americans in 1903 built the Mau Summit's tunnels and 27 bridges, spanning 11,850 feet in 73 miles. Then, however, the soft lake littoral made derailments regular throughout the 1900s. The **Nandi**, too, would keep pilfering material: telegraph wire for their womenfolk's knick-knacks, rivets for weapons and occasionally whole rails. One of the few tribes to oppose and oust the Masai, then the only one 'which actively resisted British occupation', the Nandi finally sealed their own doom by killing nine soldiers in 1905: a punitive force was despatched, this 'Nandi Rebellion' put down and the *laibon* responsible executed. Giving their name to the hills, as well as the flame-

121

Kipsigis market – baskets and pots

tree and a Yeti-like 'bear', the Nandi share the country with their **Kipsigis** relatives, formerly called the Lumbwa.

On the Kano Plains that the road next crosses the women walk upright, their burdens on their heads, no longer bent beneath back-loads like the Kikuyu. These **Ja-Luo** (p. 10) of Nyanza – north and south of the Kavirondo Gulf – are now Kenya's second largest group and influential in both government and business. (Early settlers feared them for all that as 'cannibals' who 'carried to an extreme the habit of nudity'.)

Kisumu, their capital, enters history with the Uganda Railway, which reached this then 'Port Florence' on 20 December 1901. The Luo name means 'Where one goes to get one's needs': the later nickname – Gateway to Lake Victoria – has rather lost relevance since the suspension of the railway's steamer service. With the exception of the 'Octopos Bottoms-up Club', the sights are mainly ecclesiastical: St Paul's Catholic Church and Cathedral of St Theresa, a 'Coptic Church 20th Century' and Church of Christ in Africa, a Shraddhanand Ashram temple, green and silver twin-minareted mosque and 'duolith' monument in memory of an arch-deacon. Should you be in town for a Sunday procession, the religious interest is not merely buildings but frenetic hot gospelling.

Spreading with the increasing importance of this 'Western capital', the suburbs are attractively African-administrative; Nyanza Province offices, housing estates and schools are all neatly indicated; left of the Nairobi Road in from Kericho, the **Kisumu Museum** has been on the point of opening since 1977. Lodging for visitors had scarcely improved on the 'Railway Dak Bungalow' of 1904 until in 1977 the KTDC completed the **Sunset Hotel**: left into Kakamega Road between the Wimpy and Archdeacon Owen's memorial, past the cinema, the lavish bank and the **New Kisumu Hotel** (all l.) and 1½ kms south along the shore. The town centre is a clock-tower 'Unveiled . . . in 1938 . . . in Memory of Kasim Lakha'. Though the shop-names, and atmosphere, of the streets around are Asian, Kisumu's mark on Kenya's history is as the childhood home of **Tom Mboya**.

Kisii. Running south from the Kericho road at Ahero [24], a good road – the A 1 – rises from the Kano Plains. A local attraction are ornithological colonies: the 'great **heronry** near Kisumu' recorded in 1901 and protected since 1976 is noisy with up to 1000 pairs nesting from March to July. Sacred ibis breed at the same time in an easily accessible '**ibisery**' amidst Ahero's paddies and, climbing to Kisii, you pass Oyugis [87], where a '**pelicanry**' is in season' between August and March (via the three-km. track behind the shanty-shops l.). Attractive on its well-farmed slopes, Kisii [110] possesses sundry schools, just-passable hotels, soapstone-carvers and, like Kisumu, a multitude of sects. The Bantu Kisii people, *alias* the **Abagusii**, were first subjected to a government station in 1907. In the Great War's bitty skirmishings the township repeatedly changed hands, the retreating British commander leaving drinks in his headquarters for his German counter-part and the latter leaving a note of thanks when he in turn withdrew.

Lambwe Valley National Park. Turn off the A 1 south of Kisii [110] to the C 20 (r.)[134]: 'Homa Bay 32 km'. This broad track drops from the Abagusii hills to the flatter Luo littoral: candelabra cactus and neat shambas fenced with agave. After its airstrip [162] Homa Bay appears, the view divided by two abrupt cones and framed by the lakeside peaks. Marked (l.)[166], the park is said to start 27 kms further . . . but seems to receive more attention from authors than authorities. A game reserve upgraded in 1976, 'Olambwe' has been declared but not delimited. Its approach is good in parts, skirting sisal estates and a volcanic bump [17-22 kms]. A sign 'Tolambwe Park' (l.) sends you edging along wheel-ruts, little used and unusable when wet. As the cultivated shambas continue unabashed, you soon realize that there are no boundaries, no gate, perhaps no park and probably no hope of seeing the 200-odd Roan antelope it supposedly protects.

Longer heads will disregard it and return to Kisumu via Kendu Bay: from Homa Bay [169], a seedy fishing and administrative centre redeemed by the **Homa Bay Hotel** (l.); along the pretty C 19 and (r.)[200½] by the **Kendu Bay** health centre; up past schools and the Kendu Mission Hospital (l.) to the Kisii-Kisumu road at Oyugis (p. 122)[221].

The least testing alternative is the way back through Kericho. From Kisii [0] the B 3 winds through the high country of the Abagusii and Kipsigis. Keroka [27½] is a busy dip with its market colourful and its school 'St Augustus High'. The patchwork hillsides of shambas and bandas gradually give way to larger tea estates; the road leaves Sotik to the right [52½], between the turnings to Kilgoris (p. 121) and 'Bomet 36/Narok 138 km', then high russet cuttings and steep green tea-fields are the approaches to Kericho (p. 121)[105].

Kakamega. North from Kisumu [0] the A 1 climbs past the Muhoroni turn-off (r.; p. 121). The Nyando Escarpment rises almost sheer amidst the big boulder country that characterizes the lake hinterland. After the **Equator** [14] long dips and rises take the road on across slopes thick with shambas, stands of eucalyptus and occasional tea-fields. Kakamega commences with schools and seminaries, an open-air market (r.), a prison (l.) and a suburb of municipal and Western Province offices [50]. Off left, the township's clock-tower is a masterpiece of unloveliness, erected 'by Subscriptions from all Races' for the silver anniversary in 1935 of George V's accession. A decade earlier, gold finds were making a short-lived Klondike of Kakamega. A more durable asset is the botanically 'West

Kericho country – picking tea

African' **Kakamega Forest**, known for its snakes and exclusive birds – and best entered by the track (r.) 0·8 kms after the Approved School [54]. The tarmac thereafter meets the Uganda Road [94] near Webuye, the former Broderick Falls.

Eldoret lies 67 kms on the road back (r.) to Nairobi, beyond the Kipkarren River [118], Turbo (5934 feet) and the Kitale junction (below). Perhaps because it was developed by Boers (who sailed lock, stock and barrel from the Cape and then came from Mombasa in two epic 'Treks'), Eldoret with pukka British settlers was something of a joke. The bank, they will tell you, was built around its safe because this dropped off the wagon that brought it and proved too heavy to move. The place lacked a name until 1912, being simply '64' (the number of the farm plot its first post office occupied). Unworried, it now flourishes as a market town, spacious with woollen and saw-mills and simple churches, St John's Catholic, St Matthew's Anglican. Hotels are the roadside New Lincoln and New Paradise and, off right, the New Wagon Wheel – the 'new' in fact applicable only to the **Mahindi** (l.).

The road home crosses this **Uasin Gishu Plateau** – afforestation, prairie and rarefied air – to top the Timboroa Summit – 9320 feet and the railway's highest point – and dip across the **Equator** at 9109 feet. Heaving on over deep orange hills, where mixed farms alternate with Londiani Forest, it descends past the turnings to Kericho and Njoro (pp. 121, 119) and, 160 kms from Eldoret, comes to Nakuru.

KITALE, MOUNT ELGON, SAIWA SWAMP AND KAPENGURIA

North of Eldoret [0] on the main A 104, the B 2 is clearly indicated (r.)[13] to Kitale. It crosses the ranched plateau to Soy [22], where the **Soy Country Club** is pleasantly restful with orange-pink cottages around the lawns. Farmland, mostly under maize, alternates with wattle; the Loreto Convent and Matunda – Fruit – Mission are followed by Moi's Bridge; the former Greaves Farm (l.)[58] has changed its name but still offers hostel accommodation and **camping** (Ksh. 5/- p.n.). Then comes **Kitale** [69], since 1926 the railhead capital of this **Trans-Nzoia** district. The old *Trans-Nzoia Scrap-book* gives a quaint account of its settler history, but the **National Museum of Western Kenya** is easier to find. This 'Stoneham Museum' was founded, private, by the same-named colonel in 1926. It was taken over, rehoused and renamed in 1973 by Kenya National Museums; with the Peace Corps' help, they extended his collection – 35,668 African butterflies and 21,606 African moths, trophies, birds and ethnographical objects – with displays of Pokot, Turkana, Ma'rakwet, Abaluhya and even Akamba village crafts (9.30 a.m.-6 p.m. daily, 2-6 p.m. on national holidays; entry Ksh. 1/-, schoolchildren -/50).

Mount Elgon National Park. The patchy tarmac of the pot-holed C 45 takes you from Kitale [0] to Endebess [19], whence the marked track (l. then r.) climbs – with difficulty when wet – to the finely sited **Mount Elgon Lodge** [29] and the Chorlim Gate [30] ('7000' feet a.s.l.; open 6 a.m.-6.30 p.m.; 'You enter this Park at your own Risk Good Luck'). The flora and fauna of primaeval forest, bamboo jungle and alpine moorland compensate for Mount Elgon's being the 'loneliest park in Kenya'. **Elephant Platform** [6 kms from the gate] is an easy first objective, dominating precipitously the confluence of four wooded valleys. Also marked above the Warden's offices, one km. (r.) from the gate, are the two **camp sites**, the Saito Dam and 'Koitoboss Peak 27 km'.

The **Elgon Caves** are an unusual national park feature. **Chepnyalil** lies en route to the Kimothon Gate (6 a.m.-6 p.m.). This giving on to Uganda, better follow instead the good tracks and signs to the **Kitum** Cave (l.)[5½ kms]. (The marker-post's '350 metres' means fifteen minutes on foot up a path strewn alarmingly with fresh droppings. Rocks half-block the shallow frog's mouth, its floor sloping off to an elephant-mire trough.) A one-car bridge, then the '**Makingeny** Cave 330 metres' (l.) entails an easier walk up a better beaten track: to a higher, wider cavern fronted by a waterfall, the forest pressing close on either side. Both caves are mouths of the mountain's vast network, and home no longer to the Elgon Masai but to bats and elephants, which you should beware. Elsewhere the park's 65 square miles are hazardous only with mud and rough tracks, with poachers from Uganda and Giant forest hog.

Saiwa Swamp National Park is the only place in Kenya to see with any certainty the rare sitatunga (p. 38). Because of its precious denizens – now 920 head – the swamp attracted the protective attention of the E.A. Wildlife Society in 1972, then became a national park only 473 acres small. Turning right opposite Kitale Museum [0], left at the roundabout then right into Cherengani Road [½], follow the Kapenguria and Lodwar signs (l.)[2]. On this fine new A 1, beyond Knight's Corner, a national park board points vaguely right [18½]: on the track immediately right again then left, past the police at Kipsain, the signs shape up and send you (l.)[22½] down to the three free **camp sites** and the gate [23½]. Entry is as yet also free and – again exceptionally for a national park – you walk an easy mile to the swamp and its treetop viewing platforms.

Kapenguria. The A 1 rolls on towards the **Cherangani Hills**, traverses Makutano and stops at Kapenguria [37]. Above the boma of this steep hill-centre (r.) stands an unobtrusive building: 'This Cell where H.E. Mzee Jomo Kenyatta and his five other colleagues were remanded during the famous **Kapenguria Trial** of 1952/53 has been set aside as a **National Monument**'.

LAKES BARINGO AND BOGORIA

More dramatic than Nakuru, within easier reach than Turkana, Lakes Bogoria and Baringo nestle close to the Rift's eastern wall. Touristically, as opposed to geographically, they are not so readily defined. Brochures describe Baringo as 'linked by fine new roads to Nakuru and the North': in fact the tracks both north and south have as yet next to no tar macadam. One publication reports Baringo 'so utterly secluded that even Dr Kissinger could relax without a bodyguard', another that the lake is already 'the nub of the Northern and Western tourist circuits'. While I myself find the region enticing, ecologists condemn it as a croton desolation eaten bleak by goats and gouged by topsoil erosion. (Baringo, admittedly, is much of the time mud-brown.) **Lake Baringo Lodge** was a personal favourite: after the miles of dust, a suddenly luxurious lakeside home, uniformed staff, pool on the lawns ... 'Well below par, needs upgrading', thought on the other hand Block Hotels, who took it over in March 1980 with that aim in mind.

Best simply see for yourself. Disregard the 'Marigat/Kabarnet' signs on the main road north and leave Nakuru via Showground Road (p. 116)[0]. Grassland soon yields to

sisal estates, the **sisal factory** (l.)[38] being an interesting white sight. At Mogotio [39] the D 365 veers off the B 4 (l.), which 'H.Z. & Co.' are currently surfacing through to 'Lake Baringo . . . 75 k.m.'. Both run into **Tugen** territory. Related to the Kipsigis and Nandi and speaking the same language, these Nilo-Hamites have as their most famous son President **Daniel Arap Moi**; daughters tend to leave one breast bare, and all graze their cattle and goats on this orange-soiled thornbush country. The D 365 deteriorates from average to appalling: Mugurin [60], Maji Moto – Hot Water [79] – and finally [80] **Lake Bogoria National Reserve** ('Every Adult 20/- Every Child 1/- Every Vehicle 20/- Camping anywhere 5/- p.p.p.n.').

Five kms of first-class grading usher you down to the exquisite lake: a million flamingos pink, the 2000-foot Siracho a stark escarpment behind, geysers and hot springs seething on the shore ... what J.W. Gregory in 1892 called 'the most beautiful view in Africa'. Seven years earlier **Bishop Hannington** stopped here, before moving on to be murdered in Uganda. Bogoria until recently was in consequence 'Lake Hannington'. Its waters rose dramatically in 1979, luring away

Lake Nakuru's flamingos and flooding the lakeside track. This made for better grazing on the eastern shore – 'Kenya's best place for Greater kudu' – and could scarcely make the driving any worse.

To face the dreadful rock track to Bogoria's northern gate [98½] and negotiate the 'short cut' to Baringo, you needed until recently a hired car and life insurance. Now patience is the word. With the Loboi Bridge in place [100], it may be twenty kms to the B 4 T-junction (r.). Another new bridge, across the Perakera Gorge, may put Marigat (r.) four kms further. But the current mess of road-works makes distances academic, and their one long skid-pan means that those in the back seat travel further.

Salvation comes in the shape of Lake Baringo. From the lodge you can fish, water-ski and sometimes swim. Bilharzia is absent and the crocodiles, due to defective skins, are seldom hunted so seldom molest. Giving wide berth to the hippopotami, and to the flimsy Pokot canoes, motor boats take you four miles out to Ol Kokwa – 'Meeting Place' – where the Island Camp is 25 double tents with shower and loo, bar, restaurant and resident Njemps (full board Ksh. 530/- double, 325/- single, residents 300/-, 200/-;

reservations via Thorn Tree Safaris, Nairobi POB. 42475, tel. 25641). Or to Gibraltar Island, where the Goliath heron colony is East Africa's largest (and the Njemps fear a legendary Loch Ness monster). On shore at Loimanange is the ruined Fort Baringo, a British-built outpost intended to stop slaving; near Kampi ya Samaki – Fish Camp – both David Roberts' three self-service cottages and Jonathan Leakey's Snake Farm. If only he fed its inmates the frogs that croak all night, Baringo's paradise would be unimpaired.

The drive on to Maralal brings one sharply (and literally) down to earth again. From the 'Kambi Samaki airstrip' [0] follow the murram marked 'Loruk B 4'. The former is shacks with painted façades [12½], the latter the Cherangani Hills route (p. 125), which you fork off from (r.)[13]. This D 370 up the Tangulbei Escarpment was in 1979 graded, aligned and proclaimed by Kenyans as a 'beautiful new road'. It is in fact 89 kms of 'all-weather' dirt – and sure to be corrugated by the time you arrive. Its two kms of tarmac on two steep stretches might just let the driver enjoy the fine view back over Baringo. The bridged and twisting climb terminates in the C 77 Maralal-Rumuruti (p. 128)[102].

MARSABIT, MARALAL AND ON TO LAKE TURKANA

The popularity of Kenya's northern circuit proves just how unpredictable visitors can be. Western Kenya is green, scenic and macadamed, with first-class hotels filled for all that only with officials and businessmen. The north is, on the other hand, rough: endless tracks across bleak terrain relieved solely by one mountain-oasis and one often wind-swept lake . . . and all now so alluring as the 'Great Escaperee' that flights run scheduled from the capital, land-tour operators offer 'regular departures' and an open lorry – the 'Turkana bus' – fills weekly with incurable ulu-bashing addicts.

Ideally, you should fly. As on all flights north from Nairobi you have, with luck, the unparalleled spectacle of Kilimanjaro and Mount Kenya both snow-capped below; then above the Aberdares, with distant glimpses of Lake Baringo and the Mathews Range, and down over Lake Logipi and the incredible Teleki's Volcano to Loyangalani, Eliye Springs or Ferguson's Gulf.

The drive is for motoring masochists. But as their numbers are increasing unashamedly in this day and age, the following pages give first-hand instructions on how to indulge. Note that tourists do not drive round the lake: Ferguson's Gulf entails a sortie out and back, Loyangalani likewise, but with Marsabit and Maralal as alternatives for the return.

Ferguson's Gulf, from Kitale, is just accessible (seasonally) by saloon. Though the tarmac ends at Kapenguria (p. 125), Norwegians in 1979 graded much of the 240 kms on to Lodwar. The route is not for sybarites but does allow the driver an occasional sight of the magnificent scenery: down the Kongelai Escarpment, 'ornithologically noteworthy', through the Marich Pass and on past precious few settlements but frequent, fascinating Suk/Pokot and Turkana. At Lodwar, still raided by Abyssinians in the 1900s, the simple house (l.) was Kenyatta's exile-home.

Twenty-four kms beyond the Turkana township [0] the sign points (r.) to 'Eliye Springs Fishing Club' [59]. Straight on, you cross grey-gravel plains and hills, very central Arabia, and drop to Ferguson's Gulf amid its white sand-dunes [72]. A fishing co-operative, a 1963 African Inland Mission, a Turkana settlement and erratic wire fences do not beautify the lakeside, but the guard at the jetty will flash his heliograph shaving mirror and the dinghy comes to ferry you across to **Lake Rudolf Angling Lodge**. Fishing is fantastic here almost from the doorstep. Should you not be content with the gulf's 200 species, take the lodge boat to the **Central Island** bird sanctuary, where flamingos *inter alia* breed on three volcanic lakes.

From Samburu via Marsabit. The Ethiopian Highway, according to the maps, connects these two direct, but the knowledgeable describe it as the 'worst trunk road in Kenya'. Shaking off Archer's Post (p. 110)[0], it soon curves towards the natural ramparts of Ol Donyo Sabachi. Camels, waitabit bushes, not even the Serengeti-like rock outcrops of isolated *inselbergs* make up for the track's corrugations.

The C 79, a cut **back to Maralal**, is marked 'Wamba' (l.)[21]. Climbing through a wide breach in humpy hills, fording the usually dry bed of the Namba River, it skirts that Samburu centre and turns into the C 78 (l.)[43 kms]. Through a narrower snick in more level hills, the track proceeds plumb-line straight. Zebra graze alongside cows and donkeys in the orange, thorn-tree scrubland of this Samburu outback. Lodungokwe [79 kms] is cradled by peaks, one rounded, one flat; a better route is under construction across 30 kms of the **Karisia Hills** and the track, itself better, traverses dry parkland to meet the C 77 [127 kms] from Rumuruti to Maralal (r.)[146 kms].

The Ethiopian Highway continues north across terrain more Arabia with oryx and bustard. The **Mathews Range** – Ol Donyo Lenkiyio – looms to the left; the 7460-foot periwinkle peak of Imirina (r.) turns into a Samurai hat on closer inspection. Laisamis permits this [129]. With a Catholic hospital and a Catholic church, it lies on the confines of the **Losai National Reserve** which, all unwitting, you have just finished crossing. A flow of brown basalt relieves the semi-

The 'Jade Sea': Lake Turkana

desert tedium [148]; Logaloga [179] is police and Rendille shacks, and the sandy plain gives way to hilly greenery with the **Marsabit National Reserve** [193].

Marsabit rises to 5993 feet, an upturned bowl of *gof*-crater lakes and forest. The mountain-oasis, now a **National Park**, had become almost synonymous with **Ahmed**, the bull elephant painted by David Shepherd, filmed by John Huston and featured in the *New York Times*. A 'living national monument', he received in 1970 the unique distinction of protection by presidential decree, but died none the less on 16 January 1974 . . . to be given an obituary in *Newsweek*. A post-mortem disappointed with the news that his tusks weighed only 67 kilos and his age was little over 55 years. The lore requires apparently that Marsabit have a 'king elephant': succeeding Mohammed in 1958, Ahmed was succeeded by Abdullah who, found dead in 1978, has in turn been succeeded by Mohammed (II ?).

Green segmented hills, as though of several craters, line the main track on to Ulanula and its **'Singing Wells'**, a famous watering spot for the Rendille's herds. From Marsabit 'town' [227] – boma, post office, police and (perhaps) petrol – the track (r.) climbs two kms to the national park gate (6 a.m.-6 p.m.; usual fees, plus Ksh. 5/- to camp) and two kms further to **Marsabit Lodge**. If desperate for this night-stop, use the park's 'back door', marked (r.)[215] 'Lake Paradise 6'. Four kms of boulders and bed-rock bring you to the junction of the better park track and thence (l.) to the lodge. The right-hand branch rises, treacherous when wet, through a forest dripping with Old Man's Beard. It thereafter deteriorates round the crater rim, so best stop on the top [3 kms from the junction]. On the slopes of *Sokorte Guda* – **Lake Paradise** – below, Martin and Osa Johnson (thanks to Kodak) lived for four years, photographed wildlife and entertained the Queen Mother. *I Married Adventure* by Osa Johnson gives a dated account of Marsabit. Nowadays, more prosaically, the Lake Paradise **camp site** entails 'Ksh. 300/- Un-refundable booking Deposite for this Professional Campsite only'.

From Marsabit to Loyangalani the choice of routes is between bad and worse. Tour organizers in Nairobi usually budget for the longer, safer detour through North Horr: here on the spot their drivers save time and effort by cutting due west across the Chalbi/

Koroli Desert. (This, for those travelling independently, is unwise without a guide – suicidal without water, spare tyres and petrol for as far as Maralal.)

Just north of the Marsabit park's 'back door' (above)[0] a mess of unmarked tracks veers west viz. left: 'note-taking impossible on bloody non-stop speed-bumps'. Pointless, too, in view of their profusion. The end of the national reserve [30] only means a change from mountain rock to chunky basalt. Hares streak and ostriches strut between the black-brown boulders; camels herald the softer sand terrain of purer desert. A confluence now of the tracks from Marsabit, the main route rises from a *lugga* of grey gravel to **Karigi** – police and a Rendille manyatta on the orange ridge [65]. Thereafter a clear but soft-sand track cuts across the **Koroli Desert** (which Kenyans call loosely the **Chalbi** or Kaisut) and sweeps south round Mount Kulal. After broad dry lugga river-beds [141 & 145] and the fork to the Kulal Quaker mission (r.)[159], it crosses the sere hills between Kulal's massif and the higher Ol Donyo Nyiro. Then – lighter tyre-spoor on the scree and red-grey gravel – it descends to the track from Maralal (p. 130)[175]. Inclines lined in concrete help you edge between the boulders and along Lake Turkana to Loyangalani [214].

From Nyahururu (p. 113)[0] the C 77 runs north through the **Marmanet Forest** – mostly eucalyptus and conifer afforestation – and degenerates to murram [10]. **Rumuruti** [34] is red tin roofs and a half-mile of tarmac. In the 1960s narrow bitumen, now part bed-rock and part corrugation, the track is least painful if driven fast. **Colcheccio** is indicated (r.)[62½]: 34 kms in general good and straight, but occasional outcrops of cruel bare rock and the last six kms appalling. Your reward is the ranch-house-cum-lodge. **Crocodile Jaws**, its alias, is the centre-piece of the vast panorama that drops away from the veranda: narrowing through an eighteen-inch fissure, the Uaso Nyiro falls 2000 spectacular feet. Between the 'Baringo Road' (p. 126)[97] and the 'Wamba Road' (p. 127)[131] **Adventure Trails Tented Safari Camp** (l.)[104½] is homelier but closer. True to its sign-board's '5 kms', it was started by two ex-hunters in 1979: nine double and two single tents with 'primitive showers and long-drop loos', mess tent, plastic pool, telescope and airstrip, plus vehicles, horses, camels and Shanks's Pony for 'high-savanna' game-viewing on 50,000 acres of ranch (Ksh. 600/- double, 360/- single; bookings through Nairobi POB. 14982, tel. 742926-9).

Wife with beadwork and scarification

Turkana

Veteran with lip-plug

Maralal [150] is 'capital' of Samburu District and the same-named people (p. 109). (They in fact name themselves *Loikop*, and correct the Masai nickname of 'Samburu' to *Sampurr*.) Nowadays their 'idling, blanketed moran' pose along the 'one-street township's double row of dukas'. But their traditional taboo on all non-hoofed game is the reason why elephant, rhino and the 'cats' survive in particular on Samburu land. (The considerate proximity of an army camp explains why the same now seek refuge round the lodge.) **Maralal Safari Lodge** lies 2½ well-marked kms on from the main roundabout. Rebuilt after burning in 1978, it is not only the halfway halt for Lake Turkana but a game-destination in its own right. Equally well indicated between town and lodge, the '**Kenyatta House – a National Monument**' is of rather more limited interest. Biographers and admirers of the Mzee will appreciate this featureless tin-roofed bungalow in which Mama Ngina and he were detained for six months in 1961. The general public, were entry not free, might well expect a refund (9 a.m.-5 p.m. daily except public holidays).

Maralal-Loyangalani is, put euphemistically, a seven-hour drive. 'An ordeal for man and machine' is more dramatic – but fact. The exit from Maralal [0] starts innocent enough: past the lodge (l.)[2] and up through the Leroghi forest reserve. Still beguilingly good, the track tops the crest, tips a 'Trees Nursery' (l.)[23] and crosses slopes and coppices hung with Old Man's Beard. Heaving green hills make a nonsense of this so-called Lopet Plateau which, after the 'Morijo Out Post' [39], you quit gingerly, edging down along steep rocky ledges. With Marti's wood-slat and tin-roofed shacks [62] starts the flatter swath of rock and corrugation that you bear with to **Baragoi** [105-6]. Its police, petrol and dukas with 'soda' are welcome; its 'road maintenance camp' prompts many a ribald remark. An actual traffic sign by the *lugga* as you leave, low forest balding to treeless slopes, and the long declivity of the **Horr Valley** [126-38]. The track runs, smoother sand, through lonely country but, should you stop, sudden Samburu – '*Piga picha!*' – promptly appear. Thickening vegetation next justifies the forest station of **South Horr** [149], for the

Fishing at Ferguson's Gulf

rest little more than a Catholic church and the mud-floored huts of the Mt. Nyero and Utalii 'hotels'. Any comparison with the latter would insult **Kurungu Camp** [154]: luxury cabins – and the unexpected extra of nightly *Son et Lumière* – with full board for Ksh. 600/- double, 420/- single. Steep between the ravaged sides of Ol Donyo Nyiro and Ol Donyo Mara (r.), the Horr Valley opens to lower plateau, and the track (r.)[203] from Marsabit.

The décor becomes more dramatic. First a littered battle-field, of cannon balls all in black basalt, next a moonscape of brown boulders, then suddenly [214] the '**Jade Sea**' spread before you: red hills streaked and striated green and white, the shore-line alive with flamingos and pelicans, ibis, plovers, waders, cranes and cormorants, and island-cones off shore in the blue-green waters. Such is the accompaniment as you inch along the littoral to Loyangalani and Oasis Lodge [242].

Lake Turkana is Kenya's latest touristic discovery. Rich in fish, bird life and photogenic scenery, it survives delightfully without civilization, an insight into pristine Africa. The 'beautiful water . . . clear as crystal' that Teleki 'discovered' in March 1888 remains untroubled by trippers or pollution; stark volcanic hills and islands swelter on unaltered; 22,000 crocodiles share with oryx and gazelle the once-forested shores and, until you almost collide, the countless birds see no need to fly. Nor the Turkana fishermen any point in clothes.

Prosaically, the lake measures 256 by 48 kms (but continues to contract), reaches north into Ethiopia (where the Omo River enters at a place known as Nairobi) and receives several rivers but gives rise to none. A primaeval part of the Nile system, as its fish life proves, no one knows what cataclysm cast it geologically adrift. Nor why its Nile perch grow over 200 lbs or its tiger fish fight so. Called by the Turkana themselves 'Aman', by the Gabra – confusingly – 'Galana', the lake features in early depictions as *Basso Narok*. The subsequent and late name of Lake Rudolf honoured the Austrian archduke, Teleki's patron, until altered in 1975 by presidential decree. (The nearby *Basso Ebor* was called Lake Stefanie after the archduke's consort.) The indigenous **El Molo**, a tribe of bow-legged fish-eaters once down to 80 souls, have been helped to multiply first by passing soldiers in the Second World War and recently by assimilation with their Samburu neighbours. The lake is readably documented in the *Journey to the Jade Sea* which John Hillaby made, and wrote, in 1964.

At **Loyangalani** – Place of the Trees – the well-named **Oasis Lodge** is base for boat trips to see the **South Island** birds and for camping trips up **Mount Kulal** (where the eagle-eyed find jasper, blue agate, quartz and amethyst). Hardier adventurers – well stocked with (pricy) petrol from the Consolata Mission – make for **Mount Moiti**: four hours' dusty driving on a track laid by the lodge and one day's climbing to the overnight camp. Fair-weather excursionists rest content with **Molo Bay**: following the North Horr track out past the new strategic airstrip, forking left after twelve kms and finding one km. further that the huddle of huts – balls of grass tied with string – is perhaps not so attractive as the scenery en route. And certainly less interesting than the **mineral springs**: opposite the old airstrip, four kms back on the North Horr track, just-perceptible tyre-spoor rise $1\frac{1}{2}$ kms to a slight eminence on which belch the warm and very fruit-salt pools.

Sibiloi National Park overland, for those at Loyangalani and still game, is unsuspectedly 'easy'. (By air is even easier, since Sunbird stationed at Ferguson's Gulf a five-passenger 'plane – and an intrepid lady pilot.) Forty kms north along the 'main' C 77, the left fork runs well graded through the Bura Galadi Hills before descending, rougher and roughly marked, to the **Alia Bay** park gate [c. 170 kms from the lodge]. The region is home for the **Gabra** and their herds, for the Somali ostrich, Grevy's zebra, oryx and gerenuk too. But prehistoric research, not game, is the *raison d'être* of this 700-square-mile national park. Richard Leakey recognized the area's potential from the air in 1967, conducted a survey in 1968, had the then East Rudolf National Park gazetted in 1970, and in 1972 won world-wide acclaim for his discovery of '1470 Man'. Piecing together 300 fragments of skull – a feat to equal his mother's at Olduvai (p. 16) – he established the existence of a '2-million year-old' hominid, since named from its number in the Nairobi Museum catalogue.

From Alia Bay and its **petrified forest**, the park headquarters was moved north to **Koobi Fora**. And from here the Kenyan, British and American members of the same-named **Research Project** have since discovered more major, quasi-human remains – viz. two fifths of 'Lucy, a lady 3 million years old' – and 'a variety of animals more diverse and spectacular than in present-day game parks': African, Indian and extinct elephants, 30 separate species of antelope and giant turtles larger than the Galapagos' today. In 1979 came a unique and striking find: seven human footprints, dated radiometrically as $1\frac{1}{2}$ million years old – and of HOMO ERECTUS, our first true predecessor. Here in the northernmost confines of Kenya one is on the track, literally, of the first man.

HOTELS, LODGES AND LUXURY CAMPS

The list below details those establishments used, and thus presumably approved, by Western tour operators. Though its many fine new hotels and lodges are Kenya's response to the upsurge of tourism, the result is nowhere a concrete jungle. Unlike that of many other popular vacation countries, hotel-building here is often architecturally striking and, on the Coast in particular, breathtakingly beautiful. On the other hand, many establishments that thrived on Coast or up-country settler holidays in pre-independence days have been updated or extended. The year of construction need therefore only differentiate between functional modernity or mellower cosiness, not between standards of comfort or efficiency. The high standards are in fact being made increasingly uniform by the consolidation of ownership or management. The Kenya Tourist Development Corporation (KTDC) – having merged with African Tours & Hotels (AT&H), set up the Hotel Management Company (HMC) and absorbed the hapless Hobby Hotels – now controls more than a score and, as self-contained safari 'chains' interest investors more than individual units, most of the rest are operated by the African Safari Club, Alliance, Block, Jambo and Sarova Hotels, Hotel Management International (HMI) and the Hilton and Serena groups. Their capital has ensured for Kenya a network that ranks amongst the world's finest. Some hoteliers however, by adding unnecessary amenities simply to match their competitors', overlook the fact that their function is to sell sleep. Before booking in, therefore, it is often worth checking that your night will not be noisy with power plants, discotheques, lifts and air conditioning.

Prices – for full board (FB) unless otherwise stated – are quoted in Kenya shillings. They are usually reduced for groups, and for individuals during the April-June low season. BB stands for bed and breakfast, $\frac{1}{2}$B for dinner, bed and breakfast, b. for bath, sh. for shower, tr. for triple, d. for double and s. for single (rooms). All hotels have a restaurant and bar open to non-residents, and a swimming-pool, unless otherwise stated. All Coast hotels save Mombasa town's lie on the beach: their position, and their beach-bungalow and camp-site neighbours, are described on pages 70-76. Postal addresses and telephone numbers are given in brackets. Where outlying lodges are linked only by radio, the 'Reservations' address serves not only for bookings but for urgent contact with lodge guests also. Managements provided the 1981 tariffs and technical details (or – where these are omitted – failed to do so).

AMBOSELI (pp. 92-94)
Amboseli Lodge
(Reservations Nairobi
POB. 30139, tel. 27136)

Kilimanjaro Safari Lodge
(Reservations Nairobi
POB. 30139, tel. 27136)

Kimana Safari Lodge
(Reservations Nairobi
POB. 43817,
tel. 742731-3 x 216)

Serena Lodge
(Reservations Nairobi
POB. 48690,
tel. 338656/7)

Opened in 1964 and owned, like the *Safari Lodge* next door, by the Kilimanjaro Safari Club; on a site scenic when Kilimanjaro appears; central block of bar, restaurant, reception and shop, and 54 cottages attractive in cedar-wood and stone, with pool added in 1971 and grandiose expansion plans for the 1980s in response to the popularity.

The late *Safari Camp*'s 60 tents replaced in 1977-78 with 60 d. chalets + sh., the walls pine-wood, the ceilings papyrus and the whole almost Alpine; one built around an acacia left *in situ*, and all in a semicircle on the lawns, around the camp fire, the raised swimming-pool (1974) and the makuti-roofed restaurant (1978); vehicles available for half-day game runs.

Outside the park, beyond Leme Boti on the Emali track (p. 93), and 14 kms from the Kimana Gate (p. 94); main timber-block bar-restaurant facing Kilimanjaro, overlooking an artificial water-hole and backed by 24 d. chalets + sh.; Italian owned and well managed by HMI since 1979; opened in 1976 and in 35 landscaped acres of the Masai's *Tikondo* – Spring – district; fine for families and for fishing in the Kimana River.

The park's architectural *pièce de résistance*: a discreet 'Masai-manyatta' exterior that belies a strikingly luxurious interior: entrance hall with calabashes like stalactites, wooden walkways to the poolside restaurant (where the resident weaver birds are the rare 'Taveta Golden') and everywhere a fascinating clay-buff and ochre-red décor that supposedly affords a 'built-in cultural experience'; the swampy nearness of the *Enkongo Narok* – Black Stream – ensures night-long wildlife noises; 50 d. rooms + b. in wings on either side, plus 10 + sh. added in 1978; reception shop rebuilt in 1977, another with food for Ol Tukai campers, and the terrace bar extended in 1979 (for more to watch Poaky, the orphaned bush baby, nightly?); petrol and Avis car hire on the spot, Land Cruisers for half-day game runs; opened in 1973; 948/- d., 720/- s., under 12s 277/- (1/5-30/6/1981: 615/-, 377/-, 140/-).

EMBU (pp. 112-13)
Izaak Walton Inn
(POB. 1, tel. 28)

Embu's one-time Agricultural Training Centre, made hotel in 1948 and rebuilt in 1968; 12 d. terraced rooms + b. that outclassed the reception-restaurant block until it was reworked in 1975 and rebuilt in 1978; 6 more d. rooms + sh. added in 1978 and 6 original cottages on a par with the bar (redeemed only by its beam-plaques showing various types of fishing 'fly') (and its occasional view of Mount Kenya); 8 acres of pleasant gardens, bird-viewing and trout-fishing near by (rods for hire, flies for sale, licences for 40/- p.a., 5/- p.d.); no pool.

HOMA BAY (p. 123)
Homa Bay Hotel
(POB. 521, tel. 46;
reservations Nairobi POB.
30471, tel. 336858)

A joint KTDC and South Nyanza Council venture that cost Ksh. 3 million and opened in February 1979 under AT&H management: with a plain and pleasant décor on the Lake Victoria shore (but no swimming), 19 d. rooms + sh., 2 suites + b., bars outside and upstairs for businessmen and, for errant tourists, a launch-link with Kisumu's *Sunset Hotel*; no pool; BB 280/- d., 150/- s., 350/- tr., under 12s 50/-, under 6s 30/-. After 22/4/1981: 240/- d., 120/- s., 315/- tr., under 12s 30/-, under 6s 20/-. After 1/7/1981: 240/- d., 120/- s., 290/- tr., under 12s 40/-, under 6s 20/-.

KAREN (pp. 52-54)
Westwood Park
(POB. 45664, tel. 882233)

An Austrian owner-operated 'country club' until 1973 and, after a cheerless intermission, now recovering under German management and receiving much-needed renovations; 100 beds in 'family cottages' and bungalows + b. or sh., fine gardens, sauna, horses for hire (and courtesy bus into town), tennis court, mini-golf, games room and conference/function facilities for 100, on 85 acres of Karen's quondam land (p. 52), so the bar appropriately low beams, prints and pewter.

KERICHO (p. 121)
Tea Hotel
(POB. 75, tel. 40, 280/1;
reservations Nairobi POB.
30471, tel. 336858)

Long 'the best in Kenya' and now regaining much of its former glory under AT&H management; 2 magnificent suites and 25 d., 16 s. rooms + b. or sh. in main block, very spacious cottages (1952) and the one- or two-storey 'Moi' and 'Tengecha House'; heated swimming-pool, tennis courts and putting lawns in 15 bracing acres of beautiful gardens; free visits to the tea estates (p. 121), trout-fishing (rods 10/- p.d.) and nine-holf golf at the Kericho Club (10/- green fee); conference facilities for 50, new 'Kook Bar' and the petrol station now a store for Kisii stone-carvers; BB 330/- d., 200/- s., 420/- tr., under 12s 80/-, under 6s 50/-. After 22/4/1981: 300/- d., 180/- s., 400/- tr., under 12s 60/-, under 6s 30/-.

KIBOKO (p. 99)
Hunter's Lodge
(Reservations Nairobi
POB. 67868, tel. 20592/3)

A combination of main-road motel and peaceful lakeside haven that sounds unlikely but is in fact delightful; rods for fishing and rowing-boats for hire, small pool and mini-golf, abundant birds and resident peacocks in 20 acres of acacia-shady lawns beside the dam; no longer AT&H but since 1979 under private owner-managers, whence the reworked bar, newly (but not always) opened sauna and verandas built on to the 21 d. or tr. rooms + b. or sh.; FB 400/- d., 220/- s., 520/- tr., under 12s 85/-, under 6s 55/-; ½B 360/- d., 200/- s., 460/- tr., under 12s 75/-, under 6s 45/-; BB 320/- d., 180/- s., 400/- tr., under 12s 65/-, under 6s 35/-.

KILIFI (p. 77)
Mnarani
(POB. 14, tel. 18, 26;
reservations Nairobi POB.
30471, tel. 336858)

Further to page 77; a scenic holiday centre, well run by AT&H; scuba-diving base, ski-boat, 4 deep-sea fishing-boats, 12 mini-sails, Arab dhow for creek cruises with dinner aboard and 2 goggling-boats for visits to the northward coral gardens; airstrip with aviation fuel, and petrol, available; 4 s., 42 d. rooms, with 'double beds for honeymoon couples and breakfast from 7 a.m. to midday'; FB 550/- d., 350/- s., 700/- tr., under 12s 110/-, under 6s 75/-; ½B 510/- d., 330/- s., 640/- tr., under 12s 100/-, under 6s 65/-. After 22/4/1981: FB 340/- d., 170/- s., 430/- tr., under 12s 70/-, under 6s 45/-; ½B 300/- d., 150/- s., 400/- tr., under 12s 60/-, under 6s 40/-. After 1/7/1981: FB 390/- d., 260/- s., 510/- tr., under 12s 80/-, under 6s 60/-; ½B 350/- d., 240/- s., 450/- tr., under 12s 70/-, under 6s 50/- (24-25/12 & 31/12/1981-1/1/1982: 150/- extra).

Seahorse
(POB. 70, tel. 90; reservations
Nairobi POB. 57661, tel. 338599)

True to its name, a small and curiously attractive feature/creature; 6 luxury tents and 20 d. thatched rondavels + sh., fridge-bar and extra room for dressing and/or kids, lining a narrow valley of bougainvillea, papayas and palms that opens to the main makuti restaurant-bar-games room and 2 beach-side pools; 4 mini-sails and 5 dinghies free to guests, windsurfers, 2 ski-boats, dhow and deep-sea fishing-boat ('inclusive of captain') for hire, resident sub-aqua instructor (and even an underwater scooter) for up to 12 divers; goggling excursions to the northward Horne's Pool, car hire and exclusive visits to the cashew-nut factory (p. 77); opened in 1979 in 17 acres.

KISUMU (p. 122)
Sunset
(POB. 215, tel. 41100-4;
reservations Nairobi POB.
30471, tel. 336858)

A stylish pile – all concrete, not Kenyan but attractive – opened by AT&H in 1977 to promote the Western Kenya circuit and since filled nightly by businessmen and officials; split-level reception, restaurant and public and private bars; 5 floors with 2 suites and 48 d. rooms + b., sh., central a.c. & radio, all overlooking Lake Victoria and reached by unusual lifts in free-standing concrete columns; the 30-passenger 'Sunrise' acquired in 1978 for two-hour picnic-cruises to Ndere Island, with its hippos, impalas and birds, and lunch-trips to Homa Bay; BB 370/- d., 220/- s., 440/- tr., under 12s 70/-, under 6s 50/-. After 22/4/1981: 340/- d., 200/- s., 425/- tr., under 12s 60/-, under 6s 40/-.

LAKE BARINGO (pp. 125-26)
Lake Baringo Club
(Reservations Nairobi POB.
40075, tel. 22860, 22869, 331635)

Further to page 125; built in 1968 and more country home than hotel – family photos, lounge trinkets and Visitors' Book – until bought out by UTC and Block Hotels; since April 1980 a 'unit' in the latter's chain and currently undergoing expansion and 'upgrading' – at considerable expense but not, one hopes, at the cost of its character and charm; had 10 d. rooms + b., is due to have 100, and might have any number in between by the time you arrive.

LAKE NAIVASHA (pp. 58-59)
Fisherman's Lodge
(POB. 79, tel. 5Y2; reservations
Nairobi POB. 42475, tel. 25641)

The old private house of the long-standing *Fisherman's Camp* (p. 59) recently commercialized as a 'mini-package' – accommodation for 9 – 'in separate bedrooms' – and the price inclusive of a visit to Hell's Gate, a punt-trip, wine and 'a reasonable amount of drink'; 350/- p.p., under 12s 280/-, less 50/- for no punt-trip and 50/- for teetallers.

Lake Naivasha Hotel
(POB. 15, tel. 13; reservations
Nairobi POB. 40075, tel. 22860,
22869, 331635)

The *Sparks Hotel* of the 1930s (where flying-boat arrivals recovered from the ten-day trip from Britain, p. 58); comfortable with main block and *banda*-bungalows – 42 d., 2 s. rooms + b. & sh. – refurbished and extended in 1977, in 48 acres of lakeside lawns; fishing-boats and rods for hire (50/- p.d.), with the lake's crayfish, bass and tilapia a restaurant speciality; Block Hotels' management since April 1980.

Safariland Lodge
(POB. 72, tel. 29)

A delightful lakeside property with standards well maintained by Italian owner-management; conference facilities for 100 (and Saturday feature film) in the ten-room annex (1979); cabin-cruisers, punts, bird-watching hides and even bows & arrows for hire; horses, too, for seven-hour safaris to Hell's Gate (p. 59); 105 acres of lawns, gardens and acacias scattered since 1969 with 2 tennis courts and pools, 3 luxury cottages (384/75 d., en suite with sitting room), 33 d. rooms and *banda*-bungalows, refurbished in 1977 + b., sh. and log fires (288/55 d., 247/35 s.), 5 *nyumba*-huts (215/30 d., 115/70 s.) and 18 tents (178/60 d., 96/20 s. or, without meals, 56/20 d., 28/10 s.).

LAKE NAKURU (pp. 116-17)
Lake Nakuru Lodge
(POB. 257, tel. Elmentaita 5Y6)

A former lordly farmhouse-cum-manor – of Lord Delamere's Nderit Estate in fact – partly converted in 1977 and striving to match the magnificent site, game and views; 1 d., 3 tr. rooms pristine + b., 4 d. rooms added in 1977; fully fledged in 1979, the lodge sprouted wings of 20 d. rondavels, and a 'tail' of 4 more behind; all cement-floored economical – bamboo ceiling and wall-rock dug right outside – but the bar and restaurant better under big shingled peaks; even better lake vistas from the 4½-acre grounds and especially 'Lodge Point' behind; Land-Rover, mini-bus and nearby airstrip.

Lion Hill Camp
(Reservations Nairobi POB.
48658, tel. 337916)

A 'camp' but far suaver and better appointed than many a lodge; built by an ex-hunter in 1978, luxurious and by no means 'bush', its 30 d. 'tents' being solidly floored, wooden-roofed and electric-lit, each with wood-walled hot and cold showers and flushing loos behind; all landscaped – beside log-fire bar and vast restaurant-lounge-cinema – high along the slope of Lion Hill; FB 701/- d., 467/50 s.; ½B 581/- d., 407/50 s., BB 461/- d., 347/50 s.

LAKE TURKANA (pp. 126-31)
Lake Rudolf Angling Lodge
(Reservations Nairobi POB.
74609, tel. 26623, 26808)

Further to page 127; 16 simple bungalows + sh. along the fine Ferguson's Gulf sands, with dubitable pool and economy-comfortable bar-restaurant, refurbished in 1977; astonishing fishing almost guaranteed (boats 150-200/- p.h.), abundant bird life and nude Turkana neighbours.

Oasis Lodge
(Reservations Nairobi POB.
42475, tel. 25641)

Further to page 130; the old *Loyangalani Lodge* burnt down, rebuilt, reburnt and rebuilt by Italians in 1972, as 15 d. rooms + sh. on a windy site embellished by hot (and purgative) springs trickling through 'gardens' to 2 usually warm but always welcome swimming-pools; then burnt again and the bar-restaurant block rebuilt, with 10 more d. rooms + sh., in 1978; ten-passenger canoes, safely uncapsizable, for bird-watching and unparalleled fishing (cold store for trophies) . . . when the wind permits; 745/- d., 555/- s., under 12s 187/-; residents 660/-, 484/-, 187/-.

LAMU (pp. 86-90)
Peponi
(POB. 24, tel. 29)

Built in 1932, purchased in 1946 by the Swiss who also bought out Percy Petley (p. 87) and enlarged in 1966-67 by Danish owners from 8 to 21 to 32 and now 45 beds in 1 quintuple (?) and 20 d. rooms + sh.; between Shela's mosque and the historic beach (p. 88), the site rather than the facilities justifying *Peponi*, Paradise; no pool.

Petley's Inn
(POB. 4, tel. 48, 107;
reservations Nairobi POB.
20106, tel. 25255,
Malindi POB. 20, tel. 6, 57)

Further to page 88; an early 19th-c. manor extensively and expensively restored; opened (and closed again) in 1972 and since 1974 functioning quaintly as Lamu town's best; managed since 1975 by *Lawford's*/Jambo Hotels, who reworked the popular (and Lamu's only public) bar in 1979; breezy and scenic roof-top restaurant and curious (but welcome) first-floor swimming pit; 11 Swahili-stylish d. rooms – appropriately cooled by verandahs and fans – and 3 cheaper d. rooms in the annex next door; ½B 364-550/- d., 220-325/- s. (21/4-1/11/1981: 20% less).

Ras Kitau
(POB. 76, tel. ?
Best telegraph; European
reservations c/o Blue World
Travel, 00189 Rome/Largo,
Asioli 5, tel. (06) 8445351,
850793)

Opened in 1972 on 4 blissful acres of Manda Island beach, opposite *Peponi*; part-owned and managed by Italians (whence a tropical menu predominantly *pasta*) and in 1979 suffered, like *Oasis Lodge*, the odd Italianate fate of burning down; the restaurant-reception block of coral-rock walls, mangrove and makuti rebuilt the same year with upstairs bar and Lamu arches; 5 motor boats, a 50-foot deep-sea fishing-ketch and equipment for water sports and windsurfing; generator silenced nightly but the island's thirsty game makes fresh-water pools impossible; closed annually 1 May-15 July and since 1980 a 'club', charging daily or annual 'membership'; 18 pristine d. chalets + sh. and 5 more added in 1976 in terraced rows behind; 574/- d., 393/- s. After 1/12/1981 : 630/- d., 440/- s.

MALINDI (pp. 79-83)
Blue Marlin
(POB. 54, tel. 4, 306;
reservations Nairobi POB.
20106, tel. 25255, Malindi
POB. 20, tel. 6, 57)

Malindi's first hostelry – the *Palm Beach* opened by the Bradys with 6 rooms in 1931-32, enlarged to 9 in 1934 and sold in 1954 – extended and modernized in 1965, 1968 & 1971, and Jambo Hotels' since 1975; easy-going in 4½ acres, with the cooking excellent – extra à la carte restaurant – and the 'packages' not too obtrusive; 78 d., 16 s. rooms, + b. in the main blocks, + sh. in the annex, some + a.c.; sauna (without massage . . . 20/-); ½B 332-540/- d., 188-315/- s. (21/4-1/11/1981 : 20% less).

Driftwood Beach Club
(POB. 63, tel. 155)

On 4 acres of bougainvillea, flamboyants and palms at the better end of Malindi Bay and nearest the unique coral gardens (p. 82); the once erratically-run *Driftwood*, not de luxe but successfully one of the best in its category; with no 'package' parties; seafood restaurant with a décor many a Chelsea bistro would envy; 29 d. bandas, luxury-Crusoe, to match the relaxed low-keyed mood; reception and homely bar enlarged by new owners in 1976; base for the Afro-Sub Diving School, whence an energetic clientele and the north coast's only squash court (4/- p.p. per ½-hour); closed May-June; 244/75-329/- d., 137-183/80 s., 352/50-469/50 tr., under 12s 56/80, under 5s 39/25, family cottage 536/30.

Eden Roc
(POB. 350, tel. 8, 91)

A functionally elegant 'luxury-package' main block (1970) and older bungalows that could be anywhere . . . were the efficiency expected of a stern German management not cheerfully thwarted by the Giriama staff; expanded first with a 'Tropicana Club 28' (reserved for those under that age) and now a casino club, to become a more brashly modern establishment that contrasts with Malindi's old guard of casual family hotels; 120 d. rooms and suites, all + b. or sh., some + fridge & a.c. (40/- p.n.).

Lawford's
(POB. 20, tel. 6, 57; reservations
Nairobi POB. 20106, tel. 25255)

Further to page 80; Commander L's 1934 original with many an attractive addition: one pool Africa-shaped, another added in 1977, 2 restaurants (Lamu Grill for seafood specialities) and Lamu Coffee Shop; headquarters of Jambo Hotels; in 5 acres of beach, *Lawford's* epitomizes Malindi: flowery, informal and efficient; 27 d., 12 s. simple terraced rooms, 27 d. sea-front bungalows replaced in 1977 (and equipped with solar heating), 8 d. rooms in the seaside annex and 65 d. + b. in the fine three-storey block behind (1971); ½B 314-540/- d., 188-315/- s. (21/4-1/11/1981 : 20% less).

Malindi Safari Club
(POB. 501, tel. 342)

A small, suave establishment (1978) that seems to centre on its restaurant (very Italian, like the proprietors; even full board à la carte); the reception and public rooms more opulent private villa than hotel, the 13 d. rooms + sh. a mixture of ancient and modern: Swahili wood-carved furniture with fridge bar, a.c. or fans; all with pool and tennis court in 2 acres of gardens and lawns; closed annually May-June; 220/-.

Palm Tree Club
(POB. 180, tel. 397)

The *Malindi Safari Club*'s ambitious big sister; an unusual, irregular oval of makuti that covers, in professionals' eyes, a multitude of sins: a single, communal lounge-reception area, one corner screened off as the restaurant, one unwalled pool alongside, the communal commotion and canned music crescendoing into the bedrooms built around . . . all very pleasant to look at but hopeless for privacy or peace and quiet; opened in 1980, a half-km. north of Malindi and a half-km. inland, with 'the best-stocked wine-cellar in Africa' and 16 d. rooms + b., a.c. & canopied Swahili beds; closed May-June; 350/- à la carte.

Sindbad
(POB. 30, tel. 7, 303/4;
reservations Nairobi POB. 40075,
tel. 22860, 22869, 331635)

Aspires to be Malindi's classiest and one of the township's few architectural assets: a Graham McCullough design of half-towers and high white crenellated walls, effectively arabesque (despite a red-tiled roof) and enhanced by palms and abundant bougainvillea; built in 1948 as the *New Malindi Hotel* and extended in 1967 & 1971 to 73 rooms + b. or sh. & a.c., the newest luxurious but occasionally stuffy, the oldest noisy and in need of renovation; much suaver restaurant and Jahazi Gallery; under several half-successful managements of late, its prospects improved in 1977 when it became a Block Hotel.

Suli Suli Sporting Club
(POB. 360, tel. 317, 382)

Completes Malindi's Italian trio: a smart club-house/main block with 40 d. rooms + b., sh. & a.c. and 10 villas + sh., each three- or four-roomed, in well-developed gardens; not 'in the coast', as the brochure says, but inland beside the Lamu Road north; a large pool and 2 tennis courts scarcely warrant the 'Sporting Club'; 410/- d., 307/50 s., villa 480/- bed only.

MARALAL (p. 129)
Colcheccio
(Reservations Nairobi POB.
40097, tel. 23131)

Not really Maralal but 80 miles south, and not really anywhere, since a 70,000-acre ranch starting 20 miles from the Rumuruti track ensures the delightful development's 'exclusive' seclusion; with a veranda view surpassing Kilaguni's, the restaurant-bar ranch-house dominates, at 5960 feet, the Crocodile Jaws defile of the Uaso Nyiro (p. 128); Italian owners, British Kenyan managers and, since November 1977, 7 d. bandas + b. or sh., pool, tennis court and tariffs inclusive of 2 daily game drives, manyatta visit, laundry, horses and camel safaris; FB 880/-, BB 660/-.

Maralal Safari Lodge
(Reservations Nairobi POB.
42475, tel. 25641)

The one-time Officers' Club and Government Sports Club made self-service lodge in the mid-1960s and rebuilt in 1978 as a popular stop on the 'Jade Sea Safari' and a splendid spot for game-viewing; in 19 acres of forest glade, the salt-lick become the tennis court, but the water-hole bringing game varied and close to the bar-restaurant terrace; nearby hide to take you close to several shy leopard (one black); 24 luxurious cedar-log cabins, split-level and almost A-frame, each with 2 d. or tr. rooms + b.; these with log fire and cosy extra-bed nook steep-staired between the rafters; FB 633/- d., 402/- s., under 12s 160/-; ½B 589/- d., 380/- s., under 12s 149/-; residents FB 413/- d., 264/- s., under 12s 99/-.

MARSABIT (p. 128)
Marsabit Lodge
(POB. 45, tel. 44; reservations
Nairobi POB. 30471, tel. 336858)

The last and best of the several lodge/camp projects that Ahmed and the mountain-oasis prompted in the early 1970s; completed by KTDC in 1974 and since run by AT&H, with main block of shop, reception, restaurant and bar and 24 spacious terraced d. rooms + sh. overlooking the game-rich shore of *Sokorte Dika*; 2 game-run vehicles for hire with driver; now a popular night-stop on the Lake Turkana 'circuit'; no pool; FB 850/- d., 600/- s., 1150/- tr., under 12s 150/-, under 6s 100/-; ½B 810/- d., 580/- s., 1090/- tr., under 12s 140/-, under 6s 90/-. After 22/4/1981: FB 560/- d., 280/- s., 730/- tr., under 12s 110/-, under 6s 70/-; ½B 520/- d., 260/- s., 670/- tr., under 12s 100/-, under 6s 65/-. After 1/7/1981: FB 620/- d., 450/- s., 745/- tr., under 12s 115/-, under 6s 70/-; ½B 580/- d., 430/- s., 685/- tr., under 12s 105/-, under 6s 65/-.

MASAI MARA (pp. 118-20)
Cottars' Mara Camp
(Reservations Nairobi POB. 14982, tel. 742926-9)

The original *Cottars' Camp* in Tsavo being African Safari Club 'package', the third generation of that name set up here in 1977: restaurant-bar banda, 3 d. bandas and 1 s., 7 d. tents + sh., loo & gas-lamps, all walled and roofed in Kavirondo matting, at *Ol Choro Loltokai* – Spring of the Palms – and shaded by these, acacia and *muratina* – sausage – trees; airstrip and four-wheeled drives but no pool; 654/80 d., 464/- s., under 12s 177/70; residents 392/90, 278/40, 88/85.

Fig Tree Camp
(Reservations Nairobi POB. 67868, tel. 20592/3)

Opened in 1978 but still with little publicity generally and, on the spot, direction-signs that start well but soon leave you in the lurch; 18 d., 2 tr. tents + sh., loo & gas-lamps on the oxbow bank of the Talek; Land Cruisers, no pool; 700/- d., 450/- s., 950/- tr., under 12s 150/-, under 6s 100/-.

Governor's Camp
(Reservations Nairobi POB. 48217, tel. 331871/2)

Outside the Olololo Gate (p. 120), near the Musiara Swamp – whence the management company's name – and on a scenic, 20-acre Mara River site once frequented by Sir Evelyn Baring, the governor in question; 21 d., 3 s. tents and 3 'for honeymoons, deep in the forest'; restaurant tent with fittingly superb cuisine, bar tent with cases of local butterflies and all this scale-modelled in *Little Governor's Camp* (a fly camp opened in 1977 on a 15-acre site 4 kms across the Mara and made permanent in 1979 with 15 d. tents and Masai manager); airstrip macadamed in 1977 and 2 camp sites near by (10/- p.p.p.n.); generator turned off at 10 p.m., no pool; price includes 3 daily game runs (16 Land Cruisers) and laundry; 1290/- d., 845/- s., under 12s 250/-; residents 1120/-, 745/-, 150/-.

Keekorok Lodge
(Reservations Nairobi POB. 40075, tel. 22860, 22869, 331635)

Further to page 120; the 1961 self-service camp replaced in 1965 with 47 d., 10 s. rooms, all + b. or sh. in cottages lining the lawns, and with 12 d. tents (reworked in 1977) + telephone, lighting, loo and (like the cottages now) solar-heated sh.; balloon safaris (p. 118) are a highly successful attraction; distraction – of the elephants at the pool – is the reason for the digging of another water-hole; aircraft taxi (almost) to the door and UTC vehicles make game runs; a well-managed Block Hotel.

Kichwa Tembo Camp
(Reservations Nairobi POB. 59749, tel. 334955)

'Elephant's Head', commenced in 1977 and in 1978 resited as at present amid tight riverine forest; by Abercrombie & Kent, whose hunting-era laurels might have led one to expect more than the 28 standard Selous d. tents, bar-restaurant and reception tents, 3 game-run vehicles, camp fire and tribal dancing; but there are rods for fishing, plus a game-viewing hide and 'badminton tennis quoits and frisbies', and the cost is low; no pool; 670/- d., 460/- s., under 12s 120/-.

Mara Buffalo Camp

Another Italian and initially ill-fated venture, opening and closing in 1977, and in 1978 reopening only to be inundated by the Mara floods; by 1979 the bank was decorous again with attractively beamed bar-restaurant bandas; 10 d., 4 tr. neat green bungalows with thatched (and plastic) roofs; 5 d. (or tr.) bandas of thatch and plastered mud-&-wattle and – also + sh., flushing loo & electric lights – 12 d. tents; 70-acre riverside site with airstrip, game drives, rods for hire and petrol for sale but no pool.

Mara Sara Camp
(Reservations Nairobi POB. 43230, tel. 21716)

Also Italian owned, the promoter being an ex-hunter and the name his wife's; grown from 8 bandas in 1977 to 24 d. + sh., toilet & electricity, makuti roofs and murula walls; restaurant unusual with its murula and bamboo 'big top', the site very pleasant right on the river (and alongside rapids that keep crocodiles at bay); no pool.

Serena Lodge
(Reservations Nairobi POB. 48690, tel. 338656/7)

Opened by the same-named group in 1973; 2 pastiche Masai manyattas, one a 'traditional defensive ring' of 50 d. rooms + b. and splendid view (and latterly 2 s. rooms + sh.), the other a domed, deliberately rough-finished main block, both atop the hill of Ol Donyo Oseyia and taking full advantage of the Mara panorama; balloon safaris (p. 118), hide on the Hippo Pool, 4 kms away, and Land Cruisers for half-day game runs; prices like the *Amboseli Serena*'s (above).

MERU NATIONAL PARK
(pp. 111-12)
Meru Mulika Lodge
(Reservations Nairobi POB. 30471, tel. 336858)

Built in 1973 by the Meru County Council and KTDC and managed by AT&H; 50 d. rooms + b. or sh. in attractive two-room rondavels and 16 roomier + b. & sh. in the two-floored wing (1979); main block striking with walls of local stone, tall grass 'cone' and (like Voi and Ngulia) beams of blue gum, and descending from reception and well-stocked shop to a restaurant-lounge panorama of the Mulika Swamp wildlife; airstrip near by, petrol for sale and UTC game-run vehicles for hire; same prices as *Marsabit Lodge* (above).

MOMBASA TOWN (pp. 63-70)
Castle
(POB. 84231, tel. 23403, 312296)

A prominent 1908 block, rebuilt in 1929, revived under Swiss management in 1966 and taken over in 1975 by Alliance Hotels; many-coursed lunches at remarkable prices, pizzeria and Buibui Restaurant (oriental specialities); very central but consequently noisy; no pool; 125 beds; a.c. on request; BB 207/40-244/- d., 128/10-164/70 s.

Manor
(POB. 84851, tel. 21821/2)

Mombasa's oldest – 1908 – but not quite like *Norfolk* (p. 140); 61 rooms, homely restaurant and pleasant terrace bars . . . in atmosphere, but for the a.c. units, a rambling English inn; same owners as Nairobi's *Fairview* and similarly competent African management; very central, with good private parking; no pool; BB 230-270/- d., 105-180/- s., under 12s 55/-, under 8s 45/-, under 2s 20/-.

New Carlton
(POB. 86779, tel. 23776)

Like the *Castle*, an imposing main-street period piece, but a less successful hostelry; reopened in 1977 after management and ownership mishaps, the 2 lofty floors still colonial-evocative around a central courtyard, but a.c. units now shattering the calm of its 21 d., 4 s. rooms + b. or sh.; street-front bookshop and pleasant garden bar.

Oceanic
(POB. 90371, tel. 311191)

Further to page 69; the ageing-luxurious block on the Kilindini cliffs (1958) enlivened in 1973 with an International Casino adjoining, partially reworked in 1976 and in 1977 treated to a discotheque, an à la carte Auberge Restaurant and an extension of 32 d. rooms + b. & sh.; for residents free entry to the casino, free transport to the *Ocean View* beach and nine-hole golf (15/-) near by; popular for 'functions'; 134 rooms + b., radio & breezy balcony (110 + unnecessary a.c.: + 20/- p.n.).

Outrigger
(POB. 82345, tel. 20822/3;
reservations Nairobi POB. 43817,
tel. 742731-3 x 216)

The once-exclusive 'K Boats' base and former Mombasa Sea Angling Club's headquarters 'gone public' and now British run by HMI; built in 1972, Italian owned; 3 floors of 40 d. rooms and 6 self-contained flats + b. & sh., a view of Kilindini harbour and noisome a.c.; attractive terrace for 'functions' above the panoramic pool, conference facilities for 20 and proximity of airport, station and bus terminals make for a business clientele.

Splendid
(POB. 90482, tel. 20967/8)

For accommodation, a pleasant compromise of clean, cheap, quiet and comfortably central; for evening relaxation, its roof-top bar and restaurant locally popular, and less packed than that on the ground-floor and the bars above and below; a four-storey corner block with lift to 26 d., 8 s. rooms, redecorated in 1978; no pool; a.c. on request (40/- p.n.).

Tower Hill
(POB. 80492, tel. 433470)

A 1930s pile that has possibilities – and a splendid twelve-acre site overlooking Port Reitz; after many a change of proprietor, name and fate, was resuscitated in 1977 by new German owners and management, who in 1979 renovated the pastiche, namesake towers and are currently resurrecting the hot-water system, tennis court *et al*; no pool; 16 d. rooms in the two-storey main block (3 + b. & sh.), 6 in the side-block + b. & sh., and all (unless the threat of a.c. is carried out) the quietest in Mombasa and closest to the airport; BB 233/50-286/65 d., 151/10-186/90 s. (16/4-31/7/1981: 128/70-181/35 d., 93/60-128/70 s.; 1/8-31/10/1981: 175/50-228/15 d., 122/85-157/95 s.).

MOMBASA COAST NORTH
Bahari Beach
(POB. 81443, tel. 471603)

The African Safari Club's stylish 'headquarters' (1973); sizeable pool above the white-sand beach, restaurant-bar block behind and 7 makuti-roofed room blocks around; 2 tennis courts, car-hire, goggling and deep-sea fishing-boats; 104 d. rooms + b.; a.c. 20/- p.p.p.n. extra.

Baharini
(POB. 80929, tel. 485633)

Opened by the *Ocean View* in late 1978 on an acre at the northern extremity of Bamburi Beach; 38 d. rooms + sh. in 6 blocks surrounding the small pool and sloping down through the palms to the sea-front La Taverne Restaurant; casual, clean, quiet (no a.c.) and unencumbered.

Bamburi Beach
(POB. 83966, tel. 485611-3)

Lies between *Whitesands* and the *Kenya Beach* – in both location and classiness; opened in 1970, a model hotel, compact in design, where low numbers and professional management make for high standards; accent on families . . . perhaps because the new a.c. units drown any amount of infant din; 59 d. rooms + sh. in 4½ acres; 550/- d., 400/- s., under 12s 120/-, under 6s 100/-, under 2s 50/- (24-26 & 31/12/1981: + 50/-).

Coral Beach
(POB. 81443, tel. 485221)

First of the African Safari Club's new Mombasa enterprises (1971); a discreetly attractive complex, vaguely Spanish with arches and *teja*-tile roofs, amidst lawns and bougainvillea on the cliffs of Shanzu Beach; the dining-room attractive – and instructive – with murals of named local boats, and 42 d. rooms + b. or sh. in main block and 2 wings, the simpleness of the décor compensated for by the blissful absence of a.c.; goggling, windsurfing, skin-diving and deep-sea fishing with the club's Shanzu Beach facilities.

Coraldene
(POB. 80940, tel. 485421)

The Olands' unassuming establishment – pubby bar-restaurant and 4 d. cottages – now over-awed by its side-block (14 d. rooms + sh.; 1972); camping (5/- p.p.p.n.) in the 6 acres behind the beach; no pool.

Dolphin
(POB. 81443, tel. 485802)

The 1947 *Shanzu Beach Hotel* largely rebuilt in 1966-68 with 3 suites and 108 rooms + b. & sh., some + a.c.; since 1974 the African Safari Club's 'up-market' option; stepped, steeply, down the Shanzu cliffs, whence panoramic rooms, grill and general picturesqueness; base for the club's 40-place diving school which – like windsurfing, goggling and deep-sea fishing – its Shanzu Beach hotels share.

Kenya Beach
(POB. 81443, tel. 485821)

The work, you feel, of an inspired architect who enjoyed his job; 38 unusually spacious polygonal rooms + sh. (& a.c. of just-bearable decibels) and blocks of 54 d. rooms + b. added in 1972, all sloping round a stylish and likewise polygonal main block; opened in 1971 and now the African Safari Club's, whose *Bahari/Silver Beach* sea-facilities it shares.

Malaika
(POB. 81443, tel. 485102)

Completed in 1973 as twin to Nairobi's *Boulevard* (p. 139), an ambitious V-shaped block of striking design but erratic management until taken over and slowly improved by the African Safari Club; now its quiet exception, without the usual thrice-weekly disco or band; the gardened cliffs falling straight to the Indian Ocean, resident seafarers look to the *Dolphin* next door; 90 rooms + b. & a.c. (20/- p.p.p.n. extra).

Mombasa Beach
(POB. 90414, tel. 471861;
reservations Nairobi POB.
30471, tel. 336858)

Opened in 1970 as 'the Best on the Coast': a scenic site on Nyali Beach, 20 acres of flowers and lawns in landscaped 'coral gardens'; spacious, false-marble halls and discreet central a.c.; excellent cuisine, Cave Bar, à la carte Maxime's Cellar and grill-room; UTC car hire on the spot and Marijani horses for hire on the beach; nightly programme of films, disco, conjuror, dinner dance etc.; conference facilities for 150 with secretarial and audio-visual services . . . all endorse the boast; the high standards set initially by Hallway maintained by the present AT&H management; 150 d. rooms + b. & a.c. and 2 VIP suites in main block and wings (1978-79); FB 800/- d., 560/- s., 1040/- tr., under 12s 170/-, under 6s 110/-; ½B 760/- d., 540/- s., 980/- tr., under 12s 150/-, under 6s 100/-. After 22/4/1981: FB 560/- d., 280/- s., 725/- tr., under 12s 110/-, under 6s 70/-; ½B 520/- d., 260/- s., 665/- tr., under 12s 100/-, under 6s 60/-; BB 480/- d., 240/- s., 605/- tr., under 12s 90/-, under 6s 50/-. After 1/7/1981: FB 595/- d., 390/- s., 770/- tr., under 12s 120/-, under 6s 75/-; ½B 555/- d., 370/- s., 710/- tr., under 12s 110/-, under 6s 65/-; BB 515/- d., 350/- s., 650/- tr., under 12s 100/-, under 6s 55/-.

136

Nyali Beach
(POB. 90581, tel. 471567/8; reservations Nairobi POB. 40075, tel. 22860, 22869, 331635)

Since 1946 a well-publicized institution on 18½ acres of Nyali Estate (p. 74) and since 1972 a Block Hotel, whence 2 phases of expansion and modernization that have made of it the largest on the Coast: new lounge complete with fountain, bigger bar, extended restaurant, Mvita – War – grill and Mchana – Noon – bistro (a tribute to the first owner, Mrs N.); Karibu conference hall (1975) with ancillary rooms for gatherings of 400 plus, Hole in the Wall disco, 4 shops, the a.c. quieter (slightly) and the bed total upped from 250 to 405 in 199 d., 8 s. main-block and new-wing rooms and 2 suites.

Ocean View Beach
(POB. 81127, tel. 485601/2)

The former *Ocean View Cottages* modernized beyond recognition in 1971, with pool and restaurant on 5 acres of beach beside the president's palace; the 5 surviving cottages converted + sh., a.c. & African look, but upstaged first by the 66 d. rooms + sh. in 6 blocks (those inland + a.c.) then in 1978 by the 6 two-roomed Africana bungalows + sh. & a.c.; Glenn Davies' room-décor of chequerboard floors and gay slatted wood very tasteful; the clientele mainly German; good for families with children's pool, skittles, swings and new games room (its predecessor sacrificed in 1978 for the sake of a restaurant extension); well run, together with the *Baharini* (above).

Palm Beach
(POB. 81443, tel. 485222)

So tastefully rebuilt and integrated with the African Safari Club chain in 1978 that its origins can no longer be discerned: an ex-English beach-house, converted piecemeal after 1967 to become the hapless *Casuarina*; forms, like the *Bahari/Silver Beach*, a landscaped 'twin' with the *Coral Beach* next door; narrow beach backed by caves, short walk to the club's water-sport centre on the *Dolphin* beach; 81 d. rooms + sh.

Reef
(POB. 82234, tel. 471505, 471771)

Opened in 1972, an adventurous and successful private enterprise without chain management or too obtrusive 'packages'; reception and public rooms with 'ethnic' black-beam décor; makuti-roofs swept into peaks and arched façades on the room blocks alongside: one, for the staider, in the quieter, now well-developed gardens; the other, for ravers, behind the pool and dance floor/solarium; the latter enlarged and a tennis court added in 1977, a 22-room 'West Wing' built in 1978, and in 1979 a panoramic grill-room and a conference hall for 60; 6½ cliff-top acres; the 'Reef' because that lies close to the beach below; 130 rooms + b., sh. & a.c.; 640/- d., 440/- s., under 12s 90/-.

Serena Beach
(POB. 90352, tel. 485721-4)

So self-consciously Lamu-esque as to be almost museumish: reception cool and dark with carved doors, boriti-ceilings and Arab knick-knacks; bar boldly nautical with large-scale dhow and capstan stools; their high white walls enclosing narrow alleys, the black-timbered room blocks are similarly Olde Lamoo – save that a.c. everywhere shatters the serenity; a white-washed *mnarani* (read: disguised water-tank) looks down on 112 d., 8 tr. rooms + b. and 2 modest presidential suites; opened in 1974 and one of Harper's & Queen's '300 Best Hotels in the World'; water sports, windsurfing school and floodlit tennis and volleyball courts; 941/- d., 769/- s., 1220/- tr., suite 1410/- (1/5-31/7/1981: 475/- d., 303/- s.; 1/9-30/11/1981: 713/- d., 523/- s., 905/- tr., suite 1080/-).

Severin Sea Lodge
(POB. 82169, tel. 485001-3)

Opened in 1972 on 4 acres of the northern Bamburi Beach and doubled its capacity in 1978-79 lock, stock and barrel, with a reduplicated replica of the original suave complex; whence 2 pools, 2 restaurants, 2 bars (1 non-stop), twin makuti-roofed main blocks and two-storey rondavels of 150 d. rooms and suites + b., a.c., radio and – the German owners being appliance manufacturers – electric hair-driers, electric curlers etc.; conference facilities for 100 added in 1976 and good sports amenities; tennis court, mini-golf and scuba/windsurf instruction; discreet, low-keyed commercialization but energetic management; 795/- d., 530/- s., under 12s 25% less, under 6s 50% less, suite 1350/-.

Silver Beach
(POB. 81443, tel. 471471)

Beside the *Bahari Beach*, sharing its management, tennis courts, water sports, tariff, architect and year of opening, but rather more lavish and admirably landscaped; makuti-cone atop the entrance; lounge-bar with boat-and-sail décor; grounds delightful round a central rock garden that suddenly splits for a coral ravine in which room blocks hide behind the beach; 112 d. rooms + b., sh. & a.c. units in 5 two/three-storey blocks.

Sun n' Sand
(Kikambala POB. 2, tel. 8, 55)

The *Kikambala Beach Hotel* of 1932 renamed in 1963, reviving since 1971 under new owner-management, partly rebuilt in 1972 and extended in 1979: as 53 makuti-roofed d. or tr. rooms + b. or sh. in 18½ acres of beach; public rooms enhanced by carved Zanzibar doors (each inscribed with a Qoranic quotation); informal and very good value for families, well away from Mombasa's bustle and, without a.c., more deserving the epithet 'Whispering Palms' than its noisy neighbours; 550/- d., 350/- s., 700/- tr., under 11s 110/-, under 6s 75/-.

Whispering Palms
(Kikambala POB. 5, tel. 5, 6; reservations Nairobi POB. 30471, tel. 336858)

Pricier, livelier and slightly nearer town than the *Sun n' Sand* and sharing the same shady delight of coconuts and casuarinas (even if, since 1974, a.c. in all 110 rooms makes the name a misnomer); 2 tennis courts, 2½ swimming-pools, 'fitness centre with full-time animator', bowling, mini-golf and even archery on 12 acres of white-sand beach; resident band, disco and/or films nightly, with snack bar till 3 a.m.; built in 1940, rebuilt in 1964 & 1971 and since 1975 German owned, conjointly with the *Two Fishes*, in (loose) association with AT&H; FB 550/- d., 350/- s., 700/- tr., under 12s 110/-, under 6s 75/-; ½B 510/- d., 330/- s., 640/- tr., under 12s 100/-, under 6s 65/-. After 22/4/1981: FB 340/- d., 170/- s., 430/- tr., under 12s 70/-, under 6s 45/-; ½B 300/- d., 150/- s., 400/- tr., under 12s 60/-, under 6s 40/-. After 1/7/1981: FB 390/- d., 260/- s., 510/- tr., under 12s 80/-, under 6s 60/-; ½B 350/- d., 240/- s., 450/- tr., under 12s 70/-, under 6s 50/- (24-25/12 & 31/12/1981-1/1/1982: 100/- extra).

Whitesands
(POB. 90173, tel. 485926-9)

Only devotees of the 'Olde Inn next to the Sea' will recognize vestiges in the present hotel prodigy; begun with 10 cottages in 1928, *Whitesands* grew piecemeal until 1976 when acquisition by Sarova Hotels meant wholesale demolition and reconstruction; pubby lounge-bar, low-beamed 'old world' restaurant and exteriors nostalgically half-timbered were replaced by a vast Afro-modern, makuti-roofed main block – reception, restaurant, lounge, bar and shop; still caters for well-heeled families with drivers' and ayahs' quarters (40/- p.n.) and the 20 rondavels survive beside 175 smart d. or tr. rooms + b., sh. & a.c.; a grill-room deigns neighbour the 'old' (1970) lido and pool; with 2 floodlit tennis courts on 18 beach-side acres; 650/- d., 420/- s., 900/- tr., under 12s 50%, under 6s 25%.

MOMBASA COAST SOUTH
(pp. 70-72)
Jadini Beach
(POB. 84616, tel. 01261 2021-5)

Africana Sea Lodge

Leisurelodge
(POB. 84383, tel. 01261 2011/2)

Leisurelodge Club

Leopard Beach
(POB. 34 Ukunda,
tel. 01261 2111/2)

Pemba Channel Fishing Club
(POB. 54 Ukunda,
tel. Msambweni 5Y2)

Robinson Baobab
(POB. 32 Ukunda,
tel. 01261 2026-8)

Shelly Beach
(POB. 96030, tel. 451214, 451221)

Trade Winds
(POB. 8 Ukunda, tel. 01261
2016-8; reservations Nairobi
POB. 30471, tel. 336858)

Two Fishes
(POB. 23 Ukunda, tel. 01261
2101-3; reservations Nairobi
POB. 30471, tel. 336858)

The old *Jadini Hotel* deservedly demolished and sensibly reconstructed in 1971 as main block and pool, 3 two-storey wings (129 d. rooms + b. & a.c.) and 15 cottages for foursomes; since 1974 professionally run by Alliance Hotels and again reconstructed, the reception becoming a two/three-storey block complete with conference facilities for 150; 1 squash, 2 floodlit tennis courts, 2 pools, 7 bars, nine-hole golf, 10 acres of gardens and 500 yards of beach with all water sports.

The above now adjoined – like the tail that wags the dog – by the *Africana Sea Lodge*: an 'African village' (1978) of white-walled, red-floored rondavels, 56 in a circle round the 'lawns', each with 2 d. communicating rooms + sh. & a.c.; likewise makuti-roofed restaurant and Makaa – Charcoal – grill-room, Mwamba – Reef – bar and Banda discotheque (the 'hut' being its colonial villa premises); both hotel and lodge: FB 440/- d., 220/- s., 600/- tr., under 12s 120/-, under 6s 100/-; ½B 340/- d., 170/- s., 450/- tr., under 12s 80/-, under 6s 70/-; BB 270/- d., 135/- s., 345/- tr., under 12s 45/-. After 15/7/1981: FB 590/- d., 440/- s., 775/- tr., under 12s 145/-, under 6s 105/-; ½B 490/- d., 390/- s., 625/- tr., under 12s 105/-, under 6s 75/-; BB 420/- d., 355/- s., 520/- tr., under 12s 70/-, under 6s 75/-.

Opened in 1971, an immaculate ensemble on an exquisite site; 122 identically comfortable rooms in 7 blocks facing 22 acres of landscaped gardens and coral-backed beach (which 122 a.c. units blast inexorably); main block stylishly designed with built-in coral-garden waterfall and makuti 'big top' restaurant that acoustically mutes the loudest 'package' parties; a Lamu Bar/discotheque since 1978, 4 junior suites extra (for 100/- extra p.n.) and free entry for residents to the hotel's own – and the South Coast's only – casino; 701/35 d., 462/50 s., 969/15 tr., under 12s 175/25. After 26/4/1981: 510/80 d., 372/75 s., 690/30 tr., under 12s 144/95. After 12/7/1981: 621/25 d., 483/20 s., 800/75 tr., under 12s 144/95.

Shares since early 1979 the same-named hotel's gardens of lawns and lily-ponds; 36 luxury suites + b., sh. & (suaver) a.c., spacious in one- or two-storey blocks around a separate pool; privacy rather than clubbiness assured, if only by the prices; 1051/75 d., 732/85 s., 1472/45 tr., under 12s 261/90. After 26/4/1981: 759/35 d., 552/24 s., 1104/50 tr., under 12s 214/-. After 12/7/1981: 896/80 d., 690/30 s., 1241/95 tr., under 12s 214/-.

Opened in 1974, with Italian owners and excellent African management, and boasting the distinction of bidets, radios, refrigerators, fitted carpets (& a.c.) in all 81 rooms; these in 4 blocks, with main block and 3 two-roomed cottages in 12 acres of coral and bougainvillea beside *Leisurelodge*; approaches uncannily like the latter's, public rooms spectacular and admirably cool (without the aid of a.c.); games room, à la carte grill-room, tennis court and 2 pools of unusual circular-interlock design above a beach that isn't at high tide; 530/- d., 340/- s., 758/- tr., under 12s 120/-, under 7s 78/- (1-31/8/1981: 786/- d., 463/- s., 1138/- tr.).

The Hemphills' south-coast outpost, opened in 1962, become almost an institution for serious deep-sea fishing – holds every all-African striped marlin record – and since 1973-74 less esoteric as 'base' for the marine park (p. 72); 6 d., 2 s. bandas with small pool and homely bar-restaurant; game-fishing boats + radio (July-November 1500/- for 7 hours, December-March 2000/- for 9); closed annually 1/4-15/7; 175/40 p.p. + 10/- p.n. club membership.

Promoted in 1974 by the Frankfurt-based Robinson chain, so architecturally adventurous – 150 d. rooms + sh. & quiet a.c., half in two/three-storey blocks, half in two-storey rondavels linked by catwalks – and enthusiastically sporty – 'entertainment team' for scuba-diving and water sports, games room and organized games, yoga, boxing, bowling and batik/Swahili lessons, giant chess and clay-pigeon shooting, night-club, film-shows, lectures *et al*; on a 52-acre site called locally Kigomeni between the jungle-tight Diani Forest and a beach which, now deweeded regularly, is near-idyllic.

The original homely and maternalistic owner-management replaced by that of *Lawford's* in 1973 and this replaced in 1977 by new owners and new, energetic management; whence a generously restyled, makuti-roofed reception, excellent cuisine (with à la carte menu), new approach-road and courtesy bus into town, nightly entertainment, tennis court, mini-golf and complete refurbishing (1978-79) of the 63 d., 10 s. rooms + b. or sh. & a.c. if you must; these in 1948 cottages converted in 1975, into two 'family beach-blocks (1968 & 1970), 2 'family blocks' (1973) and 40 d. rooms (1979); for all that 'the nearest beach hotel to Mombasa' remains relaxed for families rather than suave for socialites; 12 shady acres; 320-465/- d., 225-275/- s., under 12s 50%. After 23/4/1981: 220-265/- d., 110-135/- s., under 12s 40/-. After 22/7/1981: 330-440/- d., 195-230/- s., under 12s 50%. After 1/9/1981: 290-350/- d., 165-195/- s., under 12s 50/-.

The former *Sandy Bay Hotel* and favourite with a faithful up-country clientele; had become the mellowest on Diani Beach until new AT&H management brought, in 1971-72, a facelift, a fine pool and a surfaced approach-road and, in 1977-78, a larger restaurant and makuti-roofed reception, 55 more d. rooms + b., sh. & a.c., and unneeded a.c. in the 48 original d. rooms + b.; such development threatening the pubby mood and 'old world' charm, further plans were shelved . . . and *Trade Winds* is now the mellowest on Diani Beach again; water sports, weekly disco and 14 acres of sand, palms and bougainvillea; FB 675/- d., 500/- s., 870/- tr., under 12s 130/-, under 6s 85/-; ½B 635/- d., 480/- s., 810/- tr., under 12s 110/-, under 6s 90/-. After 22/4/1981: FB 380/- d., 190/- s., 490/- tr., under 12s 70/-, under 6s 50/-; ½B 340/- d., 170/- s., 430/- tr., under 12s 60/-, under 6s 40/-. After 1/7/1981: FB 490/- d., 320/- s., 645/- tr., under 12s 90/-, under 6s 70/-; ½B 450/- d., 300/- s., 585/- tr.

Mr & Mrs Fish's pleasant beach property sold several times over then reworked magnificently, beyond recognition, in 1973-74, now under AT&H management and jointly German owned with the *Whispering Palms*; vast, film-set bar-reception block, 3 three-storey wings, gardens landscaped with waterfalls, pools and 'simulated river'; water sports, horses, tennis court and discotheque; 127 d. rooms + b. or sh. & a.c.; FB 700/- d., 500/- s., 900/- tr., under 12s 130/-, under 6s 85/-; ½B 660/- d., 480/- s., 840/- tr., under 12s 110/-, under 6s 70/-.

MOUNT ELGON (p. 124)
Mount Elgon Lodge
Endebess POB. 7, tel. 36;
reservations Nairobi POB. 30471,
tel. 336858)

A hillside pile built in 1924 (the upper floor in 1939) with doors, frames and beams of striking Elgon teak in the main hall and in round 'bastion' rooms on each corner; abandoned by its colonial owner in 1963, taken over by KTDC in 1976 and extended with an annex in 1977; the last's 10 d. rooms admittedly not first-class but the public rooms, much improved, manorial; 14 d. rooms + b. or sh. in 174 panoramic acres just below the park gate and the forests of Mount Elgon; prices as at *Homa Bay* (above).

MTITO ANDEI (p. 99)
Tsavo Inn
Mtito Andei PO, tel. 1Y1)

Further to page 99; formerly *Mac's Inn*, then one of the Inns of Africa, now the African Safari Club's; 32 d. rooms + b. or sh.

NAIROBI (pp. 41-48)
Ambassadeur
POB. 30399, tel. 336803)

Very central and very popular with the bars and restaurants developed since the take-over in 1974 by Sarova Hotels (owners of the *New Stanley* and *Whitesands* in Mombasa): Safeer and Balozi restaurants, Sarova snack bar, The Arch bar and first-floor Taverna grill-room; 80 rooms + b. & radio, recently carpeted and redecorated, on 6 near-miss luxurious floors; lift but no pool; 378/20 d., 261/10 s., 529/50 tr., under 12s 50%, under 6s 25%.

Boulevard
POB. 42831, tel. 27567-9)

Practically designed in 1971, in 4 acres between Uhuru Highway and the attractively gardened banks of the Nairobi River; tour operator and car hire on the spot, popular à la carte restaurant, garden bar, 3 shops and swimming-pool games area; 70 d. rooms + b., sh. & bidet and, like the public rooms, now much improved with carpeting, murals and a more colourful décor; BB 290/60 d., 199/80 s., 405/40 tr.

Excelsior
POB. 20015, tel. 26481)

The very central corner block of the old *New Avenue* (1929) restyled from top to bottom in 1977-79: new roof, new room ceilings and fitted carpets, rebuilt reception with shop and uniformed doorman, new kitchen and – being managed by a lay preacher – a more savoury aroma; so the first-floor bars, once Nairobi's best for bachelors, changed in name and clientele, the restaurant made 'Sheridan's Grill' and the ground-floor dinner-dance Topaze hived off as shops; lift to 6 floors of 62 rooms + b., sh. & radio; no pool.

Fairview
POB. 40842, tel. 331277, 27844)

The main block a grey-stone, somehow Scottish mansion but the gardens and cottages pleasantly 'up-country Kenyan' behind; under competent African management, jointly owned with Mombasa's *Manor*; 76 rooms in main block and cottages, the 8 apartments now 'family suites', in 5 acres safe and made for children, so no pool; reception/entrance modernized in 1974; 210-240/- d., 110-170/- s., family suite 290-600/-, under 12s 55/-, under 8s 45/-, under 2s 20/-.

Grosvenor
POB. 41038, tel. 21034/5)

A recent (but dated) AT&H acquisition; very 'Kenya colony' with verandas of polished red tiles and dark wood; well out of town in Ralph Bunche Road but consequently restful in 4 acres of gardens; pool picturesque rather than olympic; 41 d., 24 s. rooms + b. or sh. in 1940s main block and 3 two-storey wings.

Hilton
POB. 30624, tel. 334000)

Since 1970 Nairobi's circular focal centre, 18 floors 250 feet high; its 4 restaurants and cafés, mezzanine swimming-pool and Watamu Pool Terrace, sauna *et al* standard Hilton-luxurious and a ground-floor Kenyan Coffee Shop popular and cheap; first-floor Tsavo Restaurant/ Ivory Bar/Amboseli Grill reworked in 1975 and the entrance hall, surrounded by shops, now shared by a *trattoria*; 5 conference rooms for 450; 274 original rooms + b., sh. & a.c., with 68 added in 1973 – beside the pool, so much sought-after; room only 430-500/- d., 340-425/- s., suite 1035/-, presidential suite 1886/-; even breakfast à la carte and everything + 22%.

Inter-Continental
POB. 30353, tel. 335550)

Eight elegant storeys dominating Parliament and the GPO, just off city centre and thus perhaps the quietest of the best hotels; sophisticated penthouse cabaret-restaurant, popular snack bar beside the pool, the 'typical pub' converted for fully equipped conferences of up to 250 and the ground-floor galleries a tourist shopping centre with bank, Avis, Kenatco taxis, travel agents and boutiques; part-owned by Pan-Am, opened in 1969 with 220 d. rooms + b., sh. & central a.c., lavishly appointed and impeccable, and since 1977 the largest, 'most luxurious hotel in E. Africa' thanks to the construction (on concrete stilts – at not quite the same first-floor height) of 220 identically immaculate rooms; room only 500/- d., 425/- s., junior suite 1000/-, presidential suite 1500/-, all + 27%.

Jacaranda
POB. 14287, tel. 742272-5)

On 4½ acres of the 'Agip estate' at Westlands (p. 55) and in fact the *Motel Agip* until renamed and revitalized as an Alliance Hotel in 1974; 130 d. rooms + b. & sh. in the original block behind the Agip restaurant and in 2 wings added along with the pool in 1973; 'pizza garden' and Quo Vadis Restaurant opened in 1977 – with appropriately Italian menu and chef – and 2 conference rooms – for 125 and 40 participants – completed in 1979; tennis court, volleyball, children's playground, typewriters loaned free and free transport hourly into town.

Milimani
POB. 30715, tel. 29461-5;
reservations POB. 30471,
tel. 336858)

A fine 'town-holiday' establishment, opened in 1972 and now AT&H; 6 storeys imposing on the hill (the meaning of *Milimani*); 75 airy and functional d. rooms + b. & piped music, refurbished in 1976 and overlooking the pool, children's pool, attractive restaurant and grill-room (live music nightly except Mondays) and 16 'short-let' flats in 2½ acres; conference facilities for 150, typewriters for hire, free transport into town; BB 370/- d., 270/- s., 480/- tr., under 12s 75/-, under 6s 50/- (22/4-30/6: 330/- d., 240/- s., 430/- tr., under 12s 70/-, under 6s 40/-).

New Mayfair
POB. 43817, tel. 742731)

A popular complex, more homely than classy, 3 miles out of town on Parklands Road; 105 rooms + b. or sh. in a 1949 main block (with reception remodelled in 1974) and in 3 two-storey wings added in 1972; 8 acres of gardens with an embryonic arboretum; 'New' since 1979, when HMI took over, reworked the now à la carte restaurant in Meru oak, adapted the old and new 'Banana Room' for conferences of 60, shut the sleazy pay-first annex and renamed the 'Oasis' the 'Mayfair Club': pool, 4 saunas, barbecue and dining/meeting room for 80.

New Stanley
(POB. 30680, tel. 333233)

Further to page 47; started in 1911, 'New' in 1959 and now so much a well-promoted institution that a 'biography', albeit badly written, has appeared: *Old Nairobi and the New Stanley
Hotel*; Blocks benefited only briefly from this blurb, selling out thereafter to Sarova Hotels
(but retaining the adjacent Bacchus Club); impressive restaurant/ballroom/conference hall
for 250, art gallery and Acacia Room (each for 50-man meetings), Tate Room (honouring
the hotel's creators) and popular Friday *smorgasbord* – though the famous (but less profitable)
Long Bar no longer functions; 10 suites and 159 d., 59 s. rooms + b., sh. & a.c. on 8 well-
appointed floors – preferable on the Kenyatta Avenue side where the din of traffic drowns
that of a.c., lift machinery, boiler room etc.; no pool.

Ngong Hills
(POB. 46020, tel. 566677)

The African Safari Club's up-country pied-à-terre; pleasantly functional with grill-room
and 35 d. rooms, 3½ kms from the city centre on the Ngong Road.

Norfolk
(POB. 40064, tel. 335422)

Further to page 46; a Block Hotel and the Nairobi favourite of many discerning visitors:
presidents, millionaires, writers – the 'great' whatever your viewpoint – have been patronizing
the *Norfolk* continually since its start in 1904; a suave, well-run 'luxury hostelry', peaceful and
not too far from town; popular for its street-front Lord Delamere (made less street, more
indoors-discreet, in 1979) and its 'period' restaurant (recently dissected by a 'function room' –
Kenya specialities Wednesday, Kenya fish Friday and Sunday curry-lunch), and distinguished
by its aviaries in 8 fragrant acres; the 'transport trio' – rickshaw, ox-cart and 1928 model-A
Ford – now made a quartet by the surrey with a fringe on top; suite and 12 d. rooms + b.
built in 1980 above the 77 d., 32 s. rooms + b. or sh. from 1972; the 1937 'Block Mansion'
converted into 8 splendid studio suites, and the 1 tr., 4 d. & 4 s. cottages immaculate though
original 1900s.

Panafric
(POB. 30486, tel. 335166)

An attractive cross between classy and practical, whence smarter 'package' parties and
regular airline crews; well run with Hallway as consultants, a British Airways Associated
Hotel; pool very pleasant with bar and spacious lawns and gardens, first-floor Simba Grill
with live music nightly except Sunday; Jambo Room and Baraza Lounge for meetings of
250 and 100 respectively; lifts to 8 almost identical storeys with a hilltop view of town; 160
rooms increased in 1976 to 172 + b. & sh., all + quiet a.c., and since 1980 all overlooked by
the 14 two-, 28 one-bedroomed service flats in the four-storey block behind; BB 470/- d.,
305-356/- s., 533/- tr., under 12s 50%, suite 686/- d., 521/- s., luxury suite 889/- d., 686/- s.

Safariland
(POB. 48119, tel. 45000)

Alongside the Club 1900 in Chiromo Road, the former *Salisbury Hotel* with a mellow,
instant-residential air; quasi-colonial cottages and terraced rooms (some 1928 original,
some added in 1948 & 1968-69) and an outsize pool (10/-).

Safari Park
(POB. 45038, tel. 802311, 802493)

The former officers' quarters of the nearby Templer Barracks became in 1948 the *Spread
Eagle* (whence the motif in the façade) and in 1967 the *Safari Park* – and Nairobi's out-of-
town best; 30 acres of mature gardens, stables, 3 pools (for adults, children & fish – but no
fishing); 2 tennis courts, sauna and 'health centre', and nearby golf; a treasure of trophies in
the public rooms and a gallery of good game photos; since the closure of the 'Casino de
Paradise' the lounge is a nightly casino – and a contrast to the very local Jackpot beer
garden's fruit machines; closest to the airport, so popular with air crews, and own Nairobi
bus to own Kimathi Street waiting room; 69 d. rooms + b. in main blocks, 13 suites and
40 flats to let, all refurbished in 1978.

Serena
(POB. 46302, tel. 337978)

Newest of the capital's luxury hotels, opened by the Mzee in 1976; aesthetically landscaped,
almost integrated into Central Park (p. 45), its Athi River stone merging admirably and its
open, flowery public rooms continuing the park's luxuriance; materials and motifs both local
– Batik Restaurant – and floral – Orchid Grill, with flowers in the room-décor and (hopefully)
cascading down the façade from each room's window-box; heated pool and five/six-floor
blocks in 3¼ acres beside Kenyatta Avenue; 3 restaurants and 3 lifts to 192 d. rooms, junior
suites and state suite + b., sh. & a.c./heating; typewriters, secretaries and photocopying for
businessmen, conference hall for 300, facilities for 380; fridge on request (10/- p.d.); room
only 659/- d., 522/- s., 868/- tr., suite 1185/-, state suite 2370/-.

Sixeighty
(POB. 43436, tel. 332680)

Opened in 1972 as Nairobi's economy-luxury compromise – and East Africa's largest until
the *Inter-Continental* grew (above); street-level arcades cosmopolitan with Japanese restaurant, pseudo-London pub, Afro-Asian curio shop and 'Kentucky Fried Chicken'; terrace-
restaurant popular daily, very central, no pool; 3 lifts to 10 identical floors, each with 34
carpeted d. rooms + b., sh. & radio; BB 473/50 d., 320/- s., 550/25 tr.

Utalii
(POB. 31067, tel. Ruaraka 2089,
2540)

Utalii – Tourism – because of the ministry's catering school adjoining; opened in 1975 as an
'application hotel' for students' in-training, so guests are pampered guinea-pigs – and pay no
service charge; intentionally exemplary under expert management/supervision; red-brick
clean and squarely functional, 8 kms from town on the Thika Road; tennis (free) and nearby
golf (Monday-Friday 40/- p.d.); lifts to 3 floors of 43 rooms, 7 suites + b., sh., a.c. & radio.

NAIROBI NATIONAL PARK
(pp. 50-51)
Masai Lodge
(Reservations Nairobi POB.
48559, tel. 334411)

The nearest game lodge to Nairobi (p. 51), so offers instant access to the Kenyan outback for
those on short visits; in the Kitengela Reserve, on a splendid site beside the craggy Kingfisher
Gorge, above the Mbagathi; 15 d. manyattas on the cliff; reception and restaurant open-plan
and panoramic above the scenic pool; FB 370/- d., 240/- s.; ½B 330/- d., 220/- s., under 12s
50%.

NAKURU (p. 117)
Midland
(POB. 908, tel. 3433, 41277)

As though displaced from a London suburb; Nakuru's oldest surviving building (p. 117),
under African management and ownership since 1977; 1 tr., 25 d., 17 s. rooms, all + b. or sh.,
pleasant terrace café-bar, passable restaurant and the Automobile Association as a useful
neighbour; no pool.

Stag's Head
(POB. 143, tel. 2516)

For slightly smarter, and noisier, stop-overs; no longer AT&H, but a locally owned property,
with carpets now in most of the 64 rooms + b., to protect would-be sleepers from the
revellers in the ground-floor beer-shop; no pool.

140

NANYUKI (pp. 106-8)
Mount Kenya Safari Club
POB. 35, tel. 2141/2)

Further to page 107; as yet unchanged by the change of owners, but with plans for expansion already publicized – 20 more rooms – and the 'policy of avoiding press and media attention . . . now waived'; 136 beds in 18 immaculate main-block rooms (1050/- d., 570/- s.), 4 garden suites (1550/- d., 1130/- s.), state or royal suites (1780/- or 2000/- d., 1220/- or 1500/- s.) and 12 luxury cottages (1900/- d., 1300/- s., 2300/- for 3, 2600/- for 4, under 12s 300/-, under 5s 180/-).

Secret Valley
Reservations c/o *Sportsman's Arms*)
Sportsman's Arms
POB. 3, tel. 2057, 2717)

Further to page 108; completed in 1961; 42 beds with sonorous loos on 2 creaking wood storeys on stilts (380/- p.p. including national park fee); under 14s (and noisy adults) discouraged; pool for animals only.

Converted from a colonial hostelry in 1954, run personally and pleasantly by the owner, Shamsu-Din; pubby atmosphere; no pool; 4 d. rooms, 26 cottages and 2 suites + b. or sh. in 10 acres of lawns; 444/- d., 247/- s.

NARO MORU (p. 106)
River Lodge
POB. 18, tel. 23)

Further to page 106; lounge-bar and restaurant low-beamed and homely, the grounds manorial – 40 delightful acres beside the Naro Moru; opened in 1966, an Alliance Hotel since 1974 and a well-equipped departure point for climbing Mount Kenya; trout-fishing on the spot or 10 kms down stream (25/- and no more than 4 fish p.d.); 7 self-service cabins spacious and characterful with log fire, kitchen, b. or sh. (192/- for couples, 420/- for 5, 504-540/- for 6, 588/- for 7) and 10 terraced d. or tr. rooms + b. or sh.; no pool; 384/- d., 288/- s., 528/- tr., under 12s 120/-, under 7s 60/-.

NYAHURURU/THOMSON'S FALLS
Thomson's Falls Lodge
POB. 38, tel. 6)

Further to page 113; the township's second homestead (1929), converted into *Barry's Hotel* in 1931 and renovated in 1971: 3 cottages and 26 d. rooms + b. & cosy log fires, with camp site (10/- p.p.p.n.), in 10 acres resounding with the falls; no pool.

NYERI/ABERDARES (pp. 103-6)
Aberdare Country Club
POB. 449, tel. Mweiga 17, 25, 6; reservations Nairobi POB. 9420, tel. 332744)

Further to page 104; a farm-house tastefully converted in 1969; manorial lounge-restaurant and 26 d. rooms + b. & sh. in luxurious log-fire cottages, 5 original, 4 from 1979; 1300 steep acres, with bushbuck frequent on the well-kempt lawns, sloping to a river restocked for trout-fishing (rods free); horse-riding, pony treks to the Aberdares and game runs to the Treetops Salient; well-stocked shop but no pool; 500/- d., 250/- s.

Green Hills
POB. 313, tel. 2687/8)

An impressive local enterprise, opened in 1979; main block red-brick and polygonal round the dance-floor (and rooms in the rondavels of the late 'Village Dancers Hotel'); caters for conferences – 150-seat hall equipped audio-visually and air-conditioned – and for entertainment: squash court, sauna, disco and billiards room; 30 d., 13 s. rooms + b. & sh.; room only 228/60 d., 127-165/10 s.

Mountain Lodge
Reservations Nairobi POB. 0471, tel. 336858)

Further to page 106; the region's newest 'hotel in the trees' and nearest to Nairobi; in fact a fancier *Treetops*, so 3 VIP suites + b., and basin or sh. in the 56 d. or tr. rooms; 14 of these built in 1978 between the stilts below, making 3 eucalyptus-wood storeys; attractive restaurant-lounge with viewing-roof and underground tunnel to bring you close to the Kihari Corridor game; AT&H; Mount Kenya often spectacular above, rods for trout-fishing near by; naturally no pool; closed by day – access 3-6.30 p.m. only (Thego Camp lunch-stop for early arrivals, p. 105); ½B 800/- d., 500-600/- s., studio 950/-, suite 1100/-. After 22/4/1981: 560/- d., 280/- s., studio 660/-, suite 710/-. After 1/7/1981: 640/- d., 370-560/- s., studio 710/-, suite 780/-.

Outspan
POB. 24, tel. 2424/5; reservations Nairobi POB. 40075, tel. 22860, 22869, 331635)

Further to page 103; the main block almost stately with timbered ceilings and galleried restaurant, its elegance offset only by a 'Treetops Waiting Room' with showers, lockers and attendant bustle; conference facilities for 50 extended by the recent conversion of the Walkers' one-time home; tennis, squash, nine-hole golf (free for residents) at the nearby Nyeri Club and rods free for fishing – from the 'River Walk' cut through a *mgumu* tree; a Block Hotel; 23 d., 5 s. rooms, 7 cottages and 7 studio suites + b.

The Ark
Reservations Nairobi POB. 9420, tel. 332744)

Further to page 104; opened in 1969, benefiting from – and acknowledging – its game-hide neighbours' experience; transport leaves the *Aberdare Country Club* (above) at 2.30 p.m., to return the next day *after* breakfast; under 7s only with the manager's permission; water-holes but no pool; 27 d., 11 s. rooms and 7 '1st-class cabins' + sh.; 780/- d., 390/- s., suite 900/- d., 600/- s.

Treetops
Reservations Nairobi POB. 0075, tel. 22860, 22869, 331635)

Further to page 103; 73 heavily booked beds in 32 d., 5 s. rooms (communal loos but no showers) and 2 suites + sh.; transport leaves the *Outspan* (above) daily at 2.30 p.m., without under 12s; no pool of course, but new ground-level hide for photographers – built to celebrate *Treetops'* 10,000th night – and a Corbett Corner in honour of the colonel who, famed for hunting man-eaters in India, was invited to join the historic royal party (p. 104); Block Hotels manage.

SAMBURU/ISIOLO
pp. 109-10)
Buffalo Springs Tented Lodge
Reservations Nairobi POB. 0471, tel. 336858)

The old self-service bandas engulfed and upgraded in this AT&H project (1979); open-sided bar-restaurant banda, more nailed-wood than 'native', with swimming-pool beside, water-hole below and – along the slope behind – 6 four-roomed bandas and 31 d. tents – Manyara under makuti – + sh., toilet & electric light; FB 700/- d., 560/- s., 740/- tr., under 12s 130/-, under 6s 85/-; ½B 660/- d., 540/- s., 740/- tr., under 12s 130/-, under 6s 70/-. After 22/4/1981: FB 440/- d., 220/- s., 570/- tr., under 12s 70/-, under 6s 50/-; ½B 400/- d., 200/- s., 510/- tr., under 12s 60/-, under 6s 40/-. After 1/7/1981: FB 560/- d., 370/- s., 730/- tr., under 12s 100/-, under 6s 70/-; ½B 520/- d., 350/- s., 670/- tr., under 12s 90/-, under 6s 60/-.

Samburu Lodge
Reservations Nairobi POB. 0075, tel. 22860, 22869, 331635)

Further to page 109; a Block Hotel; picturesque beside the Uaso Nyiro River, designed by Graham – *The Ark* – McCullough and opened in 1963 with 28 d., 9 s. bandas + b. or sh.; treated in 1972 to a wing of 20 d. rooms, extended restaurant, rebuilt reception, pool, baited leopard-platform and riverside bar where crocs are fed the left-overs; airstrip and UTC vehicles for game runs; prices like *Keekorok*'s (p. 135) and likewise complemented with a camp: 12 d. tents + sh.

SOY (p. 124)
Soy Country Club
(POB. 2, tel. 1Y1)

A post-War officers' rest-home converted in 1948 to the *Soy Residential Club*; still a 'club' (though membership is free) and still very restful with 1 s., 10 d. rooms, bar and restaurant in mellow 'up-country colonial' cottages; pool and terraced block of 6 d. rooms + b. added in 1977; 10 fragrant acres.

TAITA HILLS (p. 97)
Salt Lick Lodge
(Reservations Nairobi POB. 30624, tel. 334000)

Further to page 97; 4 miles on from *Taita Hills Lodge*, a safari-architectural extravaganza that almost defies description: 'quartets of luxurious blockhouses perched on stilts and linked by mock River Kwai bridges' probably comes closest; a mud-brick tower, half elongated Masai, half German colonial, dominates 64 d. room-rondavels + sh., and main block lounge-bar opening on to rock-pool gardens descending to the water-hole; tunnel to nearby observation bunker and drawbridge raised daily at sunset (more to keep the visitors in than the animals out); mini-bus for game runs; 800/- d., 650/- s. (21/4-10/7/1981: 635/-500/-).

Taita Hills Lodge
(Reservations Nairobi POB. 30624, tel. 334000)

A brave three-storey venture, of the lavish design and finish expected of its Hilton sponsors on an eminence of the Taita foothills; the reception and sunken bar magnificently ethnic, the rest loosely 'luxury Lettow-Vorbeck': 'sand-bagged' bunker walls and restaurant décor of askari-grill gates, Prussian-eagle plaque, high-backed chairs and pewter plates (albeit made in New York); opened in 1973 and equipped since with conference facilities for 150 in its Baraza and Mwandu rooms ('meeting' in Swahili and Taita respectively), with airstrip, tennis courts, putting green and camels, and in 1977 with a water-hole below (to deter animals from falling in the pool); 60 d. rooms, 2 suites + b.; 560/- d., 435/- s., suite 825/ (21/4-10/7/1981: 450/-, 355/-).

TSAVO EAST (pp. 98-99)
Crocodile Camp
(Reservations Malindi POB. 500, tel. 333)
Voi Safari Lodge
(Voi PO, tel. 17; reservations Nairobi POB. 30471, tel. 336858)

Further to page 98; on a picturesque site beside the Galana/Sabaki, the beauty offset in true classic grotesque fashion by the monstrous namesake neighbours; 24 d. tents luxurious with loo and solar-heated water.

Further to page 98; architecturally impressive, with entrance-hall/cave as though from some filmset 2001 city and bar-restaurant and room blocks strikingly split-level; opened in 1967 under Hallway management, now an AT&H property – and so popular for transit-stops that lunch was served in 2 busy sittings until the dining space was doubled; best for game-viewing July-March; 50 identical d. rooms + b.; FB 700/- d., 560/- s., 900/- tr., under 12s 150/-; under 6s 85/-; ½B 660/- d., 540/- s., 740/- tr., under 12s 130/-, under 6s 70/-. After 22/4/1981 FB 440/- d., 220/- s., 570/- tr., under 12s 70/-, under 6s 50/-; ½B 400/- d., 200/- s., 510/- tr., under 12s 60/-, under 6s 40/-. After 1/7/1981: FB 560/- d., 370/- s., 730/- tr., under 12s 100/- under 6s 70/-; ½B 520/- d., 350/- s., 670/- tr., under 12s 90/-, under 6s 60/-.

TSAVO WEST (pp. 94-96)
Kilaguni Lodge
(Reservations Nairobi POB. 30471, tel. 336858)

Further to page 95; Tsavo West's bustling tourist centre, so bustling in fact that the restaurant-bar (1961) above the floodlit water-holes, the 35 rooms and 2 cottages around the lawns were in 1974 relieved by a Chyulu Restaurant (with custom-built water-hole), conference centre for 100-200 and two-storey extension (16 d. rooms + sh.); AT&H; petrol, airstrip and mini-bus base for UTC, Pollmans and the African Safari Club; FB 850/- d., 600/- s., 1150/- tr. under 12s 150/-, under 6s 100/-; ½B 810/- d., 580/- s., 1090/- tr., under 12s 140/-, under 6s 90/- After 22/4/1981: FB 560/- d., 280/- s., 730/- tr., under 12s 110/-, under 6s 70/-; ½B 520/- d. 260/- s., 670/- tr., under 12s 100/-, under 6s 65/-. After 1/7/1981: FB 620/- d., 450/- s., 745/- tr. under 12s 115/-, under 6s 70/-; ½B 580/- d., 430/- s., 685/- tr., under 12s 105/-, under 6s 65/-

Ngulia Safari Lodge
(Reservations Nairobi POB. 30471, tel. 336858)

Further to page 96; 52 d. rooms + b. & sh. in wings off a spectacular, open-plan main block; this decorous in local mica-flecked stone and eucalyptus beams, its hall educational with cases explaining the bird-ringing project; 2886 feet a.s.l. and very few feet between you and the game; AT&H management, which provides an excellent wildlife talk each evening (and an earlier dinner for children to clear them off first); prices like *Kilaguni*'s (above).

WATAMU (pp. 78-79)
Ocean Sports
(Malindi POB. 340, tel. Watamu 8)

Further to page 78; 4 Sprites, 3 glass-bottoms, 1 deep-sea boat, 1 ski-boat and half of Ian Pritchard's boat embedded in the bar; petrol and shop for the Turtle Bay 'community', sea water pool (1975) for scuba-beginners; closed May-June; 1 s., 15 d. bandas + b. & sh. 372/- d., 209/- s., under 17s 110/-, under 12s 99/-, under 6s 77/-, all + 20%.

Seafarers
(Malindi POB. 274, tel. Watamu 6; reservations Nairobi POB, 20106, tel. 25255)

The late *Seafarers Aqua-club*, individualistic like *Ocean Sports*, until taken over and considerably developed by Jambo Hotels in 1977; new management and new one/two-storey blocks of breezy, spacious and characterful rooms, though the seafaring interest still strong: 3 deep-sea fishing-boats, 2 glass-bottomed, 1 ski-, 2 sailing-boats and scuba-instruction; the 38 d. (or s.!) rooms built in 1965 & 1971 now increased to 63, all + solar-heated sh. weekly films/disco/'lobster dinner-dance' *et al* to enliven the pristine restaurant-lounge-bar 20 seaside acres; ½B 408-540/- d., 242-315/- s. (21/4-1/11/1981: 20% less).

Turtle Bay
(Malindi POB. 457, tel. Watamu 3)

Watamu's plush parvenu: a functionally-luxurious establishment that looks down on its older Turtle Bay neighbours; the décor much improved since the 1971 opening, the management active and conscientious, 9½ acres of bougainvillea gardens, 3 shops, car hire and the usual sea-facilities (water-ski, mini-sail and windsurf) distinguished by the Poseidon Nemroc diving school (seasonally) on the spot (Akamba wood-carvers ensconced on the beach) mini-golf, giant chess and nightly entertainment by the pool; 81 d., 5 s. rooms + b. & sh. (some + a.c.) in 2 two-storey blocks below the hilltop reception-bar-restaurant.

Watamu Beach
(Malindi POB. 300, tel. Watamu 1)

Further to page 78; built in 1967 & 1970; owned by the African Safari Club, so its well cleaned beaches, makuti-roofed main block and cliff-top pool-bar resound the year round to alien strains; diving-school, trimaran, dhow and windsurfing, 2 tennis courts, 2 bowling alleys and mini-golf; horses for hire and car rental on the spot; grill-room – and giant chess – since 1975; 274 beds in terraced rooms and bungalows + b. or sh. (22 + a.c.: 20/- p.p.p.n. extra).

INDEX
Bold type indicates principal references

144